THE
ANXIOUS
ACHIEVER

THE ANXIOUS ACHIEVER

TURN YOUR BIGGEST FEARS INTO YOUR LEADERSHIP SUPERPOWER

MORRA AARONS-MELE

HARVARD BUSINESS REVIEW PRESS

BOSTON, MASSACHUSETTS

Copyright 2023 Morra Aarons-Mele

All rights reserved

Printed in the United States of America

10 9 8 7 6 5 4 3 2 1

No part of this publication may be reproduced, stored in or introduced into a retrieval system, or transmitted, in any form, or by any means (electronic, mechanical, photocopying, recording, or otherwise), without the prior permission of the publisher. Requests for permission should be directed to permissions@harvardbusiness.org, or mailed to Permissions, Harvard Business School Publishing, 60 Harvard Way, Boston, Massachusetts 02163.

The web addresses referenced in this book were live and correct at the time of the book's publication but may be subject to change.

Cataloging-in-Publication data is forthcoming.

ISBN: 978-1-64782-253-8
eISBN: 978-1-64782-254-5

The paper used in this publication meets the requirements of the American National Standard for Permanence of Paper for Publications and Documents in Libraries and Archives Z39.48-1992.

To Nicco, my partner,
who has made it all possible.

And to the healers in my life,
especially Dr. Carol Birnbaum,
who has seen me at my worst and
helped me achieve my best.

CONTENTS

Author's Note   *ix*

Introduction: The Open Secret and the Great White Whale   1

PART ONE
GETTING TO KNOW YOUR ANXIETY

  1. Anxious Ambition   17

  2. Anxiety Is a Double-Edged Sword   33

  3. Uncover Your Triggers and Tells   47

  4. Face Your Past   65

PART TWO
A LEADER'S TOOL KIT FOR MANAGING ANXIETY AT WORK

  5. Negative Self-Talk   89

  6. Thought Traps   99

  7. Unhelpful Reactions and Bad Habits   121

  8. Perfectionism   145

  9. Control   163

10. Feedback, Criticism, and Impostor Syndrome   183

11. Social Anxiety   201

Conclusion: Find Joy   225

Notes   *233*

Index   *239*

Acknowledgments   *249*

About the Author   *253*

AUTHOR'S NOTE

I am a leader with anxiety, not a clinician or an academic. To make sure *The Anxious Achiever* is sound from a clinical perspective, I partnered with Carolyn Glass, LICSW, MBA. Not only is Carolyn a practicing psychotherapist, she also has an MBA from Columbia Business School and is a dear friend whom I've known for over 25 years. Before Carolyn became a therapist, she and I swapped horror stories while we worked in the media and technology worlds of New York and London. Carolyn: I'm so grateful for your counsel and partnership in making this book!

THE ANXIOUS ACHIEVER

The Open Secret and the Great White Whale

The newly minted vice president of global sales closes his office door and slumps into his chair. He's worked for years to get this promotion, and everyone—the leadership team, his family, his colleagues, his friends—is thrilled. But instead of the joy and sense of accomplishment he expected and deserves, he's worried, tense, distracted, and just plain scared. He can't shake the feeling that it's only a matter of time before his new team and managers realize he might not be up to the job.

Versions of this scenario occur in workplaces everywhere, every day. Certainly, the details vary from person to person, but vast numbers of us are deeply anxious at work. Some are the last people you'd expect. The multimillionaire CEO of a famous tech company. The serial entrepreneur who's constantly in the media. The administrator at your kid's school. The social media celebrity with a devoted following. The small-business owner who lives next door.

And possibly you.

Do you ever find yourself struggling with worry and even dread about all the things that could go wrong? Are you ambitious and driven—but you also ruminate, stew, and have a hard time letting things go? Do you sometimes feel you're in over your head and that any day now others will discover you're faking it? Are you someone who avoids certain situations at all costs, like flying or public speaking, even if it means sacrificing opportunities or not advancing in your career? Do you ever find yourself micromanaging, or redoing others' work because it's not up to your standards? These are just a few of the many ways that anxiety can show up at work and affect our well-being and effectiveness.

The American Psychological Association distinguishes anxiety from fear, and the distinctions are very telling: Whereas fear is "an appropriate, present-oriented, and short-lived response to a clearly identifiable and specific threat," anxiety is "a future-oriented, long-acting response broadly focused on a diffuse threat." Anxiety can linger long past a threatening situation, or it may not even have a tangible cause. Sometimes it seems rational; other times it can arrive out of nowhere and make no sense at all.

Those of us who are anxious by nature, like me, have what psychologists call *trait anxiety*: it's just part of who we are, like a personality trait. Everyday stressors can feel threatening, so it's no surprise that many of us go to great lengths to avoid what makes us anxious. Constant or excessive worry is a defining feature of problematic anxiety, and when these feelings are persistent and interfere with our daily activities—jobs, schoolwork, relationships—they likely indicate a condition called generalized anxiety disorder. Anxiety can also be a symptom of other mental health conditions, and commonly rides along with depression, obsessive compulsive disorder (OCD), substance use, learning differences like dyslexia or attention deficit hyperactivity disorder (ADHD), and personality disorders.

Across the globe an estimated 284 million people suffer from anxiety, making anxiety the world's most common mental health ailment.[1] The true numbers are surely far higher, as these statistics reflect only the people who were able to access treatment and who received a diagnosis. Emerging data reveals that we are more anxious than ever. A study from Mental Health America found that from 2019 to 2020, the number of people seeking help for anxiety and depression increased 93 percent.[2] The Covid-19 pandemic magnified the problem, but the pandemic's aftermath is only creating more anxiety.[3] In the United States, rates of anxiety and depression were about four times higher between April 2020 and August 2021 than they were in 2019, and up to 38 percent of Americans reported feeling symptoms of anxiety in 2021. I was struck when the major public health authority in the United States recommended routine anxiety screenings for all adults under 65. I often joke that if you're not anxious, you're not paying attention. We live in a time when multiple global and local crises pop up on our screens every hour and achieving quality of life is expensive and stressful.

Research focused on mental health in the workplace paints a similar picture. Mind Share Partners' 2021 Mental Health at Work Report reveals that 76 percent of full-time US workers reported experiencing at least one symptom of a mental health condition in the past year—up from 59 percent in 2019. The most common were anxiety, depression, and burnout.[4]

Trying to juggle the demands of work with the needs of our mental health often means that both performance and mental health suffer. Unmanaged anxiety can drain our energy, wreck our concentration, and drive us to make poor, rushed, and ill-considered decisions. It can lead us to focus on the wrong things, distort the facts, and jump to conclusions, and can even result in physical pain and injury. In more extreme situations, anxiety can trap us in obsessive negative thought loops that prevent us from moving forward. It can lead us to dwell so much on the possibility of frightening worst-case outcomes that we, and thus those we lead, become frozen. In short, unmanaged anxiety can make leaders less effective, which can reduce the performance of those who report to them and of the overall organization. Above all, it makes us unhappy—and just makes life harder.

But there's another side to anxiety, which is what can happen when we learn to manage it and take advantage of its hidden gifts.

I'm a leader with chronic, clinical anxiety. I've worked in the cut-throat environment of presidential politics, corporate America, and tech startups. I've managed four corporate marketing departments and built two full-scale departments from scratch. I'm also an entrepreneur; I started my consulting firm, Women Online, in 2011 and sold it in 2021. My *Harvard Business Review* podcast (now on LinkedIn), *The Anxious Achiever*, is one of the top business podcasts in the world, which boggles my mind. I write books and articles and speak extensively on leadership to *Fortune* 500 companies, the federal government, and elite universities like Harvard University and the Massachusetts Institute of Technology. I'm also a wife, and have three kids. And I've done all of this while grappling with clinical levels of anxiety, along with periodic bouts of debilitating depression.

I know there are so many people out there just like me—ambitious, career-focused professionals who succeed while struggling with mental illness. If you're reading this book, you probably identify with this group, and the term "anxious achiever" probably resonates with you. Anxious achievers are rarely still, in body or in mind. We are goal-oriented, future-oriented, and take our work extremely seriously. We are prized team members because we go the extra mile as a matter of course and nothing less than the best will do. We create extraordinary outcomes because we are driven to *always* excel and succeed at any challenge we set ourselves.

Of course, working yourself so hard purely for anxiety's sake is awful, and it's no way to live. But because anxiety is an emotion—an internal state you can learn to manage—you can build a life that isn't ruled by it. In fact, you can even learn to rely on this complicated emotion as a loyal partner and a leadership advantage.

Because here is the beauty of being an anxious achiever: If we can align our drive with a larger purpose, we can move mountains. If we can manage our anxiety and lessen the personal toll, we can approach our work with incredible energy and ingenuity. We can be the visionaries who create bold change, the leaders people want to work for. Even if we feel afraid while doing so.

Reframing Anxiety at Work

I'm often asked a question: if anxiety is such a powerful factor in individual and organizational performance, and if it's so pervasive, why don't we hear more about it?

A big part of the answer is shame.

On *The Anxious Achiever*, I interview leaders about their struggles with anxiety and how they've learned to deal with it. The listener response has been overwhelming, an indication of how widespread anxiety at work is.

But despite my podcast's large audience, I've been challenged to find prominent executives willing to speak publicly about it. They believe that exposing their anxiety will make them seem weak. They worry that opening up about their mental health challenges will tank their company's stock price. They think—correctly, based on my experience—that people consider anxiety and strong leadership incompatible.

I speak with groups about this subject frequently, and again and again I hear the same refrain: don't talk about mental health if you want to get to the top. I know many leaders who feel they can't walk into a staff meeting and say, "I'm anxious today," and I've heard from many young people who worry that their anxiety will destroy their career dreams.

All of this happens because successful people typically hide how they feel. Despite many positive developments in leadership models and an increase in amenities for physical wellness, there is still a stigma associated with talking openly about mental health at work.

The great white whale for my podcast is a certain CEO with a raging anxiety disorder. The company they founded had an initial public offering, grew even stronger with them at the helm, and often appears on "best" lists. Yet the CEO told me that most days they wake up filled with existential dread, and they plan all work travel with enough cushion to recover from the Xanax-induced haze they use to deal with fear that the plane will crash.

I've been attempting to interview this CEO on the record for years. Every so often I check in and ask if they're ready to talk with me, trying to convince them that speaking honestly about their anxiety could change people's lives. But the CEO just can't do it. The explanation is always some variant of "It's not you, it's me."

This CEO, like many, is able to create an amazing organizational culture while assuring Wall Street they've got it all under control. After all, Wall Street prefers business leaders to never break a sweat or show much emotion beyond ruthless drive. Even though management styles and structures have evolved from command-and-control hierarchies, in many cultures leaders can't show emotion or weakness, lest their effectiveness come into question. I feel bad for these executives, honestly, and for their organizations too. Think of how much better they would feel, and how much greater their impact would be, if they were functioning at full capacity, unhindered by constantly trying to keep their anxiety under wraps.

The Anxious Achiever is a book with a mission: to reframe how we think about anxiety in the context of leadership and organizations. It tells a different, more authentic, and more hopeful story than the one society promotes—that anxiety and depression are weaknesses and prevent us from succeeding, and that we have to leave our emotions behind when we step into the office. To do all this, we're going to upend a lot of the conventional wisdom on anxiety and other mental health struggles, building a new vision around a few core messages:

- **Anxiety is part of life.** It's part of the human condition, and it often accompanies leadership, so you, your teams, and your organizations should learn how to manage it and make it a strength.

- **Anxiety is not a weakness and learning to manage it certainly isn't.** What requires more strength and courage: facing a demon, or trying to pretend it doesn't exist? Which path leads to more hope and greater impact: doing the work to address what's holding you back, or avoiding it? Looking the tough stuff in its face and uncovering years of coping mechanisms or avoidance—

what the songwriter Peter Gabriel called "digging in the dirt"— makes you really strong.

- **When you understand your anxiety and learn to leverage it, you develop a leadership superpower.** It may not feel like it now, but anxiety can enhance your leadership, ambition, creativity, empathy, communication, and vision. When you're attuned to your emotions and what they're trying to tell you, you become a conscious and thoughtful leader.

New Mindsets for a New Era of Leadership

Like every other leadership author, I want you to be super successful, be the ultimate professional, and discover the work life meant for you.

But unlike many others, I won't promise that if you follow my instructions, your career will soar. This book won't fix your life or guarantee a meteoric rise to the top. It might, however, begin a process of transformation that leads to the career and the life you were meant to have. In the long run it might just make your life easier, and more enjoyable.

On the way, though, you might feel uncomfortable. You might cry or get angry. You might even get angry at me. One of my favorite pieces of listener feedback was "I mostly love your podcast. Except it's quite raw and personal." Well, yeah. That's the point. I'm going to be raw and personal, and this book will introduce you to some pretty exceptional people who will also be raw and personal. I want you to understand that you are not alone and that anxious feelings are common. You don't need to hide them, and they don't need to hamper your leadership or your life.

Most of us will go to great lengths to avoid uncomfortable feelings. It's human nature. But when you look your scary feelings in the face, you remove their power. You discover inner truths, see the actions of those around you more clearly, and feel more powerful, energized, and on top of your game.

However, doing this requires knowing how to harness our anxious feelings. Most of us act out our anxieties mindlessly, with reactions that don't serve us or the people around us. This isn't anxiety's fault. Anxiety, itself, is good data. It can push us to check in and change things, and it can even bring extra drive, energy, and focus.

What if instead of habitually acting out your anxiety with a late night at work, endless scrolling on social media, or a Snickers bar, you took a moment and asked your anxiety, "What are you trying to tell me? Why does this person's name in my inbox make me feel so much dread? Why does that meeting coming up in two weeks make me want a shot of vodka?" Reflection is where your anxiety can be an ally. It can provide key information that's not available to you any other way. All of this is the reward for looking your scary feelings in the face!

Getting to the place where you can see anxiety in a new way—as neither good nor bad, but rather existing on a spectrum of unmanageable, manageable, and even helpful—might require discarding long-held beliefs of what strength, power, and success look like. Thankfully, the landscape of leadership is changing, and that has been accelerated by the global Covid-19 pandemic. We all realized it felt good to be more real in front of each other. Leadership in the future will not be a guy pontificating in the front of the room. Real leaders will be vulnerable and authentic, skilled at building a supportive environment that brings their teams through challenging times.

To get to that place, there are three mindsets that need to change.

The first is to give up pretending that you, as a leader, need to know all the answers—that's simply not possible or true. I hope that comes as a relief. For many of us, no longer pretending will mean letting go of a need to control things and understanding that most of us operate from an aversion to loss. If you pretend you always know the path forward in a post-Covid world, no one will believe you. Instead, adopt a mindset that's open to fresh knowledge.

The second change is to learn to tolerate discomfort. Most leadership books ask you to recognize your strengths and capitalize on them. It's the rare one that tells you to look at the vulnerable underbelly we all have, the part that most of us would rather not acknowledge—what Carl Jung called the shadow self. This book contends that you need to know your vulnerabilities and the frightening aspects of your personality you'd rather ignore if you're truly going to understand yourself as a leader *and* perform at your highest level. Leadership for the future, especially with a new generation of workers who are both more anxious and more comfortable speaking about it than previous generations, requires us to face our mental landscape and navigate it skillfully.

The third shift in mindset is to use your new awareness and self-knowledge to learn to communicate better so that you can help your people manage through uncertainty. This involves sharing the right amount of vulnerability while also maintaining professional boundaries and reassuring your team. You can't promise everything, and you don't have a crystal ball. But you're still in charge and your team is looking to you to lead, so you're going to need to put forward your best skills and best efforts.

One prominent CEO refused to hide his struggles with mental illness. He started speaking out in the 1990s and used his platform to help others until his death in 2016. His story is still so powerful—I haven't found a recent example that compares.

When Houston-based CEO Philip Burguieres went on a sudden medical leave in 1996, his company's stock plummeted 10 percent. Burguieres was the youngest person ever to be the CEO of a *Fortune* 500 company. Yet behind the scenes he was enduring panic attacks that made him think he was dying, severe bouts of depression and anxiety, and he sometimes thought about suicide.

After treatment, Burguieres used his newfound knowledge about his condition to go public about his struggles with anxiety and depression. The fact that he could stand as an equal in a room of rich white men and talk about his feelings lent authority to his words. He started a "secret CEO network" where members shared their struggles with mental health and helped each other through them. Burguieres's whisper network spread a gospel, one that I regularly hear from my podcast guests: as they sought treatment and faced their feelings, they "discovered what [those] who are bred for competition shun from an early age—that people connect not by parading their strengths but by confiding their fears, their disappointments, their hurts, as well as their hopes and dreams."[5]

We don't get through this and get better alone, in other words. Burguieres came to realize that isolation and unexpressed feelings made his condition worse, and that sharing his story and helping others was part of his recovery.

There's a key lesson here. Everything leadership gurus say about bringing your whole self to work or leading with empathy and authenticity is a lie until we talk about our experiences with anxiety, depression, ADHD, OCD, suicidal ideation, or whatever other mental health challenges are affecting us. Because, of course, we *do* bring our whole selves to work, and those selves can sometimes be in a great deal of pain—and can sometimes be real jerks.

In a culture obsessed with self-optimization, it only makes sense that truly effective leaders understand their demons, explore them, and by doing so shed those demons. When we deny our pain and our dark impulses, we can't really have any empathy, and sooner or later that repressed pain is going to emerge, probably destructively. Why is it that books telling you how to succeed don't also ask why we find ourselves repeating patterns that get us into trouble or make us unhappy in the first place?

Thus a lot of this book will be about making conscious what is currently unconscious. So much of bad leadership happens not because of incompetence or lack of vision, but because people are reacting without awareness to anxiety and anger based in experiences they had long ago. Here's an example: Your social anxiety might actually be a learned behavior that resulted from being made fun of throughout junior high school, a deeply painful experience that left you feeling shamed and excluded. When you're called on to join new groups, negative self-talk automatically arises: "I don't have anything to add to this conversation. If I open my mouth, they'll think I'm dumb. I shouldn't even be part of this group." Years of this negative self-talk have contributed to a core belief that you're not worth getting to know, or that you'll be judged harshly for your contributions. Now social events make you anxious, so much so that you avoid important meetings and networking events. The anxiety you feel about socializing has become a habit.

Reflexive reactions like these happen all the time. So occasionally I'll be asking you in this book to take a look at your family of origin and past history, because we develop our self-concept and much of our learned behaviors in childhood. We will examine how the values you were raised with and the lessons and hurts you experienced early in life carried over into your development as an adult and shape the leader you are today.

This is really about taking power back from our automatic responses and learned behaviors and then, with full awareness, making the best decisions for ourselves and our organizations. The best leaders understand how anxiety motivates their behavior and develop the skills to manage their reactions while understanding what motivates their team's actions.

Leadership is a mindset above all, and it's part of who you are, regardless of your mental health. Whether you've been an anxious achiever since childhood or your anxiety has shown up in your professional life, my job is to help you understand and better manage all the gorgeously complicated threads of your brain health and temperament so that you can build yourself into the strong, effective leader you were meant to be.

The Road Ahead

You will occasionally see people in this book referring to their anxiety as a superpower. I believe it can become one if we do the work to make it so. Yet there is a tension here: very few clinicians would call anxiety a superpower, and there is no doubt that anxiety can become disabling and render us nonfunctioning. If your anxiety is severe and disabling, I encourage you to put down the book and get professional help. The book can help to optimize your functioning, and its exercises are helpful in alleviating symptoms, but they are no substitute for treatment.

But if you're living daily with anxiety and seeking to better manage it, this book is a good complement to therapy and other mental health treatments you're doing. It is my argument that well-managed lower-level anxiety can be a powerful tool and partner in your leadership journey. You may agree or vehemently disagree that anxiety can be a superpower, but I hope that if you stick with me, you will come to see your anxiety's potential benefits.

The Anxious Achiever is divided into two parts. In part 1, I describe and normalize the problem many leaders face: how to succeed and inspire others when you're grappling with anxiety yourself. We'll discover that anxiety at work is a double-edged sword: unmanaged, it can take you down, but dealing with it and capitalizing on its positive aspects can help you see around corners, expand your empathy, and communicate more effectively.[6] I'll share stats and stories that help you understand you're not alone, and that show you how formative experiences continue to shape your current experience of anxiety and how you lead.

Part 2 focuses on specific ways that anxiety flares up at work and identifies many common reactions to anxiety, such as overwork, perfectionism, micromanaging, substance use, drinking, or unhealthy eating. It also provides an abundance of practical advice, tools, proven coping mechanisms, and exercises for better managing your anxiety, however you experience it at work. You'll hear real-life stories from leaders who've been there themselves, as well as expert guidance from professionals with deep knowledge of anxiety—what triggers it, how it manifests physically and emotionally, and, above all, how we can manage and treat it.

There is no one school of thought or treatment modality featured in the book, but rather a variety of tools and viewpoints chosen from various schools of psychology and therapeutic orientation. In general, most of the exercises and techniques stem from cognitive behavioral therapy, acceptance and commitment therapy, and mindfulness practice, because these tools are both extremely practical and effective. Many can be put to use right away and make the most sense for busy professionals.

So whether you have anxiety stemming from a traumatic episode, you've been grappling with anxiety all your life, or you're in the midst of scary change and are having your first dance with this formidable emotion, you are not alone—and there are proven tools that can help you not just manage your feelings but thrive, professionally and personally.

Having anxiety or other mental health challenges doesn't mean you can't be an effective leader, or that the pinnacles of success are unavailable to you. It means you do the work to get better and to find a way there. It means you feel the fear and act anyway. It means you persevere in spite of wanting to quit or cancel or hide or stay silent—because you remember that what you have to offer is important and meaningful.

PART
ONE

GETTING TO KNOW YOUR ANXIETY

1

Anxious Ambition

Many people can trace their earliest experiences with anxiety back to childhood, and that's definitely true for me. I had agoraphobia when I was three. I wouldn't leave the house; I clung to my mom. Hypervigilance, a state of extreme high alertness, began in my turbulent childhood and is something I still manage today. But what led me to finally get help was a massive, terrifying panic attack when I was nineteen. I was diagnosed with cyclothymic disorder (and later with bipolar II) and generalized anxiety disorder and was fortunate enough to receive treatment, mainly in the form of psychodynamic psychotherapy, cognitive behavioral therapy, and antidepressants.

Still, over the next several years I cycled between anxiety and depression, and when I entered the professional world, my anxiety brought new problems. Being with people all day left me drained, and I avoided a lot of the things that would get me promoted, like office politics. Once I turned down a lovely big office that was right next to my boss's, because it made me too anxious to know he was near all day. I drank too much at after-work gatherings to hide my social anxiety, felt nauseous before meetings, dreaded phone calls and often canceled them, hid in more office bathrooms than I can count, and lost sleep worrying over, well, all of the above. In my twenties I quit nine corporate jobs and moved to Europe and then Africa, all in an attempt to find the "right" fit, the job where I could make a significant contribution and not experience such emotional turmoil.

At the same time, I was really successful. I suffered in silence while being dependable, forward-thinking, hardworking, and ambitious. My anxiety helped me take risks that matched my ambition, and I worked in challenging jobs. At twenty-five I ran marketing for Europe's second-largest online travel company. At twenty-six I helped a US presidential campaign raise millions through groundbreaking digital marketing strategies. And at twenty-eight I was the youngest vice president at a global communications firm.

But as my career advanced, anxiety, combined with my natural ambition, pushed me to always do more. No achievement was ever enough, which is why I've also hosted two podcasts, written two books and dozens of articles, and built a public speaking career that demands a lot of travel. Some days I feel like I have three jobs, and still I worry about not doing enough.

Growing older, I found good therapy, good meds, and a powerful routine, which mostly have kept my anxiety at a dull roar. In my thirties and forties, I found more equilibrium: marrying and having children, starting a company that allowed me to set my own schedule, and avoiding people when it was all too much. I've been working remotely since 2006, way before it was cool, and I can't see myself ever going back to an office. Getting older not only gave me some healthy perspective, it allowed me the flexibility and the confidence to choose how I work and live.

Most importantly, along the way I found my life's purpose. I stopped working just to appease my anxiety, and applied that drive to define the impact I wanted to have. You can do that too. Call it your "why," your purpose, your goal—whatever resonates with you and anchors you when times get tough.

You may have a lot of goals, some grand and some humble, and they will change over time. For example, in 2010 I decided my purpose was to combine well-paying opportunities for women who write and cre-

ate content on the internet with organizations that create prosocial public policy. That became my business, Women Online. My purpose was
also to have a work life that afforded me flexibility and autonomy while
providing a great life for my kids. More recently, my purpose has been
to create a forum for successful professionals to talk about their mental
health.

In 2017, when I was on tour for my first book, *Hiding in the Bathroom*, something just snapped into place. *Hiding in the Bathroom* was
ostensibly about how to fulfill ambitions for a big career when you're
introverted and you dislike a lot of the networking and entrepreneurial
practices we think we need to get ahead. But in every talk I'd start discussing the role anxiety plays, and people would get excited. They
wanted to talk about the chapter in which I'd featured Harvard Business School professor, entrepreneur, and executive Christina Wallace,
who had severe childhood trauma and has done a lot of work to manage the aftereffects. "Situations where I feel like I can't trust the other
person or the rug has been pulled out from under me throw me into
fight-or-flight mode," she says, which can lead her to have panic attacks
and crippling anxiety. She's learned that she needs to work with her
managers and colleagues to, for example, find a way to anticipate feedback ahead of time, so she processes it and prepares instead of feeling
blindsided and anxious.

Even so, anxiety has been a gift, Wallace says, because "it's made me
an incredible manager—according to the employees I've managed across
my last three startups—because I am much more aware of how [my
employees] like feedback and how to help them show their best selves."

Anxiety is not a simple gift, though. Wallace notes that being an
"achiever on steroids" has propelled her career far and fast. But, she adds,
"I have to make sure I don't just do things for medals or résumé bul-
lets." Instead, she focuses on her purpose and anchor, "things that make
me happy and fill me emotionally and spiritually."

My audiences wanted to talk about stories like Wallace's, and they
wanted to talk about their own anxiety, how it hurt them, and how it
made them unique. Their curiosity inspired me to launch a podcast
where I interviewed highly successful entrepreneurs, politicians, athletes,

and executives about their experiences with anxiety, depression, bipolar disorder, OCD, and ADHD. These leaders have been through incredibly difficult times. Their mental health challenges travel with them every single day. They take medication, some have been hospitalized, and often they get very angry at their brains. They have built tremendous tool kits to manage their mental health. They are all purpose-driven leaders. They defy their anxiety because their values demand they show up, do the work, and lead.

Learning to tap into my purpose helps me redirect my anxiety when it's being stupid. For example, if I'm feeling performance anxiety about something that really doesn't matter, I can tell my anxiety to go away and come back another time.

When I owned Women Online, I flew almost every week to see clients or speak. I have terrible flying anxiety and hated to leave my kids, but I had to do my job to support those kids. And that was why on every runway I sat on, when my anxiety flared up and I thought, *We're gonna take off and I'm gonna die,* I could take a breath, tap into my purpose, and tell myself, *Morra, you are not doing this for fun. You are doing this for your family.* Then I'd use breath techniques and other distress tolerance tools to get through the flight.

And when my anxiety gets the better of my mood, my purpose will find me. A few months ago, I was in a dark patch, feeling both depressed and anxious. I felt unmoored because of big life changes. But then I got a message on LinkedIn from a podcast listener in South America who said, "Your work has changed my life." That single sentence allowed me to check in with my purpose and devise a plan that gave structure to my days and alleviated the hard feelings.

Because the truth is, I've never been able to become anxiety-free, no matter how many treatment modalities I've tried (and I've tried almost all of them). For me, anxiety is both a gift and a curse. It's certainly my companion in life. Anxiety has ruined a lot of days for me. It has stolen joy. But I credit much of my success to my anxiety; it makes me the unique leader I am. I'll explain why I feel this way, and you can see whether it resonates with you:

- **Anxious achievers are great at forward planning.** Anxiety is often about what lies ahead, which leads anxious people to be natural planners. We are always thinking about and anticipating what's next. This is an incredible skill for leaders because we always need to come up with creative ways to meet future challenges. The worrying that occupies my brain when applied to business planning helps drive growth. Over time I realized that my anxious nature was responsible for so much of my success as a business owner. For example, although my business started out in the blogging space was concerned enough about the rise of social media platforms like Facebook and Instagram to develop a plan to create content on them well before there was client demand.

- **We are attuned and empathetic.** Empathy is a leadership asset. It's also extremely useful when you're selling or marketing a product. How does what you're offering meet people's needs? What does your client need to feel more confident, even if they're not asking for it directly? How do they want to be seen by their colleagues? Anxious people can be very empathetic and are good at tuning in to personal and group dynamics. When we're anxious, we're concerned about what other people think about us, and we're constantly searching for clues. Sometimes this anxiety lies to us and makes us turn inward. But we can become more adept at solving problems, coming up with creative solutions, and resolving conflicts if we turn outward and ask, "I know I'm feeling the need to be heard right now. Is my colleague feeling that too, and how can I acknowledge that?" We can also manage people better. Because I knew how I reacted when I was anxious at work, I was better able to help other people manage their leadership anxiety. For example, when a client became extra demanding and was always in my inbox asking for something, I could stop and ask myself, "Does she doubt my competence, or is she just really stressed about making this strategic plan impressive to her bosses?"

- **We work hard and prepare.** Anxiety loves a goal. When you can direct your anxiety toward a specific task, you'll pour all that yearning and energy into attention to detail, thoroughness, and lots of practice. You won't miss deadlines, and you'll rock the final product. It's why we get anxious before a big speech or presentation and why we bring energy to the stage. In this book you'll learn how to create structure that supports your goals and doesn't let anxiety drive avoidance.

- **We ask for help and build infrastructure.** All good leaders know they can't do it alone. Whether it's surrounding yourself with a team you trust, structuring your days to incorporate wellness and recovery, or creating personal and professional boundaries, leading with anxiety requires creating infrastructure. We need to identify whether a pressing task feels urgent because it's anxiety speaking or because it's really a priority. Once we're clear, we can stop feeling stuck worrying and take action instead. This will help us better manage our own time—as well as others'.

Anxiety Comes with the Job

After so many years of living with anxiety and working in high-pressure environments—along with years of writing on, speaking on, and studying anxiety, leadership, and adult development—I'm convinced that anxiety is baked into effective leadership. It doesn't matter if you have a fancy title and are managing thousands of people or you're launching a tiny startup on a shoestring budget—leadership comes with a heightened set of pressures and responsibilities. When you're the one enacting a vision, setting the tone, managing people, and ensuring outcomes, much depends on you. If you're invested in the work, you're going to experience some anxiety.[1]

This is true even when things are going well and even if you don't consider yourself an anxious person or don't struggle with anxiety outside of work. While there may be differences of opinion about the nature of leadership, we can all agree that one of its defining features is an abiding concern about the future and how to prepare for it. In a real sense, then, as odd as it may sound, good leaders are paid and expected to be anxious.

When I asked Harvard Business School professor Nancy Koehn how many of the legendary leaders she studies—people like Abraham Lincoln, Winston Churchill, and John Lewis—dealt with anxiety and depression, she said, without missing a beat, "The vast majority." Koehn's research examines how leaders work from within to create positive impact in the world. "With all honesty and twenty-five years of research, all great leaders have to deal with a real variant or a real important aspect of their own fear, confusion, and often . . . borderline despair," she told me.

When leaders find themselves in pivotal moments, Koehn continued, "even if they weren't prone to anxiety, they find themselves suddenly caught up in the gales of worry and fear." But purpose and working for others "fortifies the stronger parts of you. It lowers the fear volume."

Good leaders are also paid and expected to manage teams, meaning they depend on others to achieve promised results—which comes with its own degree of anxiety. Many people struggle with relinquishing control and delegating responsibility. It's little wonder that many leaders are micromanagers, which is a common way for anxiety to reveal itself.

Further, organizations themselves can be breeding grounds for anxiety, so not only will leaders have to grapple with their individual anxiety, but they'll be expected to manage anxious people. A company's culture, for example, might be punitive, or it may expect leaders to set and meet inordinately aggressive goals, or it may reward unhealthy practices such as sleep deprivation and overwork. Organizations are also vulnerable to a variety of external threats they cannot control, such as the coronavirus pandemic or a downturn in the business cycle, which can trigger and sustain collective anxiety. This is the nature of work, and leaders will always be expected to shepherd their teams and organizations through tough times.

Systemic and ecological factors influence both our own mental health and how we react to others' anxiety at work. There is a large body of research linking experiences of systemic racism to negative mental health, including anxiety and depression.[2] Everyone in the office is a product of systemic racism, patriarchy, ableism, and economic inequality in different ways, so when your race, gender identity, sexual orientation, or educational background exists outside the majority in an organization or professional field, challenges accrue. Beyond outright discrimination, which many still face, there are psychological costs to being in an underrepresented minority group at work. In many professional organizations, people who don't fit into a cultural norm might experience the anxiety of the only, in which their difference is negatively perceived and they are expected to fit in with the dominant group.

Imagine you're the first person in your family to attend college in an office where most people seem to have multigenerational Ivy League pedigrees. You've always excelled, and now you're on your way with a promising career in a great corporate job. You like it and you're good at it, but often you feel like you don't fit in. Your background, history, and cultural identity differ from those of most of your coworkers. And then one day you're sitting in a meeting with your boss, preparing to speak, when someone makes an offhand remark about the culture of your upbringing that cuts you to the core. Was it meant for you? Was it an accident? Does it matter if it was an accident or not? A career full of such incidents creates anxiety.

Even healthy organizations generate stress and anxiety simply by the ways they are structured and managed. Multigroup and hierarchical structures trigger competition (a prime stressor) for power, influence, and status. And the almost universal practice of creating goals, plans, and budgets that are used to set direction, evaluate performance, and in many cases determine compensation naturally engenders stress and anxiety. While there's something to be said for feeling *just enough* anxiety to galvanize action and enhance performance—a theme we'll discuss throughout the book—there's no question that many people find competitive environments stressful and anxiety-provoking.

Of course, everyone in an organization brings their individual anxieties and their varying temperaments to work—it's impossible not to—
and leadership sometimes requires us to navigate difficult relationships
and manage difficult people. Even when you luck out and work with a
dream team, people are complex—"messy" might be a better descriptor—
and most of us carry unresolved issues that drive our behavior, whether
we're aware of them or not. Those of us who are anxious by nature will
react differently to stressful situations than those who are not. Some
people have neurobiological or inherited conditions like ADHD or
bipolar disorder that remain undiagnosed and produce anxiety and difficult behavior. And *all* of us act out anxieties and old hurts we don't
even realize we have. Leaders need to be prepared to guide their teams
through the baggage of interpersonal "stuff" that drives individual behavior, and thus business and organizational life.

All of which is to say: Anxiety comes with the job. You *will* be dealing
with anxiety in one way or another, directly or indirectly, on a daily basis.
So the only effective approach is to become skilled in managing it and to
even use it to your advantage. As much as we may want to make anxiety
disappear, the answer is not to try to wish it away, work it away, drink it
away, exercise it away, or hide, deny, or suppress it away.

The answer is to get the help you need when anxiety begins to undermine your well-being and your job performance, and then begin to
look deep and try to understand what's causing your anxiety to rise.
This is where a competent, caring mental health professional can be of
tremendous value, and thankfully, anxiety is highly treatable.

But I'll be blunt: if you do not look your anxiety in the face at some
point, it can take you down. So don't stop with the quick fix that
assuages your uncomfortable feelings in the short term. Instead, bravely
explore your history and inner drivers, and get curious about the factors
that are giving rise to your anxiety. How deeply rooted are these
causes? Are your anxiety and its triggers part of a larger pattern? How
do you act out your anxious impulses at work? What are the effects of
those actions?

The overall goal here is twofold: to get to a place where you're aware
of what makes you anxious and how you typically respond to anxiety,

and to create a dependable tool kit to call upon so that you can excel in your work life, no matter what challenge anxiety may throw your way. Believe it or not, you *can* lead with authority and impact even when you're feeling anxious. You can inspire and motivate others even when your mind and heart are racing and you feel deeply unsure of yourself.

If all this sounds too good to be true, all I can say is: read on. You will meet many amazing people in this book, leaders who have reached the pinnacle of success and influence while living with serious mental and emotional challenges. These leaders have learned to lead consciously, in full awareness of their anxiety triggers and go-to remedies. And in many cases, they've even learned to make anxiety their personal guide— the advantage that gives them an edge over their competitors and that fuels their drive and distinguishes them in their fields.

The Vast Range of Mental Health

To begin learning how to work with your anxiety, we should become acquainted with some basics on mental health and on how and why anxiety functions as it does. It may help to begin by picturing mental health on a spectrum. We're not talking strictly about mental *illness*, but rather any experience of mental or emotional distress. At one end of the spectrum, there's minor, everyday stress that's irritating but easy to deal with; at the other, a clinical mental health condition that leaves you miserable and nonfunctional.

In between these two extremes—which is where most of life happens—lies an incredibly vast range of mental health symptoms and experiences. Within it is everything from sadness to unease to anxiety to burnout to brain fog to depression, each of which can fluctuate in both severity and frequency. I have clinical anxiety and depression, for example, but on some days life feels wonderful and on others, especially if I'm dealing with a crisis at work and haven't slept well, my anxiety revs up and pushes me toward the unhealthier end of the spectrum.

The point is, there is a wide range of difficult mental health experiences, and we'll *all* experience some of them at some time or another. In fact, results from a recent American Psychological Association study found that up to 80 percent of people will undergo a diagnosable mental health condition, such as anxiety, major depression, or a substance use disorder. Mental illness is so common that researchers were led to conclude that "experiencing a diagnosable mental disorder at some point during the life course is the *norm*, not the exception," and that "individuals whose lives remain free from mental disorder are, in fact, remarkably few in number." How few? According to this study, which followed participants from birth to midlife, 17 percent.[3]

Now, I hope you can see the silver lining here. If you were ever worried that you were the only one struggling, you can lay that fear to rest. (Or maybe you find comfort in knowing that the unflappable colleague who always seems to have it together is probably just a very good actor.) Mental distress is simply part of the human condition. Most of the time, these difficult feelings pass once the difficult situation resolves, and even for those of us with a diagnosed mental health condition, the severity and frequency of symptoms change according to events, therapeutic interventions, and preventive measures. Some resolve with the right treatment. I find it comforting to remember that we're all in this together, that we have plenty of resources for getting better, and that what seems impossible today can look very different tomorrow.

This spectrum of experience, however, brings up some key questions: What's the difference between everyday stress and serious anxiety, and at what point does anxiety become problematic enough to be a true anxiety *disorder*?

To begin with, stress and anxiety share some similarities, but they are not the same. It's important to distinguish between the two because the differences highlight a reassuring feature of anxiety. Stress is what we feel in the face of a real threat, which is typically something *outside* us—a near miss on the freeway, the need to justify a budget shortfall, a rumor of layoffs. While the source of stress is external—events and situations that often are not under our control—anxiety's origins are *internal* and often boil down to a fear of what might happen. The Anxiety and Depression Association of America states the distinction simply: "Stress is a response to a threat in a situation. Anxiety is a reaction to the stress."

While stress and anxiety can produce identical mental and physical symptoms—worry, irritability, insomnia, heart palpitations, sweaty palms, headaches, shakiness—stress's symptoms subside once the external threat (the stressor) goes away or the problem is solved. With anxiety, on the other hand, the bad feelings can linger even after a concerning event has passed or there is no clear threat at all.

We have little control over a car that suddenly changes lanes—or just the everyday stressors and pressures that come with work—but anxiety is a different story. Because anxiety is an internal emotion that our brains create, *we can learn to manage it*, even though we may sometimes feel helpless in its grip. We can understand how and why our brains conjure internal anxiety, which gives us the power to address it and not live at its mercy.

I want to emphasize that experiencing both stress and anxiety is completely normal, and that even moments of high anxiety, such as having a panic attack, don't necessarily mean that you have an anxiety disorder.

Anxiety that has become troublesome enough to warrant a clinical diagnosis is characterized by two things. First, it's excessive and overwhelming, out of proportion to the situation. Instead of the normal jitters most everyone feels before making a speech, for example, you find yourself obsessing over how you're going to make a fool of yourself, hyperventilating and nauseous.

Second, it interferes with or prevents you from carrying out everyday activities. Being anxious about driving on an icy road is perfectly normal, but if your fear keeps you off the road all winter, you're in anxiety disorder territory. Likewise, in our previous example, if you go out of your way to avoid speaking in public, even if your dream job requires it or deep down you really, really want to have a more visible presence, that's likely an indicator of an anxiety disorder.

Missed opportunities are one of the greatest tragedies of unmanaged anxiety. If we don't learn to manage it, our anxiety can prevent us from doing the things we really want to do and being the people we really want to be.

Or sometimes, even if we're able to power through instances that make us anxious, the means we use to get through can exact too high a price. Scott Stossel, the national editor of the *Atlantic*, writes compellingly in his book *My Age of Anxiety* about his lifelong struggles, which included drinking vodka before talking to groups. Such stories are extremely common. Many of us have tried to self-medicate or have engaged in unhealthy behaviors to cope with anxiety.

If this sounds like you, try this simple thought exercise right now: Envision the person you would be if anxiety weren't holding you back. Picture that person in full, vivid detail. Who are you? Where are you? What are you doing? What's the impact you're having? Is that you, ringing the opening bell at the New York Stock Exchange? Is that you, leading a cohesive and motivated team to design a product that improves the lives of millions? Is that you, founding a series of wildly successful startups, then retiring at forty-five to spend your time mentoring young entrepreneurs? Is that you, leaving your corporate job and happily engaging in the solo business you've dreamed of operating out of your home? Is that you, getting on the plane for your business trip, sober and calm and not scared you're going to crash?

Or would you simply like to wake up each morning without a pit in your stomach?

Whatever your dream, remember that person. *This is who you are without the impediment of unexamined, unmanaged anxiety.* And this is the person to whom you'll draw ever closer as you learn how to make anxiety your partner.

Anxiety, Your Loyal Partner

When anxiety is making you miserable, it's easy to see it as an enemy that must be vanquished at all costs. But brain science reveals a different story.

The brain's main job, quite literally, is to keep us alive. It does this not only by regulating things such as heart rate, blood pressure, and body temperature, but by constantly scanning our environment for potential threats. All of this occurs without our conscious awareness in the limbic system, thought to be the oldest, most primordial part of the brain.

The area of the limbic system we want to zero in on is a complex structure of cells called the amygdala. It's here that our basic survival mechanisms meet up with our emotions—and not always favorably. Sometimes referred to as our "threat detector," the amygdala processes fearful or threatening stimuli, triggering the fight, flight, or freeze response when it perceives danger. The amygdala also plays a role in attaching emotional significance to events, which helps encode them in memory. This is why it's so much easier to remember things that are highly emotional, like the birth of a child or that epic fight with your partner—or an event that scares the crap out of you.

When your brain encodes frightening events into your long-term memory, it's doing so out of a basic survival instinct: it wants you to avoid situations it perceives as dangerous. And because the amygdala is, evolutionarily speaking, such an old part of the brain, its core training occurred in a time when humans routinely encountered life-threatening dangers like saber-toothed tigers and wolf packs. Though most of us rarely encounter such perils today, this primitive part of our brain still sometimes acts—and reacts—as if we do. Quite simply, we're wired for fear because we're wired for survival.

But here's the thing. Some of us have a hypervigilant amygdala, one that's a little too excitable and overprotective. A bunch of us have an amygdala that's both hypervigilant *and* trigger-happy, leaving us jumpy and prone to assuming that behind every rustling bush lurks a saber-toothed tiger, when it's just the wind.

Famed psychologist Rollo May observed that "anxiety is essential to the human condition," and he meant this quite literally. Anxiety exists to keep us from harm. But in the anxious individual, things can go haywire. "We are no longer prey to tigers and mastodons, but to damage to our self-esteem, ostracism by our group, or the threat of losing out in the competitive struggle," May wrote back in 1977. "The form of anxiety has changed, but the experience remains relatively the same."[4] Christine Runyan, clinical psychologist and professor of medicine at the University of Massachusetts, agrees. "When we're faced with any uncertainty, small-scale or large-scale, real or imagined, our threat appraisal system is activated," she explains.

I want to underscore a key point Runyan makes for leaders: the threat appraisal system fires in response to *any uncertainty*. And what job doesn't include uncertainty? Markets can be volatile, valued team members can resign, recessions can occur, pandemics can sweep the globe, supply chains can be disrupted. For many people, anxiety boils down to a fear of an uncertain future, and part of the responsibility of leadership is anticipating the future as best we can and making decisions that we hope will deliver desired outcomes. But, of course, there's no guarantee. With so much uncertainty baked into the nature of leadership, it's no wonder so many leaders operate from a baseline of heightened anxiety.

And there's the rub. The amygdala can't discern the difference between a threat that actually imperils our lives—the grizzly bear we stumble upon while hiking—and an event that just *feels* life-threatening, like presenting an earnings estimate to the board. Either way, if the brain detects anything it interprets as a threat, it will automatically launch the fight, flight, or freeze response. And when *that* happens, we experience the cascade of physical and emotional responses that are familiar to all of us: a pounding heart, rapid breathing, muscle tension and trembling, sweating, and possibly nausea or other digestive issues. *Fear.* This is the body's way of readying us to fight a perceived enemy, run from it, or play dead in the hopes it will move on.

All of which is appropriate and very welcome when our lives or the life of someone we love is on the line—we need an enormous influx of adrenaline, speed, strength, and heightened focus if we stumble upon a grizzly bear. But those of us who experience excessive anxiety can feel this kind of five-alarm fear in response to events that aren't life-threatening at all. Once the brain, ever on a quest for efficiency, learns the neural pathways between a perceived threat and an activated threat appraisal system, it can become habituated to experiencing an anxiety response and sending our bodies into overdrive.

The brain's automatic response creates one of the more frustrating aspects of anxiety: it is often irrational. We *know* it makes no sense to panic over the prospect of making small talk at a networking event, yet here we are in the corner, sweating and trembling and unable to rationalize our way out of it. Or we may find ourselves in a near-constant state of slightly elevated anxiety, gripped by worry and a vague sense of dread for no discernible reason.

Now, with all of this said, you may be wondering where I get off describing anxiety as a partner or a gift. It all goes back to the origins of anxiety: its very reason for being is to keep us safe. So anxiety itself is not our enemy. On the contrary, it was designed to be our friend and protector, to keep us out of harm's way.

I've found it enormously helpful to remember this basic truth and to use it as the foundation from which to begin learning how to work with my anxiety, rather than fight a losing battle against it. When my anxiety starts to escalate, I remind myself that my brain isn't broken and my anxiety isn't out to take me down. My brain is actually functioning in a way that's logical, expected, and even benevolent. It's trying to protect me from a perceived threat.

When I can put a little distance between me and my anxiety, I can treat my anxiety more calmly, thank it for overachieving in trying to protect me, and ask myself what set it off. There is great benefit in adopting this intellectual and psychological shift, from seeing anxiety as an enemy to be exterminated to seeing it as an overeager friend who's trying so very hard to help. You'll start from a place of collaboration and, on a good day, maybe even gratitude.

If you are far from that point, that's OK. Learning to live with anxiety as your friend and partner takes time. The good news is, just as your brain has learned the neural pathways for habitually launching an anxiety response, it can form new neural connections based on your choices, actions, and behaviors—a phenomenon known as *neuroplasticity*. That means we do not have to be helpless before our anxiety.

So while you're not going to think your way out of an anxiety disorder, you can take action that will change your thinking, which will in turn positively change your behavior and make your anxiety more manageable. No matter how entrenched your anxiety feels, it is always possible to change, improve, and learn new coping skills.

And that's an area where we overachievers happen to excel.

2

Anxiety Is a
Double-Edged Sword

Alyssa Mastromonaco built a long and storied career in politics, but she is perhaps best known for her White House role as the deputy chief of staff for operations in the Obama administration—the youngest person ever to hold that position. (For fans of *The West Wing*, she was President Obama's Josh Lyman.) Post-Obama, Mastromonaco became chief operating officer of Vice Media and then president of global communications strategy and talent at A&E Networks. She's also a *New York Times* bestselling author, a contributing editor to *Marie Claire*, and cohost of the Crooked Media podcast *Hysteria*. And she's accomplished all of this while suffering from both anxiety and irritable bowel syndrome (IBS), which anxiety often exacerbates.

President Barack Obama relied on Mastromonaco for more than a decade (starting before he was president) when managing everything from government shutdowns, to evacuating American citizens from Cairo after Hosni Mubarak was deposed, to helping the Affordable Care Act get passed. You could hardly have a more fast-paced, stressful, and all-consuming job, so how does an anxious person thrive in such an environment?

Well, like many anxious achievers, Mastromonaco credits her anxiety with the extreme focus and productivity that led her to be so effective. "I now understand my anxiety back then was a utility," she told me. "I think that, because I was so present, I kept it totally under control and used it to my advantage." In Mastromonaco's case, anxiety propelled her to constantly think ahead, not only anticipating potential problems but identifying multiple solutions for each of them. "Part of my anxiety makes me fastidious," she said. "Because the more that you have under control, the more you know what's coming, the less stress you have." And that translates to less stress and more progress for your team, your managers, and your organization.

While an untreated anxiety disorder will undermine your ability to lead sooner or later, living with *managed* anxiety is a different story. Managed anxiety can enhance productivity and give you a competitive edge, and anxious leaders who've learned to work *with* their anxiety can actually do better than others under stressful conditions. In a tough time, people who aren't used to processing anxiety might be up all night, while we're able to sleep. When a crisis hits, we're ready to go because we've probably mentally rehearsed the situation a million times. Data even shows that the brains of anxious people process threats in a different region than the brains of more laid-back people do—an area responsible for *action*.[1] Far from an impediment, this rapid reaction to a threat or a fearful situation is a decisive advantage. There may even be a sense of relief that the problem is here and we can put all that nervous energy to good use!

We anxious leaders who have learned to leverage our anxiety have much to teach others, because we know how to manage our fears so that they can be assets instead of liabilities. For example, I've learned that my socially anxious nature makes me an attuned, curious, and thoughtful listener, a skill that has driven my career in sales and marketing more than any number of showy presentations. Likewise, Mastromonaco's hypervigilance and her sixth sense for knowing exactly what's needed in a crisis made her the perfect person for her high-stakes, high-impact role.

Anxious people have become so accustomed to focusing on the future and what it might bring that, like Mastromonaco, we already have multiple solutions ready to deploy when something goes wrong, and we're poised to seize opportunities that others may not even recognize. In an economic crisis, the anxiety that keeps us up at night may help us fathom a way to keep our business open. We are also more comfortable sitting with uncomfortable feelings—and there are plenty of those to deal with over the course of a career. When channeled thoughtfully, anxiety can motivate us to be more conscientious, more aware of interpersonal dynamics, and more attentive to detail, as well as to produce results more quickly. It can break down barriers and create new bonds. It can make our teams more resourceful, productive, and creative, and it can make us more resilient.

So in this chapter, I'll help you understand the other side of anxiety, so you can start to see it in a new light. Far from being useless or always harmful, anxiety offers leadership advantages. The key is to make the most of its positive aspects while mitigating the negative. You may not be able to rid yourself of anxiety, or even totally control it, but you can learn to manage it in ways that benefit you and strengthen your effectiveness. And maybe you'll turn out to be one of those leaders who credits their anxiety for helping them get where they are, even though it's been a bumpy path.

The Relationship between Mental Health and Success

When I coined the term "entrepreneurship porn" back in 2014, I didn't think too much about how our obsession with business legends' highs, lows, and near misses sugarcoats and glamorizes habits that can lead to poor mental health, like chronic sleep deprivation and overwork.

What these stories mask is the anxiety, depression, and other mental health struggles so many top performers feel. There is a growing body of evidence suggesting that mental ill health—a term that encompasses both diagnosable mental health disorders and acute mental health challenges—is more prevalent among the highly successful.

In one oft-cited study that focuses on entrepreneurs, mental health issues were found to affect 72 percent of the participants in the sample group. The entrepreneurs were more likely to report having any mental health condition (49 percent), depression (30 percent), ADHD (29 percent), substance use (12 percent), and bipolar disorder (11 percent), compared with the control group.[2] More recently, 2021 data from a survey by Mind Share Partners, SAP, and Qualtrics found that executive and C-level respondents were 82 percent and 78 percent more likely, respectively, to report at least one mental health symptom than managers and individual contributors.[3] Some studies have observed that CEOs experience depression at more than *double* the rate of the general population, perhaps because the job is so high pressure, isolating, and draining.[4] For probably much the same reason, it's estimated that a little more than 10 percent of those in management positions have a substance use disorder.[5] There is even evidence of a higher prevalence of psychopathy among senior executives: while about 1 percent of the general population displays psychopathic behaviors, among senior execs the rate climbs to 3.5 percent.[6]

Why do the highly driven and successful seem to be disproportionately affected by mental ill health? It's a fascinating conundrum that scientists have yet to fully understand, but some researchers have observed that the very qualities that enable high achievers to excel have a dark side when they're taken to the extreme. For example, hyperfocus, relentless dedication, risk-taking, and outsized ambition are the hallmarks of many highly successful people, but they can come with serious mental health consequences if they're taken too far, or if they're not balanced out with mitigating habits and qualities. Without proper guardrails, for instance, hyperfocus can devolve into overthinking, rumination, or obsession. Relentless dedication can become overwork and lead to burnout, especially if you're depriving yourself of sleep and social connection. Risk-taking—if you're making leaps without the input of your team, or making impulsive decisions from a place of anxiety—can spell disaster. Outsize ambition can lead you to take on an unsustainable pace, and can result in anxiety and depression if you don't meet the (possibly unrealistic) goals you've set for yourself.

Now, obviously, having any or even all of these qualities doesn't mean you have a mental health disorder—and good leaders need each of them to some degree. The key takeaway is this: the correlation between being highly driven and successful and having a greater-than-average risk of mental ill health underscores the need for habits that support performance *and* mental health. Proper self-care, which includes things like sufficient sleep, therapy, exercise, a healthy diet, breaks from work, and social support, is nonnegotiable. This is true for every leader who's striving for top performance, but especially for those of us who are prone to anxiety or have a mental health diagnosis.

Self-care for success also includes, as much as you're able, creating the work environment that best supports your personality and your mental health. My mental health vastly improved when I got out of my corporate jobs and began to work for myself from home, where I could control my schedule and my environment. The same goes for your role: find or create work that aligns with your strengths and personality traits and, just as importantly, that minimizes exposure to known vulnerabilities and anxiety triggers. If you're a gregarious extrovert who thrives on social connection, for instance, working alone in your basement is not the best fit for your mental health or your success.

Because stress and anxiety come with the job, and because both will escalate as career gains bring more scrutiny and expectations, you'll want to make sure your supports are in place so that you're able to skillfully handle the increasing demands on your time, responsibilities, and output. When we get busy and overscheduled, our self-care practices and downtime activities are often the first things to go. But we anxious achievers need to view self-care as indispensable—as much so as our work products. Without adequate support and self-care, it's just too easy for elevated stress to morph into problematic anxiety, for exhaustion and overwork to escalate to burnout, or for unhealthy coping mechanisms to become bad habits that sabotage our success. Left unchecked, a downward emotional spiral can even trigger a serious mental health condition, and it will certainly worsen an existing diagnosis.

Alyssa Mastromonaco, who so effectively leveraged her anxious nature to produce extraordinary results, eventually reached a point where she could no longer sustain the intense pace and extreme stress of her job. Her wake-up call came in the form of frequent IBS attacks and, eventually, a physical and mental exhaustion so profound that she wound up in the White House medical unit, unable to function. It took two months for her to get back to full capacity.

But Mastromonaco's true recovery didn't begin until after she left the White House and suddenly had massive amounts of free time and nowhere to channel her anxiety. She became severely depressed and took six months off. But "instead of actually doing the decompression work I needed to do, I cried a lot . . . and became very fixated on finding a job, because I thought that the feelings would go away if I found a job and worked someplace," she says. Mastromonaco landed another high-intensity, high-stress job, now with the added difficulty of transitioning into a culture that was fundamentally different from that of the White House. Once again, her body issued an SOS. After unbearable stomach pain sent Mastromonaco to the emergency room three times in less than a month, a friend referred her to a gastroenterologist. And it was there that she finally learned what was at the root of her struggles, and how to get better.

She describes it like this: "'Here's the thing,' the gastroenterologist said. 'You have IBS, but you have severe anxiety, and you have made it so much worse.' I had just kept stuffing it down and stuffing it down till my body was like, 'Stop it. We're not OK.'" Mastromonaco got into therapy and began antidepressants, and, true to her nature, she began openly sharing her struggles with IBS and anxiety. Today she still has anxiety, but she is very much OK, because she did the work to get better and learned how to benefit from the positive aspects of her anxiety, while leaving the harmful effects behind.

Anxiety's Bad Rap

Many times over the years, I've encountered the belief that anxiety is an unproductive and harmful emotional state, and thus should be eradicated by any means necessary. A few times I've received pushback from those who believe that so-called negative emotions—such as anxiety, anger, distress, or sadness—are detrimental and do not serve us, and therefore should be eliminated (or somehow let go of). As a person who's suffered deeply and for so long from the negative effects of anxiety, I completely understand where these sentiments come from. None of us want to be in pain, and an unmanaged anxiety disorder *is* unproductive and harmful. It serves no one.

And yet I would be the first to say that anxiety has gotten a bad rap, and that trying to eradicate or eliminate it—or any other difficult emotion, for that matter—will ultimately undermine your leadership and your mental health.

If you're anxious by nature, this is just part of who you are. While you can learn to reduce anxiety's harmful effects and respond to anxiety in healthier, more productive ways, there's no intervention that will make this core part of your personality simply disappear. You don't need to feel bad about who you are, and you don't need to waste time trying to be someone you're not. Maybe you have some things to work on— who doesn't—but fundamentally, you are OK just as you are. You have contributions to offer the world that only you, with all your unique skills and hang-ups and experiences, can.

I experienced a real turning point when I accepted that I don't have to reach some unattainable goal of perfect mental and emotional health before I produce good work, and I don't have to change my nature or somehow "cure" myself of anxiety. Rather, the goal is to stop reacting mindlessly to anxiety, which so often results in poor decision-making and furthers our unhappiness, and to start responding mindfully when anxiety arrives. From a more mindful state, you can begin to uncover the advantages that your anxious nature brings.

Wendy Suzuki, professor of neuroscience and psychology at New York University, is one of the leading voices in pushing back against the conventional wisdom that anxiety is always bad. Her work in neuroplasticity—the brain's ability to adapt in response to its environment— became the cornerstone of her research on how we can take control of our anxiety and make it a useful tool rather than a negative, unproductive feeling that controls us.

The key is to find a balance between this desirable state where we're alert and poised to act, and the negative anxiety that compromises our functioning. "Good anxiety," as Suzuki defines it, is the body-brain space where we're engaged, alert, and we feel *just stressed enough* to maximize our attention and focus on what we want to do. "Think about when you performed the best," she says. "For me, it was when I was nervous, I was a little bit scared." In fact, before a big talk, if she's not nervous, she knows that she's not taking her preparation seriously enough. So instead, Suzuki actually welcomes her anxiety as "activation energy" to keep herself motivated and focused.

But what if you can't yet locate that sweet spot between good, productive anxiety, and bad, unmanageable anxiety? What if your anxiety is so painful that you just want to run away from it?

First of all, cut yourself some slack. Experiencing unpleasant feelings is difficult, and it's natural to want to run away. "We all need constant practice simply sitting with our feelings, sitting with the discomfort, and not trying to immediately mask, deny, escape, or distract ourselves," Suzuki says. Sitting with the discomfort accomplishes two things: "You get accustomed to the [anxious] feeling and realize that you can indeed survive it, and you give yourself time and space in your brain to make a more conscious decision about how to act or respond. This is exactly how a new, more positive neural pathway is established."[7] We can, in effect, retrain our brains to respond to anxious feelings in new, more generative ways. If it's easier, you can even practice accepting the anxious feelings and letting them flow through you without reacting to them. We can learn to accept that anxiety, while unpleasant, won't kill us, and we can even welcome it as a productive force.

This will indeed take some practice, but "practice is precisely why those of us who suffer from anxiety have a clear advantage of developing this superpower," Suzuki says. "Why? Because reassessment can only come when you are aware of what's not working for you, and anxiety is the emotion that pinpoints exactly that. . . . There is no better motivator to tell you what you need to work on than your own array of anxiety triggers. They can be a path forward to some of the best realizations and shifts you can make in your life today."[8]

Suzuki describes one such example from her own life, a difficult period when she was overworked, lonely, and feeling generally dissatisfied. She implemented lifestyle changes that helped her body feel better (exercise, better nutrition, and meditation), but she also began to pay attention to her anxiety, and found it had a story to tell. "My anxiety was a big red flashing sign that was really saying, *You need more social interaction and friends and friendship and love in your life! You are not a robot that only works! Pay attention to all these negative emotions I'm sending you; they are giving you a message! These negative emotions are VALUABLE!*"[9]

Anxious feelings could be your brain's way of alerting you that you need to make a change. Here is yet another way in which anxiety is our loyal friend, a way in which it offers a hidden gift. Those vague feelings of dissatisfaction and uneasiness? Maybe they're signaling that you're in a career that isn't the best fit. All that ruminating and restlessness that occurs like clockwork when you're faced with that task you dread? Maybe your anxiety is telling you that your skills lie elsewhere.

When you can become comfortable enough with negative feelings to hear and heed their message, real transformation can occur. Then, Suzuki says, you have the opportunity "to do something different, to do something in a different way, to maybe do something in a way that nobody on earth has done before."[10] Lucky you!

Once we're able to sit with that anxiety and learn from it, we've adopted what Suzuki calls "an activist mindset." This is what we'll need in order to tap into anxiety's generative powers and eventually unlock the anxiety superpowers she identifies, such as better focus, stronger physical and emotional resilience, higher productivity and performance, and boosted creativity, empathy, and compassion.

Suzuki shares the story of Monica (not her real name), a startup consultant who specialized in business development. Monica was so driven and successful that she'd earned the nickname "Wonder Woman." She'd also suffered from problematic anxiety her entire life. In her early career, her anxious nature showed up as obsessing "over every move and every last decision," and it became so burdensome that Monica considered switching careers.

Then she realized the obsessive tendencies that were leading her to worry and question every move were a business asset. Rather than trying to rid herself of the uncomfortable feelings she experienced when she was under pressure, Monica chose to train her attention to identify all the possible pitfalls of a particular situation. The resulting "what-if list" she created became "a tool to help her do a more effective and complete evaluation of any business proposition at hand." Since that realization, Monica not only expected her anxiety to surface when she needed to make a business decision, she *wanted* it to. "Embracing my anxiety has made me a much more effective entrepreneur," she says.[11]

And that, really, is the key. What are the advantages your anxious nature brings? Can you identify them, celebrate them as positives, and use them to enhance your performance?

Rightsizing Your Anxiety

David Barlow is the founder and director emeritus for the Center for Anxiety and Related Disorders at Boston University. He's an expert with decades of clinical research experience on the nature and treatment of anxiety disorders, and when I interviewed him for the *Anxious Achiever* podcast, he said something worth remembering when you're feeling discouraged about your anxiety. "I think it's important to remember that you *want* to be moderately anxious," Barlow said. "Moderate anxiety is your friend."

The best approach for anxious leaders who want to perform at their best, he continued, is to find the just-right, Goldilocks level of anxiety, not too much and not too little. "You don't want to eliminate your anxiety," Barlow said. "Anxiety is there for a reason. It's a normal human emotion, and . . . a very important part of our functioning. Without it . . . the performance of our athletes, entertainers, executives, artisans, and students would suffer. Creativity would diminish. Our crops and food might not be planted." Moderate anxiety, in short, ensures that we'll be prepared and perform at our best.

Scott Stossel, the national editor of the *Atlantic*, is a lifelong anxiety disorder sufferer, and he told me that as bad as anxious traits can be, there's often an associated good trait or silver lining. Socially anxious people who worry about how they're coming across, for instance, tend to be more empathetic and conscientious precisely because they're so attentive to the temperature of a room and the reactions of each individual. "You're probably better able to project yourself into other people's points of view than somebody who is low in anxiety, and therefore [you] may be better able to relate to people," Stossel said. "As a manager, it can make you more effective because you're better able to anticipate how something you're saying or communicating, or your company is communicating, will come across to a given individual, and you'll be better able to help them manage that."

Similarly, the anxious response of hypervigilance, in which you're constantly scanning your environment for threats, has the potential to become a force for good if you learn how to keep it in check. "In a work environment, it means you're very attuned to what's going on," Stossel said. And even if you're reading situations too negatively, "you're probably going to be more prepared for bad things that come around. You can think around corners."

The Superpower We Didn't Know We Needed

One business leader I've interviewed on the podcast who's really learned to put his anxiety to work is Harley Finkelstein, founder and president of Shopify, one of the biggest and most profitable e-commerce companies in the world. Finkelstein is an anxious achiever from way back: he's had anxiety and a gift for entrepreneurship since childhood. He launched his first business at just thirteen. When he wanted to be a DJ and couldn't get hired, he started his own DJ company. Then when Finkelstein was seventeen, just months after beginning college at McGill University, the stock market crashed and his family lost everything. The obvious next move was to drop out and move back home to work full-time. But Finkelstein thought there had to be a way to remain in school and support his family, and he found the solution in entrepreneurship. Within just a few years, the T-shirt business he launched as a freshman was selling apparel to more than fifty universities across Canada.

"That was not driven by passion," Finkelstein said. "That was not driven by interests. That was not driven by some incredible ambition. That was driven by anxiety. That was driven by this need to survive." Finkelstein's anxiety had him jumping out of bed at six every morning, raring to go. That was when it first clicked for him that anxiety could be an advantage. "This thing that I have could actually be incredibly effective in terms of achieving some sort of entrepreneurial goal or some sort of business objective," he said.

Which is not to say that anxiety hasn't negatively impacted Finkelstein's quality of life at times. When he was a kid, anxiety manifested as temper tantrums. As a teenager, it showed up as fights with his parents. As a twentysomething entrepreneur, it was the refusal to examine the roots of his anxiety and learn how to manage it in a healthier way. "Ironically, I spent [a] couple of years trying to get rid of my anxiety, because I thought that's what I should do," Finkelstein said. "It was only towards my late twenties that I realized I can't get rid of this thing. This is part of me. What I can do, however, is I can manage it better and I can make sure that this superpower gets honed."

These days, Finkelstein manages his anxiety through therapy, daily meditation, exercise, breath work, and careful scheduling that builds in work hours and protects his time with family. His deep self-awareness has enabled him to identify the tools he needs to be an amazingly effective achiever and to keep his anxiety in check when it begins to escalate—and, on the other hand, to lean on it as a superpower when the situation calls for it.

For example, if he's nervous ahead of a big public speaking event, Finkelstein does a deep-breathing exercise that activates the parasympathetic nervous system (also known as our "rest and digest" system). It's "a three-minute practice that immediately reduces my anxiety, immediately makes me more focused, and makes me less nervous," Finkelstein said. But when he needs to remain high-energy, he welcomes the presence of anxiety. "When I'm preparing for something that's really important—the IPO, for example, or an earnings call, or negotiating a very important business deal, I actually want to use some of that anxiety to anticipate all the things that could go wrong," he said. "It provides me with this incredible checklist of things that most people would never think of." Anxious achievers' ability to anticipate problems and double-check everything allows them to put guardrails in place ahead of time so that potential problems simply won't happen.

Another leader who credits her anxiety as an indispensable ingredient in her success is Andrea Parra Vera, a Procter & Gamble research and development manager based in Brazil. After Parra Vera heard Finkelstein and others on the podcast refer to their anxiety as a superpower, she reached out to me on LinkedIn. "I heard this and I laughed so hard, because it is," she said.

Originally from Venezuela, Parra Vera described growing up in a country destabilized by hyperinflation, political persecution, and a shortage of basic necessities like medicine, water, and electricity. She knew from the age of twelve that she needed "an exit strategy" for herself and her family. "I grew up scared of my life developing in this country where I had no idea if I was going to be able to have a future for myself," she said. "I grew up anxious and worried that anything could happen at any time."

Parra Vera put that anxiety to work by becoming an overachiever in everything. "I started every language that I could, I graduated top of my class," she said. "I tried to find the absolute best job that I could. So overall I felt like I had to be the very best I could be. I had to be like, if there's a bone in my body that has potential, I'm going to squeeze it out because I need to get every opportunity that I can so I can leave this situation and also be of help to everyone that is around me." Parra Vera took it upon herself to complete her education and earn enough money to move her parents and brother out of Venezuela. She acknowledges that such an enormous endeavor—and believing that it was up to her alone—came from the anxiety-driven story she told herself. But she also credits her anxiety with the perseverance to be a trailblazer who changed her family's lives for the better. "I don't think I would have done it without that ambitious overachiever mindset," she said.

Now that her family is safe and Parra Vera is in a demanding leadership role, I was curious how her anxiety shows up in her work life and how she handles it. She described experiences that will be familiar to so many of us: bouts of impostor syndrome, worry about whether she's doing enough, worry over being prepared for the next crisis, worry over "the worst possible outcome." What helps her? Therapy, herbal tea, journaling to externalize and process her emotions, and being transparent about her anxiety at work. In fact, when Parra Vera asked for flexibility in her schedule that would better support her mental health, she received not only full support but help from HR to launch a program about mental well-being at work. "My personal mission is to bring that message of, we're human beings, it's OK to have struggles in your day-to-day," she said. "Everyone at work is not perfect. You can have challenges and you can learn how to deal with them, and that doesn't make you less of a professional."

Though most of us won't experience the extreme circumstances Parra Vera did, many anxious achievers have put their anxiety to work to create better lives for themselves and their families, and every leader will be called upon to negotiate high-stakes, anxiety-provoking situations from time to time. What Parra Vera has done so well, and what all of us can learn to do, is what psychologists sometimes refer to as *defanging our anxiety*. Anxiety doesn't disappear, but you can learn to take the bite out of it and render it less damaging. Parra Vera defanged her anxiety by talking about it, and in turn she helped a lot of other people at her company defang their anxiety as well.

Anxiety *is* a superpower, Parra Vera said. "We just have to tone it down so it doesn't take that much out of us."

Instead of a harmful impediment to leadership, anxiety is a helpful ingredient. The key is learning how to manage it so that serves us, while leaving behind the kind of debilitating anxiety that can undermine our leadership and inhibit our growth.

3

Uncover Your Triggers and Tells

Let's face it: Anxiety is weird. It's inconsistent and often makes no sense. What one person experiences as threatening another barely registers, and it's not uncommon for seemingly contradictory anxiety responses to exist in the same person. I've talked to so many leaders who have no problem delivering a keynote speech before thousands, but suffer panic attacks over the mere thought of dinner-party small talk. Others find high-contact jobs invigorating but decompensate when they're alone, feeling intense bouts of anxiety or depression; still others thrive alone and become drained, anxious, and depressed from lots of face time. Even people we traditionally think of as brave—skydivers, cliff jumpers, fearless investors—are sometimes beset with crippling internal anxiety.

In some cases, anxiety actually *drives* people to take on risky behavior that most of us would avoid. The stakes feel so high that risk is the only way to for them solve a problem and reduce anxiety. Shopify president Harley Finkelstein, who we met in chapter 2, has been anxious *and* entrepreneurial since he was a young child. Investor and startup consultant Andy Johns, who has worked at or advised *eight* early-stage companies that became worth more than a billion dollars, says anxiety "contributed to my ability to perform well at work while simultaneously also making it very hard to keep my head on straight."

Your experience of anxiety can be tightly focused on a certain situation or area—a phobia, for example—or it could manifest as a pervasive sense of unease or dread. Anxiety can also come in the guise of behaviors our society and work cultures reward: perfectionism, overwork, excessive concern for the well-being of your family or team. It can coexist with other mental health challenges, such as depression. It can be a constant companion, always simmering on the back burner, or it can flare in response to certain triggers or situations.

The point is, anxiety's forms are legion. It is highly specific from person to person—what causes it, how it manifests in our bodies and in our emotions, and how we respond when we're triggered. So in this chapter, I'm going to ask you to take a hard look at yourself and how your anxiety plays out at work. Identifying and facing your anxieties can be difficult and even painful. You may feel that focusing on them will only make them stronger or cause an anxiety attack. Or you may fear that recalling anxieties that arose from some humiliating public failure may take you back to relive the agony.

Have faith, though. Decades of research have shown that those who understand their feelings have higher job satisfaction, stronger job performance, and better relationships. They're more innovative, and can synthesize diverse opinions and deescalate conflict. Their self-awareness makes them knowledgeable about what gets to them, enabling them to prevent anxious situations at work. They're able to respond to anxiety and stressors in a far more effective manner for themselves and their team, leading to better outcomes for everyone. Why? They understand themselves and what triggers their anxieties. They have created strategies to manage anxiety instead of just coping as well as they can and pushing through. They are no longer trapped by acting out automatic behaviors that punish themselves and their team.

Moreover, social psychology research has shown that people respond best to leaders who project a combination of competence and warmth—

and warmth comes first. Warmth requires a willingness to be vulnerable and transparent. It helps leaders quickly connect with those around them, facilitate communication, and establish their trustworthiness.

It's really quite simple: leaders who understand how anxiety motivates their behavior and who have developed the skills to manage their reactions are better leaders and deliver better outcomes for their organizations.

Playing Detective

Getting to know your anxiety will require you to tune in and take an honest look at yourself and your behavior. Approach this exercise with as little judgment and as much compassion as you can. You may have an obvious form of anxiety, such as panic disorder or glossophobia (fear of public speaking). Or maybe you wake up every morning with a pit in your stomach and an undefined sense of dread about starting the day. You may have a fear of death or personal loss that impacts your business leadership. Whatever your experience, start right there, in the moment, and play detective with your experience.

Rebecca Harley, a psychologist at Massachusetts General Hospital and assistant professor of psychology at Harvard Medical School, helped me learn to examine my experience, and it starts with turning inward and noticing what's happening in the present moment. Like a detective who's simply observing and gathering information, tune in to whatever is happening and see what you discover. Playing detective is a fact-finding mission. Your job isn't to judge what's happening or *do* anything about it at all. It's to observe impartially.

Once you've observed what's happening, see if you can put some words to the most prominent experience. It may be a thought (*This presentation is going to be a disaster*), a physical sensation (dizziness, nausea, dry mouth, racing heart, excessive sweating), or a behavior (mindless scrolling or snacking).

Note how you react when anxiety is present. I call this reaction a *tell*, and it can take many forms—from tightness in the chest or a stomach flip, to impatience or irritability, to insomnia or indigestion, all the

Quick and Easy Body Scan

Physical tells can function like the check-engine light in our cars: they're the early warning sign that anxiety is taking over. A body scan is one of the simplest and most reliable ways to begin gathering data about how your body processes anxiety. You can inconspicuously do a body scan at your desk in the middle of a busy day, even in an office with an open floor plan, making it an ideal exercise for work.

Three times during the day (perhaps morning, noon, or evening, or before meetings or events—you choose), conduct a body scan by following the steps below.

1. Sit upright in a chair with your feet flat on the floor and your hands in your lap. Keep your chin neutral. If possible, close your eyes.

2. Note which part of your body you feel most immediately.

3. Scan through the following body parts. (If you like, record yourself speaking each one, and then you'll have a guided body scan ready to use at any time.)
   - Your head
   - Your jaw
   - Your neck
   - Your shoulders
   - Your wrists and forearms
   - Your upper back

way to a bout of depression (a loss of interest in life, for example). Your tells may not always be negative behaviors with harmful consequences. For instance, many of us connect more often with friends and family during stressful times. When I'm very anxious, I cook and freeze meals. Others exercise or fidget or organize their workspace.

A physical experience is often the first tell for many people. This is because our bodies will register anxiety even if our minds aren't con-

- Your lower back
- Your stomach
- Your hips
- Your hamstrings and rear
- Your calves, ankles, and feet

4. Note what feels tight, painful, or otherwise uncomfortable.

5. Breathe into that feeling, into the specific area that feels uncomfortable. If you like, add in a countermeasure: take slow, diaphragmatic breaths, adopt a gentle smile, and visualize the discomfort dissipating. (For example, picture your jaw unclenching, your heart rate slowing, your shoulders relaxing.)

6. Over the course of the day, notice how each of these areas feels different with each scan.

Anxiety is a total body reaction. You might be familiar with feeling a racing heart or shallow breathing, but anxiety can also manifest in the short term as chest tightness, clenched jaw muscles, or frozen shoulders. Over the longer term, you may experience gastrointestinal symptoms, hypertension, skin breakouts, appetite changes, or a marked increase or decrease in energy levels. By learning how your body experiences anxiety, you can get to the root of the problem instead of only treating the symptoms.

sciously aware of it yet, or if we simply aren't ready to admit our anxiety to ourselves. One of the first signs that my anxiety is ramping up is that my shoulders are bunched up under my ears. Much of the time, I won't even notice that it's happening until I stop and check in. If I don't, my neck and shoulders will eventually tell me in the form of pain and tension. (To learn more about your tells, read the "Quick and Easy Body Scan" exercise.)

When I was the head of marketing at an international company, every Thursday I felt nauseous and developed a migraine, plus I was exhausted because I couldn't sleep the night before. It took me a long time to realize that the lunchtime staff meetings I had to run on Thursdays triggered terrible feelings of performance anxiety, impostor syndrome, and social jitters. My body was broadcasting the news, but I hadn't yet learned to connect my physical experiences to my emotional landscape.

During a therapy session in 2021, I realized where the roots of this experience lay. When I was in high school, I ran for school president. Not because I had a grand leadership vision or because I even *wanted* the role—I did it because I thought I should, and because my worries about getting into a good university were escalating. Now I know that my anxiety created impulsive behavior. I threw my hat in the ring without much thought, and was shocked when I won. But I had no plan and no agenda. So every Thursday of my senior year, I presided over a lunch meeting of the student government, during which I'd just sit there and flail. The grown-ups in the room, including two of my favorite teachers, made snide comments about it being "such a quiet year" and did nothing to help. I was seventeen and couldn't advocate for myself, and the more ashamed and anxious I felt, the more paralyzed (and miserable) I became.

Fast-forward a decade. I was in charge of the marketing department, but I found myself freezing up at our Thursday lunchtime staff meetings. In that case, I enlisted the help of my deputy, a man who was only too happy to take over and run the meetings. Even though I was his boss, I was too anxious and ashamed to step in, so I gave away all my power.

Now fast-forward again. I was trying to fit into someone else's management structure for the first time in many years. Two Thursdays in a row I had to have very difficult conversations with the CEO, and I became so overwhelmed that I simply lost the ability to speak. It was my therapist who pointed out the connection between all of these experiences, and that these Thursday meetings were a serious trigger for me. At the root of each was shame. The kind of shame that said, *You're in over your head and everyone knows it; you're in a seat you shouldn't be in; you don't deserve this role, and no one is going to help you.*

My therapist observed that when I was seventeen, I was set up to fail because I was so young and in over my head, and no one stepped in to mentor me. The current situation triggered me because it summoned all those memories of shame and feeling like a fraud. But feelings aren't facts, and now I am an adult with self-awareness and agency. I can create a different outcome. I met with my boss and said I didn't think we were communicating well.

Was I anxious going into the meeting? Of course. But this was manageable anxiety, and it felt great to advocate for myself and not give my power away. It turned out to be an incredibly productive meeting for both of us.

Know Your Triggers

Trigger is a term often thrown around colloquially to indicate feelings of discomfort, but in psychology a trigger is a stimulus such as a smell, a sound, or a sight that we react to. Triggers can make us recall or even reexperience feelings of trauma. Far beyond mere discomfort, triggers can spark feelings of anxiety and panic, and can sometimes cause flashbacks of a past traumatic event. Despite the word's misuse in popular culture, I choose to use it because it's clear and familiar. Many in the fields of medicine, psychology, and social work now refer to triggers as *activating events*. Triggers, or activating events, are the things that set us off, that spark our anxiety and provoke a physical and emotional response.

Marc Brackett, founder and director of the Yale Center for Emotional Intelligence, notes that leaders and managers are triggered *all the time* at work—which we may not even realize because so many triggers occur subconsciously. What sets us off could be anything: the way someone talks or acts, or the way a team member is habitually late. Over time these triggers build up inside of us and, as Brackett puts it, "accumulate in a debt of anger or anxiety." That mounting debt can then show up in situations and in ways that, on the surface, have no apparent connection with the trigger: yelling at a colleague or a family member, drinking too much, binge-watching Netflix. But in reality, the reaction that seemed to come out of nowhere actually has an identifiable cause.

Many of us think we know what makes us anxious or stressed at work, and sometimes it's abundantly apparent. But often what actually triggers us is specific and surprisingly small: An email from a client you haven't gotten back to. A message from your boss. A news notification. A colleague who coughs too close to you. Or it might be bigger: A dip in the market. Rumors of a reorg. Or even something that isn't likely to happen. When unemployment numbers skyrocket, for example, you might feel nauseous and unable to focus even though your job isn't in jeopardy.

So, think about it—how does anxiety show up for you most often at work, and what triggers it? Common anxiety-inducing situations include:

- Conflict or difficult conversations

- Public speaking or presenting

- Cryptic communication from a colleague, manager, or client

- Social gatherings or networking events

- Meetings (running them, participating, providing feedback)

- Remote work and performance on camera

- Feeling a need for face time or being more physically present

- Balancing work/home responsibilities

- Work travel

- Financial news

- Promotions or new jobs

The list is endless and is different for us all. The key is to identify what situations make you anxious and how you feel when anxiety kicks in. Our goal is to move from feeling anxiety and reacting on autopilot, to understanding what triggers our anxiety and managing how we respond. Knowing what your triggers are can improve your ability to handle your anxieties, which research shows can lead to higher job satisfaction and stronger job performance, not to mention greater well-being all around.

Sometimes we can discover our anxiety triggers by working backward from the unhealthy response. "Once you acknowledge that something is not working and is no good for you, you can look one step before it to find out what triggered that feeling of urgency," psychotherapist Carolyn Glass told me. "What was the quick response that was unconscious, the one that may not have solved your problem but that you felt compelled to do?"

Think about the last time you did something mindlessly, barely aware of what you were doing until the deed was done. Who ate that entire package of Oreos, clicked "buy now," fired off that snippy reply, or posted an impulsive screed in the Slack channel? Not anyone you know, I'm sure, but just for argument's sake, let's say that shortly after checking your email one morning, you found yourself scrolling through Twitter and Instagram, and before you knew it, a full hour had vanished.

But instead of beating yourself up for it, you decide to play detective and get curious: Why did I do that? What set me off and sent me into the no-man's-land of social media? By carefully examining the events of the day and examining your thoughts and feelings, you discover that on this occasion it was your colleague's overnight emails, which left your inbox jammed with to-dos, that triggered your anxiety. And not only that, it was hardly the first time this person had contacted you during off-hours—nor was it the first time you responded by avoiding the emails.

So here's a challenge: When an interaction or a situation sets you off, stop and examine the situation without judgment. Simply notice your response—your thoughts, your emotions, your behavior. Then rewind the clock and see if you can identify what triggered you. Read the "Identify Your Triggers" exercise to get started.

Identify Your Triggers

With this exercise you'll practice identifying the triggers that set off your emotional reactions.

Three times during the course of the day (perhaps morning, noon, or evening, or before meetings or events—again, you choose), stop to examine how you're feeling.

1. Begin by naming your emotions. What specific feelings are you experiencing now? (You can see a categorized list in table 3-1.)

2. Now, think about what triggered those feelings. Can you name specific people or situations that brought them on? Does knowing your trigger help you think differently about how you feel?

Once you know your typical responses as well as your triggers, you're more likely to be able to deal with the trigger without responding hastily or in a state of high anxiety, and without letting the trigger hijack your mood and your entire day. When you start to notice patterns and source why you're reacting, you start to get control.

Your Greatest Hits

In ways large and small, we're all triggered at work. When anxiety strikes, how do you typically react? Are those behaviors helpful or not?

Do you ignore or suppress anxiety? Do you power through? Pile on more work? Duck out of responsibility? Vent with a colleague?

At home, how do you deal with stress from the office? How often do you rely on a drink, a muscle relaxant, a sleep aid, or an over-the-counter analgesic throughout the week?

Our typical responses to anxiety are what I call our greatest hits. Most of us tend to respond with one or two typical greatest-hits coping mech-

TABLE 3-1

A list of emotions

Go beyond the obvious to identify exactly what you're feeling.

Angry	Sad	Anxious	Hurt	Embarrassed	Happy
Grumpy	Disappointed	Afraid	Jealous	Isolated	Thankful
Frustrated	Mournful	Stressed	Betrayed	Self-conscious	Trusting
Annoyed	Regretful	Vulnerable	Isolated	Lonely	Comfortable
Defensive	Depressed	Confused	Shocked	Inferior	Content
Spiteful	Paralyzed	Bewildered	Deprived	Guilty	Excited
Impatient	Pessimistic	Skeptical	Victimized	Ashamed	Relaxed
Disgusted	Tearful	Worried	Aggrieved	Repugnant	Relieved
Offended	Dismayed	Cautious	Tormented	Pathetic	Elated
Irritated	Disillusioned	Nervous	Abandoned	Confused	Confident

Source: Susan David, "3 Ways to Better Understand Your Emotions," hbr.org, November 10, 2016, https://hbr.org/2016/11/3-ways-to-better-understand-your-emotions.

anisms. And once you turn to those coping mechanisms multiple times, they become habitual.

Let's say a certain person's name pops up in email or Slack (your trigger), and your stomach immediately flips (your tell). In response, do you shut your laptop and go get a cup of coffee, pretending the email isn't there? That's avoidance.

Do you drop everything you had planned for the start of your workday, and spend half an hour writing an exhaustive reply instead? That's perfectionism.

Do you stare blankly at the screen and engage in some truly creative fantasies about all the ways the project you're working on with this person could fail? That's catastrophizing.

Your reactions may not always be negative: You might exercise. You might reach out to a trusted friend or family member. I know one leader who works on a classic car restoration project when his anxiety spikes: fifteen or twenty minutes of tinkering in the garage zaps the anxiety spiral, and then he returns to his home office. My practice of cooking and freezing meals when I'm anxious is one of my healthiest coping strategies. Later, when my mind is clear and my body is calm, I can address work issues with much greater impact.

Coping mechanisms are a fascinating set of responses. Not to be confused with *defense mechanisms*, which generally occur at an unconscious level and are ways to avoid experiencing emotions you're not ready for, coping mechanisms are typically conscious and purposeful. They're how we respond to and manage situations that make us uncomfortable. Psychologists refer to healthy and unhealthy coping mechanisms respectively as *adaptive* and *maladaptive*.

Glass offers a useful distinction: Adaptive coping mechanisms give us a way to move through a hard moment and *toward* health. Maladaptive coping mechanisms offer quick relief in a hard moment but take us *away* from health. Eating a cookie in response to anxiety may soothe us, but only while eating the cookie. Afterward, we may feel guilty, ashamed, or physically uncomfortable—and regardless, this unhealthy form of self-soothing offers only temporary comfort.

Examples of adaptive coping, on the other hand, are grounding techniques such as belly breathing or progressive muscle relaxation, or a physical activity such as going for a walk, doing yoga, or dancing. Adaptive coping mechanisms help you feel better in the moment *and* for the long term, and because they help you progress through a hard moment rather than avoid it or numb yourself, they help build distress tolerance and resilience.

Identifying your maladaptive and adaptive responses is powerful, regardless of whether they're mapped to avoidance or problem-solving. It may take a little detective work to identify your typical coping mechanisms, as some reactions can be subtle and may play out over time, rather than acutely when we're triggered. For example, you may not realize that anxiety is why you've been on email until 10 p.m. every night until you fall asleep on your laptop. Or your reactions may feel mild or trivial at first, such as popping an extra Advil PM or watching more TV than usual. But when you start to notice recurring patterns of behavior, this is your cue that you are reacting to anxiety. And when you can begin to source why you're reacting in these ways, you get control. To understand your responses better, read the "Check Your Reactions" exercise.

Check Your Reactions

While there are a multitude of things that can make us anxious, and they're highly idiosyncratic from person to person, responses to anxiety actually tend to be fairly typical. Let's practice being aware of our reactions to anxious feelings.

1. Think of a time you felt anxious. This could be a situation in the past that sticks with you, something you identified during the "Identify Your Triggers" exercise, or something you're experiencing right now.

2. How did you react to that anxiety?

3. Think about the effect your reaction had, starting with how it affected you personally. Did it alleviate your anxiety? Exacerbate it? Neither? Now think about the effect it had on others. How did your reaction affect your colleagues, team members, or direct reports? How did it play out in a meeting?

4. Repeat this exercise throughout the day as you experience anxious moments. Examine your self-talk around each response. Are there themes or thoughts that are driving the behavior patterns, such as a fear that you'll lose everything, a fear of negative feedback, a fear of being found out or shamed, or a fear of letting others down?

Uncovering Automatic Reactions

Do you ever have unexpectedly strong reactions at work, or reactions that seem to come out of nowhere? Do you find yourself repeating the same unhealthy patterns or winding up in the same predicament over and over again, despite sincere intentions to change for the better? When scenarios like these occur, it's likely that automatic reactions are having an outsize effect on your behavior.

When I kept quitting jobs in my twenties, it had a lot more to do with an underlying need to prove that I was good enough than it did anything happening on the job. I hadn't yet done the work to discover the unhelpful automatic thoughts driving my responses, so I just kept falling back on the same coping mechanisms—mainly overwork and drinking—which weren't working. Until I cultivated the self-awareness that enabled me to see what was going on beneath the surface—and, importantly, used that awareness to change my behavior—I kept being miserable at work, and I just kept quitting.

Just as with triggers, we're acting out automatic learned behaviors all the time, and they have concrete, real-world consequences. I'll give you an example from my own life. I have always been a highly competent person, and growing up I took on a great deal of the household responsibility before I was ready. I became pretty controlling about household management because I learned in childhood that if I don't take charge, no one will. When I got married and had children, this pattern repeated. Negotiating the division of labor at home with my husband, I felt that I took on an undue burden. Anger and anxiety built up. Why was I always the one who had to do everything? I grew to resent my husband, and something like a minor dish infraction could make me say nasty things that were way out of proportion to the situation. I was acting out automatically due to a learned behavior from my childhood.

Now translate this dynamic to a work context, where triggers provoke automatic behaviors all the time. For example, have you ever worked with someone who insists on their own agenda, devalues others' ideas, overthinks every decision, or encourages a culture of overwork? (Have you ever been *that* person?) On the other hand, have you ever accepted less money than you're worth, taken a job beneath your capabilities, failed to enforce the boundaries you need to thrive, or missed an opportunity to negotiate on your team's behalf? Though the first group of examples represent abuses of power and the second abdications of power, chances are, automatic reactions are behind *all* of these unproductive and harmful responses.

It would be great if we could check our old wounds, unresolved issues, and maladaptive coping mechanisms at the door when we show up for work, but they're with us wherever we go. If we don't attend to them, they'll play out on a daily basis in ways large and small. So it behooves us to cultivate the self-awareness we need to get to know what's behind our behavior—and then make changes that support the growth and well-being of us and our teams.

I'm a firm believer that everyone needs to do this work. Because leaders are in a position of power and their actions always affect others, they bear a special responsibility to become aware of their automatic reactions. Many examples of bad leadership are actually examples of unhelpful responses to anxiety by leaders who are reenacting unproductive patterns of behavior.

By contrast, excellent leadership comes from those who have the self-awareness necessary to create a culture that sets up their team for their best chance of success. Study after study has demonstrated that leaders who've put in the effort to gain self-awareness are, by and large, simply better leaders and empower their teams to produce better outcomes. Leaders who are self-aware are more confident and more creative, and they're better communicators. They make better decisions, build stronger relationships, earn more promotions, and have more-satisfied employees *and* more-profitable companies.[1]

If you're ready to look beneath the hood and become better acquainted with what's at the root of your behavior at work, refer back to the responses you identified in the "Check Your Reactions" exercise. Look for patterns of behavior, the reactions that keep showing up. Now, go a little deeper and play detective with what's driving those particular patterns. What self-talk is showing up? Just note what you find, without judgment. It might take a while to find the theme or thought that's catalyzing this behavior.

Microsoft senior executive Danny Bernstein told me he used to be "a terror as a manager" because his anxiety led him to push his teams very hard. When preparing them for the annual ritual of performance reviews, Bernstein's method was to overprepare and hold himself and his teams to an unreachable standard. "I did that for years, and I would get negative feedback on it universally," he said. "But I was very stubborn about it because I was saying, 'No, I'm just trying to prepare you!' It took me a very long time to let go of that approach and to realize that what I actually should be doing is boosting people's confidence in those smaller discussions and helping improve psychological safety."

It's awareness *coupled with action* that makes all the difference. Psychologist and self-awareness expert Tasha Eurich cautions against *only* trying to figure out why you behave the way you do. "Why" questions, she says, can actually be unhelpful when it comes to increasing our self-awareness. That's because we tend to come up with the wrong answers to introspective questions—we're biased toward what feels like a new insight and often miss what's objectively true. Further, why questions can invite unproductive negative thoughts and ruminative patterns rather than uncovering the objective information we need to propel us forward. "For example, if an employee who receives a bad performance review asks, *Why did I get such a bad rating?*, they're likely to land on an explanation focused on their fears, shortcomings, or insecurities, rather than a rational assessment of their strengths and weaknesses," Eurich writes.[2]

Far more effective, she says, are "what" questions, which help us stay focused on objective information and actions that orient us toward future growth. They help us act and improve, rather than leaving us stuck and ruminating. So instead of asking why you got such a bad rating, ask, "What steps can I take to improve my performance and get a better rating next time?"

From Honest Insight to Effective Action

As much as we may try, we cannot control every outcome or ensure that every day will go flawlessly. But we absolutely can understand how anxiety motivates our behavior and how our automatic anxious thoughts and reactions directly contribute to that behavior, both positively and negatively.

Whether you're a leader who's anxious by nature, like me, or your anxiety springs from a situation at work, you can develop the skills to manage how you react to triggers. We can learn to create the working conditions that propel us to our highest achievement—and to prepare ourselves for the moments when triggers and anxiety-provoking circumstances arrive. When they do, we can remind ourselves that these feelings are part of life and that the healthiest thing we can do is allow ourselves to feel them and to respond with self-compassion. We can tell ourselves that these difficult feelings will pass, just like they have a million times before, and that we will show up and do our thing, just like we have a million times before.

Having this knowledge not only gives us personal insight and deeper self-awareness; it gives us freedom, agency, and the ability to leverage our anxiety as a leadership superpower. It returns a sense of control that we may fear was lost forever. It allows us to take power back—and keep it. No longer must we settle for reacting on autopilot, letting the chips fall where they may. We can respond thoughtfully, skillfully, and with full awareness of how our decisions will impact our teams, organizations, and careers.

4

Face Your Past

Jason Miller had always driven himself very hard—the first in his family to go to college, an excellent student, a senior executive at a global company—until he ended up in the emergency room at the age of forty, convinced he was having a heart attack.

Miller grew up in Sandusky, Ohio, surrounded by men who were living with potent yet hidden anxiety. He still remembers coming home from school one day to find that his dad had been laid off from his job at General Motors. At first, eight-year-old Miller was excited about having his dad at home more often. "But that wasn't what really happened, because he was working too hard to find a way to make money," he says. Miller's dad eventually started his own business, but the family continued to struggle. "It got to a point where we were literally not sure when there would be food on the table next."

Miller vowed to go to college and find a career that ensured feeding his family would never be a concern. But as he advanced in the corporate world, old self-doubts resurfaced. He responded by working even harder—and getting more stressed out. He even changed roles in the hope that the stress of working in a 24/7, always-on global environment would dissipate, but it didn't. He was losing sleep and was constantly stressed, but still Miller tried to ignore his discomfort and power through. "I just thought, 'I'm tense. So what?'" Miller says. "It's just the way it is, because I grew up in an environment where people are stressed all the time."

One day he found himself suddenly short of breath, dizzy, and with tingling in his left arm. Knowing these were all symptoms of a heart attack, Miller, his wife, and their five-year-old son rushed to the hospital. After a full workup, a neurosurgeon told him the tingling in his arm was due to a stress-induced back condition and a pinched nerve, but there were no signs he'd suffered a heart attack. Then the neurosurgeon told Miller that if he didn't get his stress under control, he was going to die young.

That was the first time that Miller realized that someone could literally die from uncontrolled stress and anxiety. He'd wound up in the emergency room, fearing for his life as his wife and son looked on, because in effect his body had dialed 911.

As a leader, you bring your past with you into every meeting, every negotiation, and every activity. It's true even if you're unaware of how your past is influencing your present behavior and how it's affecting others.

That's why, when an interaction or a situation triggers an anxious response at work, you should examine why.

Anxiety Is a Signal

Symptoms of illness or disease provide us with vital information. Fever and fatigue, for example, alert you that something is amiss in your body. Acting on that information can restore your health or even save your life. Anxiety—a symptom of dis-ease, if you will—works in much the same way.

Amanda Clayman, a financial therapist who frequently counsels people through their anxieties about money, describes how this works. "Anxiety is a signal, it's information," she says. "Its purpose is to bring our attention to something, to shock us out of automatic thinking and say, 'What is this thing that feels yucky, that I need to attend to?' [Anxiety] is there to keep us safe."

Clayman distinguishes between "signal" (helpful) and "noise" (unhelpful) anxiety. "Anxiety is supposed to alert us to danger, but its job is to alert, not to assess," she says. It's our job to sort the signal from the noise. Signal anxiety provides reliable information; it alerts us to true threats. Noise anxiety, on the other hand, is the unhelpful, irrational anxiety that impairs our functioning. Though noise anxiety does get our attention, it's a distraction. "It's a drag on our ability to process and make good decisions," Clayman says. This kind of anxiety can often be traced back to childhood or to a traumatic experience. "We learn through experience what we think we need to be afraid of in the future," Clayman explains. "So anxiety is almost always reactive to something that's happened to us in the past."

Marc Brackett, founder and director of the Yale Center for Emotional Intelligence, agrees that anxiety is a key provider of information, and he expands this to include all emotions. Brackett says we should learn to be "compassionate emotion scientists" rather than "critical emotion judges." Why? "Because emotions are information," he says. "They're a guide." Brackett recommends that we label our emotions—because each one is an invaluable clue—and then, acting as compassionate emotion scientists, question each feeling's merit. Is it helping us with the task at hand, or is it hindering?

"By way of example, being granular and specific about my feelings [provides] information that says, 'Marc, maybe this is the wrong path for you,'" he says. "But don't just go with your gut instinct—really dissect it. Is it just your fear of failure showing up here, or is this really something that you don't want to do and believe is a dangerous way forward?"

The night Jason Miller realized his stress and anxiety had reached life-threatening levels, he made a list of all the things that were worrying him. The list quickly filled the page, vividly demonstrating why he'd landed in a hospital bed. He says,

> This is what's happening inside of me, which is all the stories
> I'm telling myself about how I am a phony and a fake, and
> I'm worried about being caught and not being taken care of,
> and failing and losing money, and losing security, losing the

house. That was a really, really hard moment, but it was my wake-up call. I literally said to myself, "If I have the power to do this to myself, I have the power to do anything I want."

Miller acted on the information his anxiety yielded by taking a three-month leave of absence, during which he got into therapy, started working with an executive coach, learned mindfulness meditation, and began yoga and physical therapy. He spent more time in nature and prioritized time with his family.

At the end of his leave, Miller went back to work, though it felt "scary as hell" to return to a high-pressure, high-stress environment. "I wasn't stress-free," he says. "Stress never goes away, but now I had all these tools and capabilities to manage it more effectively, and I stayed with it." Beneath all that stress and worry and acting out of old patterns was a true self waiting to emerge, one that led Miller to a sustainable lifestyle and a more fulfilling career. "My limiting story I was telling myself was keeping me from giving my gifts," Miller says. "And that was a big part of the racket I had going on. . . . My true nature was being suppressed into this identity I felt like I had to manage and keep up."

Anxiety is one of our most valuable messengers, signaling that we're headed down the wrong path or are about to make an unwise decision. You can parlay the information that anxiety yields into all sorts of improvements and better outcomes: higher productivity, increased empathy, better communication, deeper motivation, maybe even a career that's a better fit. And that's a good start—but don't stop there.

For anyone who wants to get to the bottom of their anxiety and gain the sort of self-awareness that's required for deep transformation and healing—and a leadership journey that brings personal fulfillment as well as the kind of skill that inspires teams and organizations to be their best—you'll need to look to the past.

The Legacy of Childhood Experiences

Leadership coach Jerry Colonna believes that many of the leadership problems we face—anxiety, avoidance, impulsivity, denial, anger, toxic relationships, and sometimes things like drinking or drug use—spring from our fundamental childhood experiences. This is unwelcome news for many people, and I get it. *Do I really have to examine my relationship with my mother*, you might be thinking, *in order to be a better leader?*

Well, probably. Think about it: It's not as if our personal histories vanish the minute we arrive at the office or log on. Each of us has a long and detailed history that we carry with us wherever we go. We're all products of our past circumstances and the complex set of influences that shape us, so at least some of our experiences and influences are bound to have an effect on our leadership. We might be able to build successful careers while engaging in bad behaviors and unhealthy reactions, and we've all known people who have done it. But understanding how your childhood shaped the adult you are today allows you to be a great leader.

Our early influences are usually a mixture of positive and negative, but the negative influences have a way of being "stickier"—more memorable, their effects more enduring. Psychologists refer to this hardwired tendency as *negativity bias*. It's thought to be an evolutionary advantage that is rooted in our basic survival instinct: remembering encounters with negative stimuli helps us avoid those encounters in the future. But in our present circumstances, negativity bias can sometimes trigger disproportionate responses. It can cloud our judgment, causing us to miss or discount a positive development because we're so fixated on the negative, and it can make us *too* cautious, unwilling to take risks or move ahead in an attempt to stay small, unseen, and safe.

Groundbreaking research on adverse childhood experiences (ACEs)—those that occur before the age of eighteen—demonstrates how negative events that happened in the past affect us for years to come. In the original study conducted in the mid-1990s, researchers identified three types of ACEs that led to negative outcomes: *abuse* (physical, emotional, or sexual), *neglect* (emotional or physical), and *household dysfunction* (divorce, an incarcerated parent, or witnessing violence, substance use, or mental illness in the home).[1] Since then the categories have expanded to include community and systemic adverse experiences, such as racism and chronic poverty, and dozens of studies have been conducted using ACE data.

Among the findings, two key points emerged. First, ACEs are very common, occurring across all demographics. More than two-thirds of study participants reported experiencing an ACE, and nearly one-quarter have experienced three or more. Second, there is a "powerful, persistent correlation" between the number of ACEs a child experiences and the risk of negative outcomes later in life—and those outcomes affect all areas of life. Researchers found "a dramatically increased risk of heart disease, diabetes, obesity, depression, substance use, smoking, poor academic achievement, time out of work, and early death," and more recent research revealed a clear link between ACEs and financial stress in adulthood.[2] Experiencing ACEs can increase the likelihood that you will be an anxious adult.[3]

Systems clearly matter too. The experience of growing up Black in the United States, for instance, a country operating from a racist social system, can create anxiety that begins in childhood and builds into adulthood. A 2016 study found "experiences of individual, cultural, and institutional racism may constitute a culturally specific factor that is linked to anxiety in Black American populations."[4] Relatedly, there is data showing that members of lower castes in the Indian system of social ranking have worse emotional well-being than members of higher castes, and that women suffer more than men in these systems.[5] The impact of trying to get an education, build a secure life, and develop a career in racist, patriarchal, rigid social systems can create anxious achievers. After all, as psychologists Akshay Johri and Pooja V. Anand write, "an individual's well-being cannot exist in a vacuum. It is dependent on various social and structural processes larger than the individual."[6]

Susan Schmitt Winchester, a C-suite HR leader and coauthor of *Healing at Work*, believes one of the best places to unlearn and recover from the harmful effects of difficult experiences from our past is the workplace. Winchester acknowledges that this is the last thing many of us think of when it comes to working on our psychological stuff, but she points out that unlike our families of origin, work brings choice on both sides: we choose our employer, and our employer chooses us. And let's face it, as most of us spend the majority of our waking hours at work, our unresolved issues and old wounds are bound to show up there.

All of our triggers from the past, Winchester says, "may be sneaking into our workplaces every day and causing havoc."

She calls this "living the unconscious, wounded career path." Often people assume they don't have issues from the past to deal with because they don't have a history of trauma or ACEs. But both Winchester and Colonna point out that we are all wounded in some way—which is to say we've all experienced dysfunction in our early lives. For example, someone who lived with a parent who was overly critical, overbearing, or unpredictable experienced some of the same limiting beliefs and adverse effects as someone with a history of trauma.

In search of a term broad enough to encompass this group of adults, Winchester and her *Healing at Work* coauthor Martha Finney came up with *adult survivors of a damaged past*, or ASDPs. In the term itself are important clues to how we can heal—and even find hard-won advantages from our old wounds.

As adults, Winchester says, our choices are no longer dictated by parents or other caretakers, and on a deeper, psychological level, we no longer have to react to the impact of past adversities. "We don't have to be prisoners to the past," she says. "'Survivor' is, I think, a hopeful word of resilience that whatever dysfunctional dynamic you experienced when you were younger is also a great gift in teaching the ability to manage difficult situations." The opportunity for ASDPs is to realize that we don't have to live with whatever heavy burden our past experiences left us. "Damaged," Winchester is fond of saying, "isn't doomed."

If the first step is to recognize that gaining new insight and understanding of our past will make us happier in the present, the second is to realize that we have the power and the agency to do so. But how do we actually engage in the work of healing at our workplace? One of the most effective ways to heal *and* to become a more effective leader is to pay attention to what triggers us at work. "What I've noticed about myself and others is that when someone has a reaction to something that's occurred in the workplace, and it seems to be a much stronger reaction than the facts of the situation would suggest . . . that's a clue that the person may be having a response that is fueled from something that happened in their past," Winchester says.

The Rapid Power Reclaim Method

Susan Schmitt Winchester developed a three-step strategy she calls the "rapid power reclaim method" for when someone is feeling anxious and overwhelmed at work. We'll use a classic tough moment—receiving negative feedback—as an example. Here's how to keep yourself from "spiraling down on that unconscious wounded career path," as she says, and stop yourself from overreacting.

- **Step 1: Create choice.** Remind yourself that you have the power not to get lost in the trigger and to respond with old, automatic patterns—you're an adult now and can choose how you respond. You can also give yourself the space to manage an intense response. If you're in the middle of a meeting and get flooded with emotion, it's OK to ask for a ten-minute break. When the meeting is over, Winchester recommends finding some way to purge the physiological and emotional energy you're feeling so that you'll be less reactive and see more clearly. Deep breathing, drawing or journaling the feelings, hitting a pillow—anything to get the emotion out of your system.

When you find yourself reacting in such a way, Winchester advises asking yourself, "Am I sure?" For example: Am I sure my boss is angry with me? Am I sure my colleague's silence means they disapprove of my work? Am I sure I need to recheck my work ten more times? Answering this question often reveals that our triggered reactions are out of proportion to the scale of the event—a sign that old hurts and unresolved issues are influencing our present behavior. (To learn a helpful technique for these tough moments, read "The Rapid Power Reclaim Method" exercise.)

But here's the thing: not all of the effects of old wounds are negative. Just as anxiety can be a superpower if we learn to tap into its generative aspects, many of the negative lessons and experiences we had in childhood can manifest in positive leadership skills.

- **Step 2: Elevate action.** Here's where you implement a new, healthier response. In the case of negative feedback, elevating your action may mean approaching the feedback with an attitude of open curiosity. "Rather than going into defense [mode], I'm going to ask questions to understand it," Winchester says. "I'm going to really focus on what I can learn from this feedback versus beat myself up with it." If you're especially triggered, simply responding with "Say more" opens up the conversation and prevents you from shutting down. "What advice do you have for me?" is another way to elevate your action in the moment and respond in new, more productive ways.

- **Step 3: Celebrate and integrate.** Having a different response to an old trigger is worthy of celebration! Mark the occasion with a positive activity you find rewarding. Celebrating successes integrates this new response into your identity, Winchester says. The more you pair a new response with an old trigger, the less powerful that trigger becomes.

Colonna explains one way this can work. When a child grows up in an environment in which a parent or caregiver is absent, unavailable, or unreliable, sometimes the child must assume responsibility for the physical and emotional well-being of other family members. It's not a desirable scenario, but one of its silver linings is that the child receives early lessons in developing resilience and in being a caring leader who is responsible for each member of their team. "This is a really important message," Colonna says. "These wounds don't necessarily result in only negative behaviors, like, say, conflict avoidance as a result of growing up with violence. They result oftentimes in very, very powerful positive experiences, such as the ability to step into uncertain situations and to craft a vision and a way to be." In the best-case scenario, Colonna says, adult leaders who've experienced early adversity are left with "the inner resources to be able to withstand shocks because they've already experienced them."

One of the most helpful lessons I've learned is that when present-day circumstances stir up unresolved hurts from childhood, we re-experience the same level of fear we felt as a child. For example, if you've ever wondered why even a slight rejection can leave you shaky and near tears, or why the edge you think you detect in your boss's voice can make you ruminate for hours on what you did to make them angry, look to your past. How would four-year-old you feel if the parent you depended on for survival rejected you, or the caregiver you relied on for safety launched into a rage? If we've never dealt with these early negative experiences—which truly are terrifying to a child with no power and no agency—we can succumb to automatic reactions and misperceive the level of threat we're encountering in the present.

So now, when my anxiety seems especially irrational—when I know there is no true threat to my survival but it *feels* like there is—I address the past instead of the present. I remind myself to pause, do some deep breathing, and look inward at the small, frightened child who still lives within me. I picture her in detail: five-year-old Morra, defenseless and hypervigilant and desperate to please, peering up at adult Morra, who has so much more power, experience, and wisdom. How can the adult me help the five-year-old me feel better? Sometimes I picture adult me bending down and scooping up child me as I would one of my own frightened children, holding her until she calms. Sometimes I gaze at her with all the compassion and gratitude I can muster, and tell her she's OK now, that she doesn't have to work so hard to keep me safe any-more. Sometimes I simply picture adult Morra grasping child Morra's hand and leading her to some better, safer, happier place.

I've found these visualizations to be powerful and deeply trustwor-thy. If you feel silly trying them out, just remember two things. One, this is a private exercise; no one has to know. Second, and more impor-tantly, you are healing yourself. Think of how powerful this is—you need real strength to face your fears and do this type of work. "War-riors are not unafraid," Colonna says. "A warrior acknowledges there's wisdom in the fear. Fear is the wish to keep you safe. It's reckless and foolhardy to deny fear. The strength comes when we choose to act in the face of fear."

No matter how damaged or helpless you feel, you have the power to face your fear and heal yourself. And like a muscle, that power grows stronger the more you use it.

Your Workplace as a Family System

We often joke that our offices are like families . . . large, dysfunctional families. It is funny, and yet we all know how complex and difficult it can be to maintain healthy relationships among any group of people, be it a family, a community organization, or a team of coworkers. Bowen family systems theory is one of the many frameworks for understanding the ways in which familial dynamics can get replicated at work.

Bowen theory, developed by the psychiatrist and researcher Murray Bowen, says that the best way to understand people—their characters, motivations, personalities, behaviors—is within the context of their family relationships. Bowen believed that the bulk of the problems we experience in adulthood stem from the negative ways we learned to manage stress and anxiety in our families of origin.[7] As adults, we automatically replicate behaviors that we adopted in our family, where we all played certain roles. (If anyone has ever referred to you as a "golden child," for example, that's a role you played.) Others expect certain behaviors of you, and you expect the same of them. Whether we're aware of it or not, those early lessons and roles recreate themselves at work, which is why it behooves us to understand our role in the "family system" that is our workplace.

In short, systems theory (or systems thinking) proposes that everything is a part of a larger, complex system, and that each part of that system—whether it's a member of a family or an employee at an organization—is interdependent and interrelated. Thus, changes to one part of the system affect all the other parts of the system, as well as the system as a whole.

It's easy to see how systems thinking plays out at work, as organizations are made up of divisions, departments, teams, and individuals.

Even small businesses and independent contractors are part of a complex system, as they operate with particular products or services. So effective leadership will always require not only individual self-awareness, but group awareness, as any group of people in relationship to each other becomes a system.

Paul English, the serial tech entrepreneur and philanthropist who cofounded Kayak, has taken a systems-thinking approach to management, and believes that one of his CEO superpowers is his ability to observe human dynamics at play. This involves listening with full attention to everything that's being said, but also tuning in to the unspoken interplay between people in a room. English describes how growing up in a tiny house with nine people made him hyperaware of dynamics by necessity. "I think that trained me to really focus on interactions," he says. "And I would say 5 percent of the time I spend in each of my companies is watching interactions."

English first became aware that he was noticing people at work the same way he noticed family members at home shortly after he made the transition from computer programmer to manager. It was a difficult transition, he concedes, in part because the old playbook he used as a successful programmer—being prolific and fast—didn't translate to managing people. For that, he needed to dial back into his early, informal training in human dynamics. "I learned in my first few years [of management] that if you pay attention to people and see what's on their mind, you can make them happier and more productive," he says.

English took this skill all the way up the chain. "I think the biggest skill for a CEO, particularly for a high-pressure startup where you're really going for it, is removing stress and trying to develop a team which has the mojo," he says. "And if you want a team which is exciting to work on and to work with, you have to become observant of interactions."

If you can understand the dynamics that drive your team, and the forces that affect their collective mental health and trigger anxiety, you can work toward building a cohesive, high-performing team that can accomplish extraordinary things—in English's words, a team with the mojo.

We need that more than ever in the wake of the Covid-19 pandemic, as psychotherapist and author Esther Perel points out. "A collective trauma, a collective event, a global pandemic like this demands collective resilience, not individual resilience," she told me. "And that means that you tap into the collective resources that lift all boats and reach out to the coping strategies of the group in a way that involves mass mutual reliance."

She advises that we examine the ways our teams and organizations made it through the pandemic (and, I would add, any experience of collective anxiety or trauma). What new ways have you learned to rely on each other? What new insights and practices do you need to retain in order for the entire group to continue to develop? "That degree of interdependence is what allowed us to continue to work as well as we have," Perel said. "Let's not lose it."

Using Systems Thinking to Refresh Your Leadership

One of the most important principles in Bowen family systems theory is *differentiation of self*. It refers to the ability to think and act independently while staying connected to others. Differentiation goes back to your family roots. People who are less differentiated have trouble separating themselves from the emotions, wants, and needs of their families. Their emotional boundaries are porous—if their mom is sad or anxious, they get sad and anxious too—and thus they live at the mercy of feelings, theirs as well as others'.

Not surprisingly, people with a poorly differentiated self depend heavily on the acceptance and approval of others. Bowen observed that they either quickly adjust what they think, say, and do to please others (he called this group "chameleons") or dogmatically insist on what others should be like and pressure them to conform (he called these people "bullies"). Interestingly, bullies depend on approval and acceptance just as much as chameleons do, and conflict threatens them just as much. The difference is that bullies push others to agree with them instead of with others.[8] In both cases, the less differentiated person is using others to seek reassurance that they're OK and to gain a more solid sense of self, rather than generating a sense of "OKness" from within.

In contrast, people with a well-differentiated self recognize their dependence on others, but can separate their own thoughts and feelings from those of other people. In the face of conflict, criticism, or rejection, they can stay calm and clearheaded enough to distinguish thinking rooted in a careful assessment of facts from thinking clouded by strong emotion. They're able to respond thoughtfully, rather than react automatically, and those responses emerge from their internal values and desires, rather than from the pressure of outside forces, such as a person or group they're trying to please. Because their sense of self is differentiated and well developed, they live less at the mercy of feelings, and they can be with others in the midst of strong emotion and not absorb that strong emotion themselves.[9] They don't need to jump in and fix things or rescue people, because they have a greater ability to tolerate discomfort.

These are broad descriptions, of course, but I bet you can already see how varying levels of differentiation of self can play out in the workplace—and how having a higher degree of differentiation can make you a more effective leader. When you are differentiated, you are able to work from a sense of your true self. You can anchor in your core beliefs and values and can operate out of a firm foundation, rather than reacting reflexively or being swayed by the constantly shifting conditions that characterize so many work environments.

I reached out to Kathleen Smith, an expert on Bowen theory, to learn more about how we can use family systems thinking to enhance our leadership or just improve everyday office dynamics. She explained that at lower levels of self-differentiation, anxiety in any group context gets expressed in two main ways: overfunctioning or underfunctioning. These two strategies are what we learned from our family of origin, and they represent the quickest means we have of calming ourselves and everyone else down when anxiety strikes. They're autopilot *reactions* rather than thoughtful *responses*.

I've found the concept of overfunctioning or underfunctioning roles one of the most helpful guides to navigating not only my leadership anxiety but my marriage and my role at home. I'm a classic overfunctioner.

When it comes to anxiety in the workplace, overfunctioning is more common, especially among leadership, and can even be prized. But Smith points out that in Bowen theory, both overfunctioners and under-functioners are considered to be at the same level of differentiation. Both offload the responsibility for managing their personal anxiety.

The overfunctioner responds to anxiety by taking on too much responsibility. They direct people, maybe even to the point of being controlling. They tend to believe that nothing gets done without their advice or assistance. Because the boundary between the overfunctioning leader's sense of self and others' is porous, they see others as extensions of themselves and assume they know others' thoughts and feelings. Especially in anxiety-provoking situations, they can misjudge others' capabilities, leading them to jump in and resolve a problem or "rescue" colleagues rather than trusting them to get the job done. It's easy to see why: fixing the problem relieves their anxiety.

It's also easy to see why the classic overfunctioning leader can look really successful and be highly valued by a team or organization. But Smith cautions that overfunctioning is actually "a pseudostrength" and can come with a high price to pay. "If they aren't able to direct others, or if others don't go along with [their directions], all of their capability has a steep decline," she told me.

As does their self-esteem and their confidence. When we're over-functioning, Smith went on, "we get propped up in our own function-ing by acting as if other people are an extension of ourselves, by functioning for them. And often that's what leads to burnout." It can also lead to frustration and disappointment when the people who stand in as extensions of ourselves don't perform well or become less capable. It's a huge burden to carry others' thoughts, feelings, and behaviors! All of this is why overfunctioning is a pseudostrength, and why it isn't sus-tainable in the long term.

Underfunctioning, on the other hand, can look like passing the buck, playing it safe, or depending on others to solve problems rather than getting involved yourself. Underfunctioners underestimate their abilities and are more than happy to let others take over when things get difficult. Which brings up an important point: Overfunctioning and underfunctioning are reciprocal. Overfunctioners cope by getting involved in others' problems. Underfunctioners cope by getting others involved in *their* problems. These two dynamics can't exist without each other.

Notice, too, that both are trying to resolve their anxiety through other people. The overfunctioner's attitude is "I need to get overly involved and problem-solve for others so I can calm my anxieties." The underfunctioner's is "I need someone to get overly involved and problem-solve for me so I can calm my anxieties." The Bowen response is that both the overfunctioner and the underfunctioner need a stronger differentiation of self—and developing it has nothing to do with changing the behavior (or thoughts or feelings) of others, and everything to do with learning to regulate your emotional functioning. (To start becoming more differentiated, read the "Questions to Help You Develop a More Differentiated Self" exercise.)

The leader who can regulate their emotions and remain clearheaded and calm in the midst of a challenge is the one who can lead a team through any experience of collective anxiety and inspire them to perform at their highest capability, rather than "infecting" the system with their personal anxiety and squandering time and energy doing others' jobs for them. "This is why self-regulation is such a key component of leadership," Smith writes. "Leaders who are running around trying to put out anxious fires, instead of staying calm themselves, are largely ineffective." But leaders who can manage themselves and inspire calm, she says, can communicate to each member of the team that they're capable enough to "find a path through the chaos."[10]

I love this advice, and no matter what our role is, we all need to take responsibility for our emotions and behaviors, which affect each member of the "family system" at work, whether we're aware of it or not. When we're operating without awareness, it's so easy to get caught up in automatic reactions that, at best, reduce anxiety only for the short term and, at worst, lead us down a dark path of unhealthy coping mechanisms that become bad habits.

Questions to Help You Develop a More Differentiated Self

The following reflection questions come from Kathleen Smith's writings, where they appear in slightly different forms. Use them as an aid to begin developing a stronger, more differentiated self in your relationships.

Defining Your Self

- What are your core beliefs? What do you stand for?

- What does good work look like to you? What about being a good colleague?

Observing Your Thinking and Behavior

- When do you adopt beliefs and values from others without doing your own thinking?

- Where have your underdeveloped beliefs caused conflict or anxiety?

- In what relationships is it hard for you to think for yourself or communicate your thinking? How can you develop your own principles?

Are You an Overfunctioner?

- Do you rush in to solve problems, even if it's not your responsibility?

- Do you prefer to just get something done your way rather than taking the time to teach someone else?

- In a meeting, do you speak carefully in case colleagues get hurt feelings or anxiety, or soften someone else's statement if you can see they hurt a colleague's feelings?[a]   *(continued)*

Questions to Help You Develop a More Differentiated Self

Are You an Underfunctioner?

- Do you avoid stressful situations, hoping that someone else will dive in and fix things?

- In a shared project, are you content to let another person drive and to give them more credit for the end product?

- Has anyone ever told you, "You have great ideas; you just need to take more initiative!"

Planning for Change

- What behaviors would you have to interrupt to become more differentiated?

- What people would you need to work with and be with to practice defining yourself? How would you do it?

- How can you prepare for pushback and people's discomfort when you define yourself?[b]

a. Kathleen Smith, "Are You an Overfunctioner?" *Psychology Today*, October 17, 2019, https://www.psychologytoday.com/us/blog/everything-isnt-terrible/201910/are-you-overfunctioner.

b. Kathleen Smith, *Everything Isn't Terrible: Conquer Your Insecurities, Interrupt Your Anxiety and Finally Calm Down* (New York: Hachette Books, 2019).

Perhaps you grew up in a household where your mother was always in a panic. Your brain learned to think "Fire!" all the time, even though there wasn't a fire. As an adult, your panic button may still be easily triggered. Being less differentiated can create more (and exhausting) reactivity, because you're always at the mercy of other people's emotions and the unfiltered effect other people's emotions have on you. A terse email from your boss causes you to lose a night's sleep because you instantly go into panic mode. Or if a colleague is upset, you assume it's your fault and your responsibility to fix it . . . and *boom*—you are anxious. All of this makes perfect sense, given the family system in which you grew up.

But you're an adult now, and you don't have to repeat old patterns. You can step back from the automatic thought, ask yourself, "Is there really a fire?" and then tell your anxiety, "Thanks, you've done your job, but there's no fire and you can be quiet now."

Being a responder rather than a reactor lowers the tension throughout the entire group. Reactors build off other reactors, so things can easily escalate. Think about the urgency of a client situation when two anxious reactors are in charge, and how good it can feel when someone calm comes into the room and brings the temperature down. Imagine if you could be that calm person for yourself!

It's Never Too Late

Fortunately, thanks to the brain's amazing neuroplasticity, there's plenty of opportunity to get better at self-differentiation as an adult. "You actually are not locked into these mechanisms 100 percent," Smith says. "If you can begin to observe them, you have an opportunity to step back and ask yourself, 'Is this really what I want to do?' When the chips are down, is there a different, more flexible, more creative way of responding to an anxious person, to a challenging colleague, to an impossible family member? Can I put up with the discomfort of not doing what I normally do?"

Learning to tolerate discomfort—your own as well as other people's—is a key aspect of differentiation of self. It allows us to pause before acting—to not assume we know what others are thinking, not make impulsive decisions, not take on too much responsibility, and not operate on autopilot in the face of anxiety. "That's what it means to work on one's own differentiation," Smith says. "To operate a little bit outside the emotional system while still being in the thick of it."

For the overfunctioner, who has trouble tolerating another person's distress, a good first step is to plan ahead: Instead of the automatic reaction of taking over and managing someone else, what could a more differentiated response look like? That may mean having "to watch people flail a little bit," Smith says. Rather than immediately rescuing them, a healthier response would be to "slow down and let people do things less efficiently" than you would, and to listen to their thinking even if you disagree with them or think they're flat-out wrong. Doing others' jobs for them and refusing to hear their points of view undermines their autonomy and denies them the opportunity to step up, grow in their roles, and become more effective. The more differentiated response, Smith says, "opens up the space for you to be surprised by other people's capabilities. . . . Sometimes the best gift you can give someone . . . is to step back and let them function for themselves."[11]

Whereas overfunctioning can stem from an inability to tolerate another person's distress, the inability to tolerate your own distress can lead to underfunctioning. Underfunctioners tend to believe that their thinking isn't as important or as effective as other people's, so the challenge for them is to trust themselves and not shut down when things get difficult. In a work environment where there are lots of underfunctioners, there may not be a lot of conflict, but there's not a lot of progress, either. Underfunctioners, Smith says, can practice taking a stand for their thoughts and opinions, and taking a position on an issue when there might be pushback, instead of falling silent or avoiding it.

This is a lesson I'm still working on. Until recently I was entirely caught up in being reactive, because I didn't trust myself. Even though I had run my own business for over ten years, I didn't listen to my instincts or trust my work product. Everything I produced, I ran by a staffer. I constantly jumped through hoops and pleased everyone else, because I was so scared of rejection. External accolades and money became the metrics by which I judged my success, because that's what mattered to my family of origin and to me. A single negative comment from anyone could ruin my day. I avoided people who I thought might be mad at or disappointed in me. My emotions completely ruled my life.

On the one hand, being so insecure helped me because I hired people who were smarter than me. I delegated often and had tremendous faith in my team. My radar for client or staff unhappiness became so attuned that I created a workplace culture of overservicing clients. Our clients loved us, but we were all running on empty.

Although one of my mantras is "always consult before doing," in this case I realized my desire to please others and not myself was limiting. So I decided to get curious about what a more differentiated response would look like. How could I better tolerate the anxiety I felt over the quality of my work, and not rely so heavily on external reassurances?

Well, ironically, those external assurances gave me an excellent place to start. I could look back on years of successes, great and small, and remind myself that they were real and trustworthy; it was my anxiety that was the unreliable narrator. From there, I began to practice evaluating my work and speeches based on my criteria of quality—not others'. And do you know what? I liked what I saw, and it was far less exhausting—and far more efficient—not to involve so many others in evaluating the merits of my work. That doesn't mean I don't seek out feedback. But this technique has made for a far less anxious and more enjoyable work environment for me and my colleagues.

When we can anchor into our core self, the birthplace of our values, the self that knows what a good work product is, we not only calm our anxiety—we become a more effective leader and a better teammate. This is why we need a differentiated self.

"The greatest strength, the greatest dignity, comes from the internal knowing of our own self-worth," Colonna says. "That is the greatest source of risk. It's the thing that gets attacked. It's the place from which the warrior springs." And you can't get to the place from which the warrior springs, the place where the most effective leaders are forged, without becoming a differentiated self. "I fail every day, but I will get up tomorrow and I will try again, regardless of what the external world thinks of me," Colonna says. "It took me a long time to grow up in that way. I think that *that's* the opportunity that leadership presents for us."

The past will always be with us, and no one shows up to work a blank slate. But we have so much choice and agency in how our past affects us. When we understand how our past created our current thinking and the ways we interact with the world, we can choose how we show up, and not just react to old patterns. Other people are showing up loaded with their pasts too. "Their pasts, just like yours, may inform their expectations of the present," says psychotherapist Carolyn Glass. A better understanding of your and your team's past patterns and formative influences helps develop the crucial self-awareness you need to manage anxiety and be the leader you were meant to be.

A LEADER'S
TOOL KIT
FOR
MANAGING
ANXIETY AT
WORK

5

Negative Self-Talk

In my twenties I worked in a toxic environment on a national political campaign. I developed a reputation in my department for being disorganized. On a political campaign everyone runs around like mad, trying to prove how hard they're working and how much they're getting done (whether it's true or not). For some reason, my bosses loved to pick apart my writing and use it as proof of disorganization. One day the department director, Doug, decided to make fun of how I wrote memos in front of the whole team. "Have you ever read one of her memos?" Doug asked. "They make no sense!" Everyone laughed.

The truth is, I was twenty-six years old and in over my head. I wrote bad memos because I didn't know what I was doing. I was inexperienced and needed help and mentorship. And frankly, memos aren't my strong suit.

Over the years, I came to learn that I'm actually a good writer with a nonlinear brain. I don't process information in memo format, so I need to structure my memos carefully, because I see things as circles where others see straight lines.

But sometimes I still hear my boss's voice. When I found myself in another difficult work environment, guess what: My memos again became a source of criticism. My manager picked apart everything I wrote, even down to criticizing my font choice. My negative self-talk went on full blast: "You are so disorganized! You make no sense! You've written books and published articles—why can't you write a clear memo, for chrissake! You really don't know what you're doing."

Until recently, this kind of negative self-talk sparked a spiral of anxiety and self-loathing that left me feeling bad for days and triggered all kinds of unhealthy behaviors, from exercising to the point of injury, to both binging and severely restricting my food intake—all while I was barely aware that this critical voice existed.

The first step in dealing with negative self-talk—that inner litany of condemnation and criticism many of us know all too well—is to simply become aware of what it's saying. As with playing detective to identify your anxious thoughts, feelings, or behaviors, at first that's *all* you need to do: just become aware. You don't need to fix the negative self-talk, try to ignore it, or talk back to it. This will feel counterintuitive because overachievers are so accustomed to strategizing and problem-solving. But for now, simply note what that voice says, and—this is important—do it with zero judgment. *Ah*, your more mindful, mature inner voice will say, *that's interesting.*

Then, from a less reactive state, you can start to do some investigating. Have those words and the attitude they reflect always been with you? Does this voice and what it's saying sound like anyone you know? Where did you first notice it? Does that voice pipe up under particular circumstances? Can you see any patterns here?

For many years, cognitive behavioral therapy, or CBT, has been the gold standard in the treatment of problematic anxiety—and its genesis sprang from the need for an effective treatment for the negative self-talk that was at the root of many people's depression. In the 1960s, while conducting research on severely depressed patients, psychiatrist Aaron Beck noticed that they all displayed what he referred to as a "systematic error" in their thought patterns: a negative bias against themselves. Through "faulty information processing," he observed, they tended to see everything that happened to them—past, present, and future—through a negative lens. They expected the worst to happen and were prone to "a massive amount of self-criticism."[1]

From these early observations, the entire field of CBT was born. Beck's insight was that our thoughts determine our emotions and our behavior, and that if we learn to change our thinking—from unhelpful perceptions not based in reality to more objective, reality-based ones—then we can become free of the self-defeating thought patterns and negative self-talk that exacerbate our anxiety, depression, and limiting behaviors. In short, CBT helps people learn how to identify and change the harmful thought patterns (cognition) that have a negative influence on their actions (behavior) and the way they feel (emotions). This framework distinguishes CBT from other forms of psychotherapy, and it puts much of the power for getting better in the hands of the individual.

One of the hallmark principles of CBT is learning to become aware of your self-talk—the internal monologue that "speaks" throughout the day. Often our self-talk is so spontaneous, ingrained, and subtle that it influences our mood, well-being, and performance without us even knowing.

Self-talk can be positive ("Nailed it!" or "This jacket looks great on me"), neutral ("Don't forget to pick up the dry cleaning") or, as it tends to be for anxious and depressive people, negative ("That was so stupid!" or "How could I have said such a thing?"). Pause for a moment and tune in, and you'll likely find that your inner voice has plenty to say. Once you can identify your negative self-talk, you can start to confront and question it. You might ask, Is the story I'm telling myself or the observation I'm making about myself really true? Even posing the question is a huge step forward, as awareness begins to break the hold of negative self-talk.

Writer Anne Lamott refers to our "always-on" inner monologue as radio station KFKD. In one ear is the voice of self-aggrandizement that tells you how special and brilliant and amazing you are, and in the other is the voice that relishes pointing out all your failures and shortcomings and doubts.[2] If you're like most anxious achievers, you're very familiar with that negative voice. Most of the cognitive distortions that assail us come from negative self-talk we haven't stopped to examine. Not surprisingly, negative self-talk has been associated with anxiety, depression, post-traumatic stress disorder, aggression, and low self-esteem.[3]

Now that I'm well-therapized and well-acquainted with my negative self-talk, I can handle it more lightly, and not get bamboozled by its harsh words or waste so much time trying to deal with it. I can also examine my negative self-talk under the light of truth: Am I actually bad at writing memos? Well, yes, but who cares—I can get better. Am I actually disorganized? No, I just work differently.

So where does that voice come from? Whose is it?

Well, as so often happens, we can trace the roots of most self-talk to childhood, and this is the case even if you didn't have a harsh, cruel person in your life saying the words you're hearing now. In my household, there was a myth that I didn't work hard at school and that I simply coasted on my natural intelligence. Being called disorganized or unfocused triggers a very particular kind of inner voice for me: my mother's. More specifically, it's my mother's insistence that I didn't try hard enough and that I deserved my failures because I bullshitted everything—versus my sister, who tried so, so hard. (And if we want to go a level deeper, I'm also hearing the voice behind *that*, which says my value lies in achieving perfection.)

When that monologue begins to play on a loop, I'll stop whatever I'm doing and say, "Hi, mom!" That little moment of lighthearted awareness—calling out that voice as the long-ingrained pattern it really is and, importantly, distancing myself from it—is usually enough to arrest the stream of negative self-talk and bring me back to the present moment. Back, as it were, to reality.

That's not to say that being criticized for writing bad memos doesn't hurt. It does. But I can wave to my mom and to Doug and my other critical bosses and say to them: just because you say I am doesn't mean it's true.

This is one of the very best things about ongoing adult development. You have agency and awareness now, and you are finally able to distance yourself from those old patterns. That voice, the one saying you're a fraud and you can't handle leading a company? That voice is an unreliable narrator, and you don't have to believe it, trust it, or base your behavior on its claims. You can even stop and thank that voice for trying to protect you, but you can also tell it that you don't need that sort of full-throttle protection anymore. This technique—of externalizing your anxiety and separating yourself from it, and even summoning some gratitude for its good intent—is one of the most powerful ways of defanging anxiety.

But sometimes the most appropriate reaction is to tell that voice to buzz off.

Emmy-winning celebrity makeup artist Andrew Sotomayor has a brilliant way of dealing with his negative self-talk: calling the voice a chipmunk. He strips it of its power by naming it as the squeaky, cartoonish little beast it is: "OK, chipmunk," he says, "go away." The technique works even when his negative self-talk takes a dark turn and says things such as, "You're a piece of garbage, no one likes you, you're terrible at this, you're never going to be loved, you're unworthy of being loved." Those instances are "a little harder to battle," he says, but he recognizes that untruthful inner voice for the unreliable narrator it is and responds in the same manner: "OK, chipmunk, we're fine, just go away. I'll deal with you later."

What Sotomayor is doing so capably is getting distance from his negative self-talk and separating his authentic voice from the unreliable narrator that threatens to undermine his work and self-worth. He's able to tune out radio station KFKD and render his destructive self-talk less scary by reframing it as a teeny-tiny, powerless chipmunk.

Alice Boyes, a former clinical psychologist and the author of *The Anxiety Toolkit*, recommends coming up with a funny character, as Sotomayor did, or an obnoxious character to differentiate that anxious voice from your own. The aim, she says, is "to externalize your anxiety a little bit and have a lighter relationship with the anxious voice." It's in this calmer, less reactive state that you can begin to examine that anxious voice objectively and recognize where it's leading you astray.

The sooner you can separate *your* voice from that of your inner chipmunk and bring yourself back to reality, the sooner you'll be productive and the better your decisions will be.

The Necessity of Self-Compassion

One of the most fascinating aspects of negative self-talk is why it exists in the first place. Why do we have an inner voice that seems to chatter away of its own accord? And why does it so often tell us harmful, untrue things about ourselves that undermine our confidence and make us less happy and less effective?

Believe it or not, the answer goes right back to our primitive brains and our basic survival instinct. It turns out that, like anxiety, the primordial function of negative self-talk is to protect us from harm. If our ancestors made a mistake that threatened their survival, there was value in remembering that mistake and scolding themselves for it. Think about it: you're far less likely to repeat a mistake if you judge yourself harshly for it and feel ashamed for committing it. Over time, that self-scolding, self-shaming impulse grew stronger as evolution selected for and encoded it in our deep memory. Today it still shows up even though the mistakes we make don't often threaten our survival. Once again, it's an evolutionarily adaptive response that, in our modern context, has gone awry.

On the podcast *Hidden Brain*, psychologist and self-compassion expert Kristin Neff explains that negative self-talk, which she refers to as our inner critic, "comes from a simple desire to stay safe." It taps into the body's fight, flight, or freeze response. Because making a mistake or failing at something feels threatening and scary to us, the brain launches an anxiety response, just as it would if we heard something go bump in the night. At that point, Neff says, "we either fight ourselves, thinking we can control the situation and be safe, or we flee in shame from the perceived judgments of others, or we freeze and get stuck in rumination. And these are all really natural ways we try to stay safe, so you might even say the motivation of the inner critic is a good one, even though the consequences are anything but."

The shame we feel as a result of the inner critic's words is especially pernicious, a huge factor in dysfunctional behaviors such as addiction, eating disorders, and suicidal ideation. And self-criticism doesn't just hurt ourselves. When we're beating ourselves up, Neff explains, the stress hormone cortisol becomes elevated, and we have a shorter fuse with others. Further, because it's easy for people to pick up on each other's internal mindsets, emotions are somewhat contagious. If you're grumpy and agitated and stressed, your team is more likely to be grumpy and agitated and stressed. When that's our mindset, Neff says, we're not as patient, not as effective, and simply not as present, because shame and self-criticism are actually "incredibly self-absorbed states."[4]

So how do we get ourselves out of the downward spiral of negative self-talk, anxiety, shame, and the maladaptive behaviors we turn to in an attempt to quiet the inner critic? One powerful way is to practice self-compassion.

Now, if you're already rolling your eyes, no judgment here; I used to be one of you. But that was before I understood how revolutionary self-compassion is—and how difficult it can be to practice, as so many of us have become accustomed to the critical inner litany that plays on a loop. I also understand how extending compassion to ourselves, especially when we've made a mistake or failed to reach a goal and feel like we've let others down, can feel counterintuitive or just plain wrong: Isn't this *exactly* the time we should be criticizing ourselves, so we won't make the same mistake again? And isn't self-compassion tantamount to letting ourselves off the hook, or sweeping a problem under the rug?

On all counts, Neff's research reveals quite the opposite.

Similar to the unreliable narrator voice of anxiety, the self-critic, according to Neff, *resists reality*. It "somehow believes that perfection is possible if we just try hard enough," she says. But the reality is, everyone makes mistakes, and perfection is an impossible standard with an ever-moving goalpost. And while self-criticism can work as a short-term motivator, Neff says, "it works in the way corporal punishment works with children. It gets short-term compliance, but it causes a lot of long-term harm."

Being an Inner Ally to Yourself at Work

This exercise is based on Kristin Neff's well-known "self-compassion break" exercise, modified slightly for use in the midst of a busy day at work.[a]

When a work situation occurs that revs up your inner critic, carve out three minutes for yourself. I find that it helps to change locations, since the physical movement can quell my inner critic momentarily and cues my mind to reset. If you can't leave your desk, don't worry; this exercise is internal, so you can do it anywhere without others noticing.

Now, take a deep breath and say to yourself:

"This is a moment of anxiety." (Or pain, or stress, or suffering— whatever feels right.)

"Anxiety [or pain, stress, suffering] happens at work, and everyone experiences it sometimes."

"May I give myself the compassion I need in this moment."

Feel free to adapt this last statement to the situation. I once used this exercise after I'd blurted out a thoughtless comment in a meeting and couldn't let go of the guilt and shame—even though the group immediately accepted my apology and laughed off my gaffe, saying it was no big deal. My self-compassion statement was "May I forgive myself." At other times, it's been a simple "May I be kind to myself."

The exercise is effective because it evokes what Neff calls the three components of self-compassion: *mindful awareness* rather than over-identification with your negative thoughts and feelings, *common humanity* rather than isolation, and *self-kindness* rather than self-judgment.

a. Kristin Neff, "Exercise 2: Self-Compassion Break," self-compassion.org, n.d., https://self-compassion.org/exercise-2-self-compassion-break.

Neither does self-criticism improve your performance. "When you have a lot of anxiety, it actually undermines your ability to perform at your best," Neff explains. "If you have a lot of shame, shame actually shuts down our ability to learn and to grow." It leads to depression and lack of motivation, which means it's actually counterproductive. And rather than ignoring their mistakes or shortcomings, Neff's research found, people who are more self-compassionate take more responsibility for their mistakes, are more conscientious, and are more likely to apologize.[5] Turns out that not practicing self-compassion backfires all around.

For most of us, self-compassion will be an acquired skill, something we have to practice many times before we get into the habit. And that's OK. Have compassion for yourself even as you're learning self-compassion, and keep your endgame in mind. (To get better at practicing, read the "Being an Inner Ally to Yourself at Work" exercise.)

Self-compassion is not about letting yourself off the hook or being self-indulgent. It's about learning to stand tall, approaching your work and your role as a leader with a clear-eyed, accurate stance. It's about not getting hoodwinked and disempowered by the unreliable narrator voice of anxiety or the biased voice of the inner critic.

Don't forget: Buying into what the inner critic tells you *does* let you off the hook. If you believe you're a fraud, that you're incapable, that you don't deserve to be here, that you'll never be *good* enough . . . then you will sit down and won't step into your role as a leader.

Don't let that happen. Stand up and claim your place.

6

Thought Traps

In early 2021 I was asked to join a prestigious, invite-only group for business authors. This was the kind of company that triggered instant impostor syndrome. Bestselling writers, household names, mega TED speakers, even a four-star general . . . you get the idea. What the heck was I doing here with these impressive people? When I wrote an email to introduce myself to the group, I confessed that even saying hello created intense anxiety. To my delight, one of the group's most prestigious members replied, "Feeling impostor syndrome is a qualification to be in this group." And lots of other members jumped into the email chain and said they felt the same way. This was a big "Aha!" moment for me: so many of us feel like we don't belong, even—or especially—the most ambitious among us.

Impostor syndrome, the inability to believe that you deserve your success and that it's a result of your skills, is a prime example of what psychologists call a *thought trap*. You may also have heard thought traps referred to as cognitive distortions, thinking errors, or automatic negative thoughts. Though these negatively biased and untrue patterns of thinking do indeed distort our perceptions and become so ingrained that they arrive automatically, I prefer the term thought trap, as it gets at that sense of being ensnared.

Thought traps tend to run on repeat, and they are more prone to occur when we're distressed. It's no surprise, then, that anxious and depressed people tend to experience thought traps more frequently. Just consider: If all you can think is, *I'm a fraud, and any day now people will find out I actually don't know what I'm doing,* your mood and self-confidence are going to plummet and your anxiety will escalate. And from there, the thought trap will influence your behavior. Some people may turn to overwork to combat the feelings of fraudulence; others may turn to a maladaptive coping mechanism such as substance use, avoidance, or passive-aggressiveness. Whatever the feeling or the behavior, it's the distorted *thinking*—the thought trap—that's steering the ship.

When thought traps occur, we can't see clearly, communicate effectively, or make effective, reality-based decisions. Often the consequences of the ill-advised decisions we do make negatively affect us and the teams we lead. That compounds our anxiety and can lead us into further thought traps. It truly becomes a vicious cycle.

Becoming aware of your thought traps can take some practice, as they're so habitual and automatic that we often don't even notice them—they feel like parts of our personalities. Here's an exercise to try: Think of a time when you felt anxious. It could be a situation from the past that sticks with you, something that bubbled up recently during a tense negotiation, or something you're experiencing right now. How did you respond mentally to that anxiety? Did you automatically assume the situation was your fault? Assume the worst was going to happen? Think that this always happens to you, and no one else? Become fixated on what went wrong, unable to let it go? These are all examples of thought traps and of your anxiety speaking up!

Rest assured, you're in good company—we all become ensnared by thought traps from time to time. Moreover, they're so common that there's a wealth of guidance we can draw on for help.

Why Do Thought Traps Occur?

The simplest—and least satisfying—reason thought traps happen is that we're human. *Everyone* engages in thought traps, and it's surprisingly easy to make illogical connections or unhelpful assumptions, or to default to biased attitudes or old patterns of thinking.

One explanation for why this occurs is a story that will seem familiar by now: Our errors in thinking can be traced back to a survival instinct that's been wired to make snap judgments. The brain, writes clinical psychologist Paul Gilbert, has evolved a "better safe than sorry" threat appraisal system that privileges efficiency over accuracy. It has a tendency to assume the worst and overestimate the level of threat, and to launch a threat response immediately in an effort to make sure we're safe.[1] *If I always assume the worst will happen*, your brain says, *I can always be prepared for it.*

Cognitive behavioral therapy, or CBT, teaches us that the particular types of thought traps we're prone to is a result of the core, fundamental beliefs we learn from childhood *plus* our attitudes and assumptions as we get older and try to make sense of the world around us.[2] Here's an example. If you grew up in a household where your parents were overprotective and tried to shelter you from any harm or disappointment, your core belief could be that the world is a dangerous place. From the bedrock of that core belief, attitudes and assumptions such as *I must stay small to survive* or *I can never let my guard down* can emerge. With this anxious orientation to the world influencing our perceptions, it's easy to see how we can succumb to irrational thoughts and beliefs.

Psychiatrist David Burns, an early student of the late psychiatrist Aaron Beck, who we met in chapter 5, says that when we're upset, we often tell ourselves exaggerated or untrue stories about the world and about ourselves. It's only when we can become aware of this "mental con" that we can shift our thinking, which will shift our feelings. And then, of course, we can shift the way we act.[3]

Letting go of thought traps, or toning them down, is one of the biggest acts of leadership you can take. Why? Because leadership is about taking risks. When you're stuck in thought traps you will find it almost impossible to take risks, because the price of failure seems fatal. But that's the mental con! The reality is, your threat appraisal system is overreacting because that's what it has been wired to do, and the things you're telling yourself in reaction to that perceived threat are not true, or at least are greatly exaggerated.

Common Thought Traps of Anxious Achievers

Let's look at the top ten thought traps that most commonly affect us at work and in the context of leadership. Most of these examples come from Burns's classic book, *The Feeling Good Handbook*. I've included a few others—catastrophizing and overthinking—that seem to particularly affect anxious achievers.

All-or-nothing thinking

Burns described this one as the tendency to see things in black-or-white categories. If a situation falls short of perfection in your eyes, for example, you see it as a total failure.[4]

All-or-nothing thinking, also known as *polarized thinking*, robs us of the chance to experience life in its full variety and complexity. It leads to poor self-esteem, bad decisions, and, like all cognitive distortions, a focus on the negative. A classic example is the typical job interview. The all-or-nothing thinker will leave the interview focusing on a single blunder they committed or the one thing they wish they'd said, and conclude that the entire interview was a bust and there's no way they're getting the job. A healthier, more nuanced stance is to consider the interview as a whole: sure, there are a few things you wish you'd done differently, but by and large the interview went OK. One of the best ways to respond to all-or-nothing thinking is to replace the "or" with "and." There were positive *and* negative moments in the interview. The experience was a mixture of good *and* bad.

When you're convinced it's all a disaster, reach out to a trusted adviser. For me, this is usually my husband or my former business partner. They know me well, and as reliable narrators they bring a dose of reality into whatever situation has triggered me. Sometimes that will mean helping me see in shades of gray rather than in my rigid, perfection-versus-failure mindset. One important note: Consulting a trusted adviser is a healthy coping mechanism as long as the person you're reaching out to doesn't feel dumped on and is capable of providing that objective view. Otherwise you're just passing on negative feelings.

Labeling

Labeling, Burns says, is an extreme form of all-or-nothing thinking. "Instead of saying, 'I made a mistake, you attach a negative label to yourself: 'I'm a loser,'" Burns writes. We each have our own go-to labels when it comes to criticizing ourselves and putting ourselves down; hurtful labels like *failure*, *incompetent*, *unqualified*, and *undeserving* seem to show up frequently in the negative self-talk of anxious or depressed individuals. Just as you'd imagine, these labels only exacerbate the problem. Burns calls them "useless abstractions that lead to anger, anxiety, frustration, and low self-esteem."

Of course, we can engage in labeling when it comes to other people as well. If your boss makes a poor decision, you can automatically think, *What an idiot!* even though nine times out of ten he makes good decisions.

Burns points out that labeling is inherently irrational because people are not the same as what they do. In other words, there is a distinction between our core identities and our activities. The thought trap of labeling erroneously ascribes the source of a problem to a person's entire character or essence, rather than to their thinking or behavior.

Once again, such an error in thinking gets you off the hook when it comes to improving a situation. If you think you're inherently bad (*I am a failure*), rather than a normal person who makes mistakes or bad decisions (*I occasionally fail*), you've essentially given up before even trying. The same thing occurs when you label other people. "You see them as totally bad," Burns writes. "This makes you feel hostile and hopeless about improving things and leaves little room for constructive communication."[5] Labeling makes it difficult to create a workplace culture with constructive communication and teams committed to improving performance.

One of the best ways to combat any thought trap is to examine the evidence for and against your error in thinking. I think this works particularly well for labeling. Let's go back to that example of your boss. He makes a poor decision, and your automatic thought is, *What an idiot!*

First, what's the evidence demonstrating that he's an idiot? In this case, your evidence is that he made a poor decision today. Is there anything else? Write it all down. Now, examine your evidence for truthfulness. Is a single poor decision really proof that your boss is an idiot? Of course not. Writing down the evidence for the opposing view helps, too. What evidence do you have that your boss is *not* an idiot? I'll bet there's plenty! You can do this same thing for yourself, and once again, I bet you'll find that an isolated incident caused you to attach a negative (and untrue) label to yourself—and find plenty of things to attest to your competence and skill.

You may feel silly or embarrassed by your thought traps once you've exposed them to the cold light of day. And that's OK! It's so easy to get caught up in irrational thinking when we're under pressure or depressed. Bringing these thoughts out of our minds is often enough to release their hold on us.

Jumping to conclusions

There are two forms of this familiar thought trap: *Mind reading* occurs when you arbitrarily conclude that someone is reacting negatively to you. When you're *fortune telling*, you predict that things will turn out badly, even if you have no proof that they will.

Mind reading can lead us to believe that others are thinking things that they really aren't. ("He doesn't think I deserve my promotion." "I'm sure she's angry with me.") Fortune telling can lead us to inaction: if you convince yourself that things aren't going to get any better, why bother trying?

In addition to the harmful effects that jumping to conclusions can have on our self-esteem, productivity, and relationships, this thought trap presents a special danger: it can seriously impair our decision-making. If we make a decision based on insufficient evidence, we're very likely to be wrong. All leaders need to make quick decisions from time to time, but when you're under pressure—or if you're anxious by nature and have a tough time tolerating uncertainty—that's a great time to assemble a group of trusted advisers to make sure you're seeing all the evidence, and to run your thinking by them.

Another great way to counteract this common thought trap is to hit it with a dose of truth. First, ask yourself: Do I actually have access to someone else's inner thoughts? Can I *really* know exactly what's going to happen in the future? Next, test your conclusion. What evidence do you have to support it? Write it down. Often, we come up with a pretty paltry list! I once thought a colleague was angry with me because she didn't smile when we passed each other in the hallway, but turns out her worried, unhappy expression had absolutely nothing to do with me. Both of her kids were sick, and she was on her way to pick them up from school. You can also remind yourself of the times you jumped to the wrong conclusion in the past. Is it possible it could be happening on this occasion as well?

Catastrophizing

One of the most common thought traps, catastrophizing is jumping to the worst conclusion based on little or no evidence. That little blemish must be melanoma; an argument with your significant other signals the end of the relationship; the less-than-perfect performance review means you're getting fired. A catastrophist might always assume the worst-case scenario, no matter what the issue at hand is.

Catastrophizing isn't just about irrational fears. Telling ourselves that a task is so huge or so awful that we simply can't do it can quickly undermine our performance. Take the example of running a cash flow analysis for your business. When you open up the accounting software, your mind might go to a dark place, and all of a sudden, a month's worth of figures has spiraled into a belief that the business will tank and you will lose your home. Even if you're fully aware that what you're telling yourself isn't true and you have plenty of evidence to the contrary, when your anxiety is high and you're in the grip of this particular thought trap, even the most outlandish "what if" scenarios seem plausible.

The award-winning author Ashley C. Ford incisively captured the sham logic that's inherent in this experience: anxiety and depression are unreliable narrators. You can listen to them, but you don't have to agree with what they're telling you. They are liars. "That's what they do," she says. "[Their function] is to lie to you and tell you that everything is going to go wrong all the time and that you are always going to make a bad impression." But Ford has learned to discern when a feeling comes from her true self, and when it's being fueled by the lies her anxiety and depression are telling her. "You have to just stop and go, 'That is how I feel . . . but that is not reality. That is a feeling, and feelings are not facts.'"

Back in March 2020, when the stock market slumped and people's fears about Covid-19 spiked, one of my biggest clients canceled its work with my small business. I quickly convinced myself that our company was doomed. *We'll never survive this*, I kept telling myself. But then I consulted with my business partner (a more reliable narrator than I), and she suggested we adjust our forecast based on the numbers—the facts, in other words, and not my feelings. The facts revealed that we'd lose half our revenue for the year. This was upsetting, but it was a far different scenario than going out of business completely. Armed with the facts, we could adjust to make up for the loss.

Catastrophizing isn't rational, so you can't reason your way out of it. The far more effective way to get free of this thought trap is to take a small, meaningful action to stop the mental spiral. Sometimes it will be as simple as consulting a more reliable narrator. Sometimes it will be moving the needle just a tiny bit forward. This may seem minor, but making even a small amount of progress will ease anxiety and give your brain the nudge it needs to refocus and get back to productive work. It will also get your attention off of your fretful imagined scenarios, and onto something productive.

In general, focus on the near term whenever you can. You may not be able to tell your employees what will happen next year, or even three months from now. You can't promise everything will be OK. But you can help your people, and yourself, feel safe this week. Focus on that and deal with the big questions when you feel calmer or when you can get input from trusted colleagues. Sometimes you have to turn off the future for a little while in order to manage through the present.

Filtering

Burns describes mental filtering in terms of its negative presentation: "You pick out a single negative detail and dwell on it exclusively, so that your vision of all reality becomes darkened, like the drop of ink that discolors a beaker of water. Example: You receive many positive comments about your presentation [from] a group of associates at work, but one of them says something mildly critical. You obsess about his reaction for days and ignore all the positive feedback." But it works both ways: you can fixate on a single positive detail while discounting more critical or negative information.

Either way, you see how the error in thinking clouds your perception of reality. We fixate on a very narrow slice of experience and ignore the rest, missing our chance to benefit from the preponderance of evidence to the contrary. When we dwell on the negative, we miss out on capitalizing on all the things we do well, and it's so easy to become discouraged, or even hopeless. When we dwell on the positive at the exclusion of hearing constructive feedback, we miss the chance to hone our skills and up our game.

A practical way to confront this thought trap—as well as the next one, discounting the positive—is to keep a record of your accomplishments. Keep a running collection of emails, tweets, messages, compliments, or other forms of positive feedback—objective proof that you're doing good work—and review it when you're feeling overwhelmed or doubtful of your accomplishments. (Bonus benefit: an achievement log makes self-assessments and performance reviews a snap.)

Discounting the positive

This thought trap is very similar to filtering, but I want to mention it specifically because it shows up so frequently in anxious achievers. It's the fallacy of rejecting positive experiences by insisting they don't count.

I've heard so many leaders discount their successes in this manner, and I've been guilty of it myself. You attribute a success to an instance of luck or good timing, calling it a fluke. Or maybe you dismiss a job well done by saying it was nothing special, anyone could have done it.

While at first glance, discounting the positive doesn't seem to be as harmful as some of the other thought traps, think about what happens if it prevents you from repeating a success or trying something new. A former colleague of mine has a phobia of public speaking. While she has delivered well-received presentations, she believes each one is a fluke that can't happen again, and thus she passes up desirable opportunities that would require a more public role.

"Should" statements

"I should be further along in my career by now." "My boss shouldn't be so stubborn and set in her ways." "It shouldn't be so hard to get ahead at this company." "I should know better." There are endless examples of this very common thought trap. Be on the lookout when words like *should, must, ought to, have to,* and their negative forms come up.

"Should" statements are a thought trap because you're telling yourself that things should be the way you hoped or expected them to be. Should statements don't reflect reality as it is. As our examples above attest, they can be directed at yourself, others, or the world in general. Trying to motivate yourself by using should statements usually backfires, Burns says, because you're treating yourself as a delinquent who has to be punished before you can be expected to do anything, and it leaves you feeling rebellious and more apt to do just the opposite.

Should statements can also be toxic at work. Should statements aimed at yourself can be damaging to your mood and motivation ("I should never have presented that proposal in draft form. Now my boss thinks I can't spell or write!"). Should statements aimed at colleagues can feel punishing and shaming to them. How many times have you thought something like, *He should know better than to contradict our boss in public. What's wrong with him?!* Should statements aimed at the world or at systems can lead to anger and frustration, rather than real change.

Then there is the thought trap of comparative shoulds. Some research-ers consider social comparison its own separate cognitive distortion, especially when the comparison results in a negative self-assessment ("He'll always have higher sales than I do," or "She'll always earn more money"). Sociology professor Jessica Calarco highlights a specific iter-ation of comparative shoulds that can be pernicious at work. "If you feel like everyone else in your workplace is putting in seventy hours a week, and you feel like you're only putting in thirty-five because that's all you can possibly do, or even less than that, then you're going to feel out of place and awkward and like a failure," she says. "[You'll feel] like you're not living up to the standard that is set for everyone else." This kind of competitive, unhealthy work culture is common, and it creates both individual and collective anxiety.

When you find yourself engaging in a should statement, try writing it down and then reframing it in a gentler, less demanding way. For example, rather than "I should be further along in my career by now," try reframing it as "I'd like to be further along in my career." Now, are there actions you can take to make that happen? Sometimes the answer is yes. And sometimes you'll find that the belief behind your should statement is unrealistic. For example, "I should always be able to antic-ipate my boss's needs" isn't realistic. You can let go of this impossible standard.

Personalization and blaming

Personalization and blaming are opposite expressions of the same error in thinking. Personalization occurs when you hold yourself responsible for external circumstances and actions that aren't under your control. Even if the action is committed by someone else, you take the blame for it. Blaming is the opposite.

Here's an example. One of your direct reports is struggling with their workload, and you take this as evidence of what a bad manager you are. That's how personalization works: it's *your* fault they're struggling. With blaming, on the other hand, you place all the responsibility on your direct report: it's *their* fault they can't handle their work.

The healthier response in both cases—for you and your direct report—is to meet with this person and ask them what's causing the problem, and then strategize on solutions. Note that this response gets you out of your head and requires you to listen to the other person, which shifts your attention from the private realm of distorted thinking to the external, where you can hear reality.

Self-blame, by the way, is a big one for anxious achievers. We assume things are our fault even if they're systemic or way beyond our control. Why are we so eager to take the blame for things that, examined logically, can't possibly be our fault?

Psychologists offer three general reasons, and they all have to do with self-protection. First, self-blame may offer an illusion of control—and we know how anxiety-inducing it is to feel uncertain or out of control. If we take responsibility for a negative event, it means this outcome was potentially controllable or avoidable, which means we convince ourselves that we retain some form of control. Second, self-blame can be a way to avoid conflict. If we take on the blame ourselves, it relieves us of the need to confront others or even retaliate against them, which runs the risk of prompting a counterattack. Either way, we avoid the stress and anxiety of a direct confrontation. Third, self-blame may be a learned response to old childhood wounds or past trauma. When you were a child and relatively powerless, it may have been safer to blame yourself when something went wrong at home and to act submissively, rather than to confront a parent and risk their anger. Learned early, this can become a lifelong habitual response.

With this thought trap, applying self-compassion techniques can be powerful. Refer back to the "Being an Inner Ally to Yourself at Work" exercise in chapter 5 for more.

Ruminating and overthinking

Ruminating is a type of obsessive thinking that involves repetitive thoughts or themes. I call it stewing. Often these thoughts center on negative events that happened in the past, but it's just as easy to become fixated on problems in the present or that we anticipate in the future. Whatever the object of our ruminations, this thought trap is a huge anxiety amplifier, and it can undermine mood, performance, and productivity.

Ruminating is such a common thought trap that we can all come up with a litany of personal examples. Who hasn't dwelled upon a careless comment, a time you were slighted or insulted, or that time you were embarrassed back in sixth grade? Or who hasn't become so fixated on a problem at work or in a relationship that we constantly turn it over in our minds, playing it on a loop?

I asked anxiety expert Alice Boyes why we do this, as ruminating causes us so much more anxiety.

"Anxious people like to resolve uncertainty as soon as possible, and often they can end up rushing into situations that don't need to be rushed into," she told me. "People will end up accepting worse outcomes over potentially better ones because they don't want to tolerate uncertainty." And the rumination? Turns out, in its own weird way, your brain is trying to solve a problem for you. "Recognize that you've got some emotional pain there and your brain is trying to help you figure it out, but it's just not doing that in a way that is actually helpful," Boyes said. The reason goes back to what we've learned about how our brains try to protect us against perceived threats.

Ruminating reinforces anxiety. Psychologists tell us that what distinguishes rumination from helpful processing is that rumination doesn't generate new ways of thinking, new behaviors, or new solutions. Instead, it covers the same territory over and over and over again, keeping us locked in a negative mindset, with no movement toward a solution.[6]

In a perverse way, overthinking and rumination can actually feel good to us: it feels better to do something rather than nothing in an anxiety-provoking situation. "People often think that worry has some sort of protective benefit so that it helps them make good decisions," Boyes said. Our minds say, "'If I don't worry about something . . . I'm going to let things slip through the cracks. I'm not going to foresee something that might go wrong.' People end up believing that they need to think through everything in advance." But if anything, she said, the opposite happens, leaving us feeling more confused, more stuck, and eventually languishing in a pattern of inaction.

I'll admit, this one is really tough for me, and I'm still working on it. But one way I've found to interrupt ruminating at least for a while is to write down my thoughts. This is another way of "exposing my thoughts to the light" so that I can better see when they're irrational or illogical. When I can see them for what they are, it gives me motivation to move on.

Emotional reasoning

Emotional reasoning can be summed up as "I feel it, therefore it must be true." For example: "'I feel terrified about going on airplanes. It must be very dangerous to fly.' Or 'I feel guilty. I must be a rotten person.'"[7] According to CBT, emotional reasoning gets it backward: feelings are actually a *product* of thoughts and beliefs, and if our thoughts are biased, the emotions we experience because of them don't reflect reality.[8]

An example of emotional reasoning that commonly affects performance happens when you feel overwhelmed by your workload: "I feel really overwhelmed, so it must mean I'm not capable of handling my job." And as feelings and thoughts affect behavior, what will happen if you react in an unhealthy manner? For example, if you react to your feeling of overwhelm with avoidance or procrastination—two classic unhealthy reactions we'll examine in chapter 7—you compound not just your anxiety, but your already overwhelming workload.

What's a healthy response? As with many thought traps, do what you can to get out of your head. Talk to a therapist or other trusted adviser, and run a truth test on these instances of emotional reasoning. Your feeling of incompetence, for example, is temporary and very likely to be exaggerated, or probably even false.

Thought Traps and Your Leadership Style

Of course, living in your thought traps is stressful and painful for you. But now imagine how your coworkers and direct reports feel. Leaders' behavior—everything from your general demeanor to your tone of voice to your moods to how you react under pressure—has a disproportionate effect on employees. If your anxiety is palpable, it's most certainly affecting others, and if you're relying on thought traps to quell anxiety, chances are everyone feels less safe and therefore can't perform at their best. No one can think clearly or deliver peak performance when they're walking on eggshells or are constantly triggered.

We joke about Debbie Downers and Nervous Neds, but the truth is, it's deeply challenging to work for someone who always assumes they're the worst or that anything that goes wrong is their fault, or who can't accept mistakes and shortcomings as anything less than epic failures.

In contrast, psychologically safe teams are able to make mistakes openly and talk about them afterward. We all crave psychological safety at work, and it's so crucial for doing good work, but it's hard to come by. Most of us fear making mistakes because we fear looking foolish, unqualified, or incompetent. We fear shame. Psychological safety is hard to achieve when you feel your job rests on being right.

I had an "Aha!" moment a few years ago when my kindergartener told me that he'd learned a big lesson in school that day. He proudly relayed, "When I make a mistake, my brain grows! So it's a good thing to make mistakes." That felt like a radical concept to me. And I wondered: Does my team feel that way around me? Are they scared to make mistakes? Well, am I scared to make mistakes? (Yes.) Like many adults who fear shame and looking foolish in front of others, do I work extra hard to look like I always know the answers? (Yes.)

So I asked Harvard Business School professor Amy Edmondson, who brought the concept of psychological safety into public consciousness, to clear up some of the myths around psychological safety.

First of all, Edmondson told me, psychological safety is "not being nice. It's not 'safe space.' It's not a trigger-free environment. It's not a guarantee that everything you do will get a round of applause." So what is it? "It *is* a sense of permission for candor. [It's] the belief that you can be yourself. You can speak up, ask for help, disagree with an idea, admit a mistake—and you won't be rejected or punished in some way."

A psychologically safe environment, she said, is one "where your focus is on the task or on other people. Not on yourself, not on, 'How do I look? How am I coming across? Am I OK? Will I get rejected?'"

In short, it's an environment free of the fear of being shamed.

I asked Edmondson if working in a psychologically safe environment is the opposite of walking around with social anxiety. She affirmed that: "It's the opposite of social fear, and it's really important for teamwork and knowledge-related work of any kind that forces us to take risks and get some things wrong on the way to discovery and advances. We want to make a contribution, we want to be among people whom we like and respect, and we don't want to feel that anxiety that we might be rejected."

Chris Yates, chief talent officer for Ford Motor Company, and a guest on my *Anxious Achiever* podcast, once held a failure party with one of his teams, complete with a DJ. Yes, they celebrated a massive organizational failure with fancy dress, cake, and cocktails. "We celebrated the hell out of the failure because it was a great learning moment," he said, adding that he told the team, "We're going to wring every single learning we can out of this catastrophe, so it will never, ever happen again." And they did. Nothing close to it has ever happened again. "In fact, the excellence of that team directly came from the experience of that moment," Yates said. It was a pivotal bonding experience.

If a failure party is a bit much for you, here are a few things you can do if you're craving a more psychologically safe team environment but struggling to get there: Admit you don't know something, and laugh about it. Own up to a mistake, and brush it off. If a team or organization experiences a failure, ask a bunch of good, nonjudging questions about what everyone thinks has happened.

Our heroes don't fear feeling shame, and I think if we want to get our teams to a psychologically healthier place, we have to be open to the fear too. Your brain will grow if you make a mistake!

How to Loosen the Grip of Thought Traps

OK, let's say you've recognized some thinking patterns in our list of thought traps. Welcome! You're in good company. But what do you do now? I will always tout the enormous value of working with a good therapist, but there are small effective actions you can take right now to begin loosening the grip of your thought traps. Here are some practices that work.

Work on your mindset

The right mindset is essential, so before you try to address a thought trap, shower yourself with self-compassion. I know this won't feel natural to many of you—believe me, I get it. But you're not going to get anywhere by beating yourself up, and *you can't think your way out of a thought trap.* Just remember: we all experience thought traps, and if you can regard yourself with a little bit of lightness and humor, you're going to feel so much better so much more quickly—and you're going to be more productive and effective more quickly too.

See the humor

If your self-compassion tank is full and you're able to see the humor in your thought traps, have a good, healthy laugh at yourself. Some of our thought traps are so absurd! And they can be truly funny if we follow them to their logical conclusions: Do your typos actually mean you're going to get fired? Could it possibly be solely your fault that your company didn't meet its sales goals? Of course not! Distorted thinking can lead us to believe some outlandish things. Recognizing that absurdity, and treating it with a dose of lightheartedness, immediately loosens the grip of a thought trap.

Get moving

Your mind is the source of the thought trap—so get outta there! Do something physical to break free of the thought trap's hold. Go for a walk. Grab coffee with a colleague. Reach out to a trusted adviser. Stand up and stretch. Listen to some music. Get up and dance. Even if you're posing reality-check questions to yourself ("Does this one mistake really mean my entire career is tanked?"), don't just think about them—physically write them down.

Give guided meditation a try

Try guided, rather than silent, meditation. I've found that when my anxiety is really high or a thought trap is entrenched, my meditation practice quickly turns into a session of ruminating (or catastrophizing, or filtering, or whatever the thought trap *du jour* is). It's helpful to keep up your meditation or mindfulness practice for all sorts of reasons, so try switching it up to guided meditation for a while. Focusing on another person's words takes the focus off of you and distracts you from your unhelpful thinking.

Find the shades of gray

When you realize you're engaging in black-or-white (all-or-nothing) thinking, look for shades of gray. Write down the two extremes in your thinking—for example, perfection or failure—and then list descriptions that more accurately reflect your performance. (Your achievement log will come in handy here. And if you can't yet see the shades of gray, do this exercise with a trusted adviser.) You'll find that your list contains successes *and* mistakes, victories *and* setbacks. Now look at those two extremes again. Are they realistic? Is anyone perfectly perfect? A complete failure? No, not even you.

Try balanced thinking to sift fact from opinion

One of the key tenets of cognitive behavioral therapy is that facts are not opinions. That may seem obvious, but when you're anxious, depressed, or triggered, it can be easy to forget that your opinion about something isn't necessarily factual. So write down your thoughts and see if they're facts or just opinions that shift based on your mental state. Then you can offer yourself an alternative to your thought trap, a *balanced thought*. For example, if your thought trap is "Because I messed up the numbers on that slide, my team will lose respect for me," a more balanced thought could be: "Yes, I got the projections wrong. That was embarrassing. But it's the first time in three years I've ever done something like this. It's not a big deal in the long run and it was only an internal team presentation. Overall, my staff really trusts me, and I know this because I saw my recent 360-degree review."

Sometimes you find that your anxious thoughts *are* based in reality. If you're willing to be brave, looking at your mistakes can help you better understand your fears. For example, do you always choke in high-pressure situations, or just sometimes? Or maybe you did bomb a presentation—but does that really mean you'll be fired? When you can differentiate fact from opinion, you can let yourself off the hook and relieve yourself of a great deal of anxiety. And you can identify what needs attention and what you can actually improve.

Just say no

This one is deceptively simple, but sometimes it's exactly what's needed. When you recognize that you're in the grip of a thought trap, literally say "no" or "stop" aloud. Use whatever pithy response suits your personality and mood: "Nope!" "No, thanks." "Not today!" The point is to quite literally interrupt the thought trap. The more you engage in this healthy habit, the stronger it becomes. Your brain will learn this cue to break free of a thought trap before it spirals out of control.

What If the Worst *Does* Happen?

I'll be honest with you. My original conclusion for this chapter was a more traditional take: a summary of key ideas, along with some heart-felt encouragement to help you let go of thought traps so that you won't be held back from realizing the fullness of your leadership.

But I want to tell you about a time when my thought traps were actually right.

Once I started a big job that quickly became a source of constant conflict and of conversations so tense that I cried. My boss and I soon agreed that I needed to leave when my contract ended. I would be unemployed and starting over—which was definitely not my plan!

For months, thought traps ruled my life. Catastrophizing: *I'm going to lose everything and be broke.* Shoulds: *You should have done more due diligence on the organization before leaping into this new role.*

And so much ruminating. Dwelling on details, on comments, on emails. I couldn't eat or sleep because all I did was dwell, try to mind read (*I'm sure everyone at the new company thinks I'm stupid or a fraud*), and predict the future (always with a doomsday scenario). I was a poster child for every cognitive distortion in the book, and I acted out my anxiety.

I was the queen of all-or-nothing thinking. Starting over when I'd had such big dreams was hard. But the funny thing was, all the experienced businesspeople to whom I told my story sort of shrugged it off. Like this was just a normal part of life, instead of the catastrophe it felt like.

Then one day my ninety-one-year-old stepfather, who'd had a very long career in business, told me, "Welcome to the club." The club of people who've gotten fired, made bad decisions, fucked up, lost a lot of money, had all their plans change. Yes, if you're in business long enough, you'll do all these things. My stepfather was telling me, as Burns notes, that I, like everyone, have the right to take risks and not succeed. In a way, I had to get over my inflated self-image and accept my weakness.

And then I realized I still had to lead. People needed me to show up. My team, my clients, and my reputation called for me to accept this difficult change and illustrate the path forward. I had to put my anxiety aside and tune in to what my colleagues needed from me as I transitioned out of the company. I understood that they too were anxious, because I had hired them and now I wouldn't be there anymore. As I approached my end date, I had to create a communications plan that broke the bond but provided assurances.

And guess what: everyone is fine without me!

Anxious achievers, perhaps even more than most people, need to look our egos in the eye and realize: We don't have to be perfect or always be better than others. We have the right to fail and carry on anyway. "When you no longer need to be special, life becomes special," observes Burns's colleague Taylor Chesney.[9] There's great freedom in letting go of (or, in my case, having wrested from me) the compulsion to be perfect, or special, or better than.

Later, after some of the anger had burned off and I could regard the situation with more clarity, I saw that my thought traps weren't telling the entire truth after all. I was still the skilled professional who'd gotten the job in the first place. The very worst *hadn't* happened. My original plan had failed, sure, but I wasn't left with nothing. My staff was settled in. The company was thriving without me. I wasn't destitute, my family and friends didn't love me any less, and I came away with an abundance of hard-won lessons that changed my leadership for the better. I even feel respect and admiration for my former boss.

It took a long time to manage the feelings, but the process of experiencing such disruptive change actually quelled a lot of my go-to thought traps. By accepting that I'm no smarter or better than anyone else who might make a bad decision and pay the consequences, I'm not just a better leader, but a better person to be around.

And if I ever decide to throw my own failure party, you'll be the first to know.

7

Unhelpful Reactions and Bad Habits

Jason Kander, a veteran of the war in Afghanistan, became a rising star in the Democratic Party. He was a state senator in Missouri by his mid-twenties and its secretary of state at thirty-one. Later he ran for the US Senate, launched a campaign to become mayor of Kansas City, and was forthright about his ambitions to one day become president. Because of his charisma, connections, and media appeal, politicians constantly asked him to host fundraisers and make introductions. He said yes to every request and flew all over the country to deliver keynotes and raise money, even though behind the scenes he was suffering excruciating nightmares, terrible guilt and shame, and panic anxiety.

It was only when he began to entertain thoughts of suicide that Kander sought out help and began weekly therapy through the local Veterans Affairs facility.

Kander learned that he'd been suffering from undiagnosed, untreated PTSD, and reacting to it by trying to be a hero to others, always rushing in to help and pushing himself relentlessly. He now realizes that his ambition was fueled in part by the attempt to self-soothe through some of our most socially acceptable and rewarded unhealthy coping mechanisms: overwork and people-pleasing.

Many anxious leaders rely on unhealthy reactions that may be soothing in the short term but ultimately become habits that make them more stressed, deplete their energy, and undermine their leadership. The problem is, once the temporary relief wears off, whatever was making them anxious is still there—and often it's grown worse while they were avoiding it.

Ironically, unhelpful reactions can help people advance in their career. Overwork, for example, is frequently lauded. Kander's drive led to a life filled with accolades many of us only dream of and a fast-track career in public office.

But at some point, our bad habits will exact a toll that is too high. Work can become an addiction for many of us—a way to avoid issues we don't want to deal with, people we don't want to confront, or internal demons. If you want to truly manage your anxiety for the long haul, you need to understand the origins of your drive to work too hard and examine if the plaudits are really worth the price.

Why Do We Form Habits?

Our brains are constantly searching for the most efficient means to complete a task and will convert almost any routine process or task into a habit, because habits save time and metabolic energy. Habits allow the brain to operate on autopilot, relieving us of the burden of thinking through routine tasks step-by-step. Habits are behaviors we adopt to give our anxiety something to do. If we're drinking a martini instead of feeling anxious about that looming deadline, our brain thinks that's a win.

Research has shown that, like all animals, we are more likely to revert to heavily ingrained patterns or coping behaviors when we're under stress.[1] When a job disruption throws you off a comfortable routine, you may feel tremendous anxiety and lack of control. One executive, suddenly working from home during the Covid-19 pandemic, told me he mimicked his morning commute by driving to Starbucks every morning in an attempt to make things feel more normal, even though he'd hated his commute for years. This habit frustrated him and wasted time, but he kept it up because it was a deeply ingrained pattern and brought him relief from anxiety in the short term. Notice your desire to turn to familiar patterns, whether harmful or helpful, when you're triggered. No doubt your employees feel the same.

But what alerts us that a habit is no longer serving us, even if it consistently delivers a reward? We experience some sort of negative consequence that outweighs the reward. Avoiding your work results in missed deadlines and poor performance reviews. Or maybe you exercise so much that you sustain a stress fracture. Maybe you realize that automatically worrying each time you're given a new deliverable is a habit that isn't helping you create excellent work.

Whatever has brought you to this point, you're aware that you want to make a change. And that's what we're focusing on in this chapter: the unhealthy reactions that become habits that threaten our leadership and exacerbate anxiety over time.

Common Unhelpful Reactions

Let's take a look at some of the most common negative reactions to workplace anxiety. Some of them take place within us; we may be the only ones aware of the internal struggle. Others play out in our interactions with others.

Micromanaging

Micromanaging and hovering over employees are common anxiety reactions (remember the overfunctioner in chapter 4?). Now that so many of us are working remotely, and team members can't be summoned, controlled, or rallied around for feedback, you may be even more present in your employees' inboxes and Slack channels. Sometimes we're aware that we're micromanaging, and other times we're acting out our anxieties habitually.

Poppy Jaman, who runs the UK's City Mental Health Alliance and was CEO and founder of Mental Health First Aid England, says that when she catches herself micromanaging, it's a sure sign that her periodic depression is flaring. This is very important to notice, she says, not only because it's a signal that she needs to take care of her mental health, but because she doesn't want her employees to feel pressured.

Jaman, a trained ambassador for mental health in the workplace, is very aware of her anxiety and depression tells. But what about the rest of us? How can we recognize when we're stepping in too often and are actually impeding progress with our frequent check-ins?

Here are other telltale signs that you're micromanaging: you insist on being cc'd on everything; you tell team members to run everything by you; you assign yourself to projects that don't need your input; you refuse to delegate; you spend a lot of time correcting employees' work; or you're convinced that your way is the best way to get things done. There are many more, but what they have in common is an underlying need to control things. And that, of course, arises from anxiety.

The best way to tame micromanaging tendencies is to address your anxiety—much like Jaman's method was to take care of herself before depression gained too much of a foothold. But there are also leadership techniques you can use to dial back on your micromanagement and let your employees thrive. One is to use the tried-and-true 80/20 rule. In this case, that means letting your employee complete a task in their own way 80 percent of the time. For the remaining 20 percent, *guide* your employee—but even then, remember that your role is to motivate, not to check in frequently or do the task for them. Another technique is to focus on beginnings and endings, rather than middles. That means you issue clear objectives, expectations, and deadlines, and then throughout the middle of the work, make yourself available for guidance—but otherwise, resist the temptation to check in. At the end, when the employee has met their target, you can assess the outcome.

Procrastinating

Seth Gillihan, psychologist and host of the *Think Act Be* podcast, says that two forms of self-talk tend to drive procrastination: (1) "This is going to be a pain" and (2) "I might not do a good job."[2] With one (or both) of those narratives playing on repeat in our minds, is there any wonder we put off a task we'll find unpleasant or that we fear we won't do well? For the anxious achiever, this is prime anxiety-trigger territory, and procrastination is an understandable response.

The bad habit of procrastination is an excellent example of what psychologists call *negative reinforcement*: negative in the sense that we experience a reward in *not* having an unpleasant experience, and reinforcement because it makes the behavior more likely in the future.[3] It feels good in the moment *not* to make that call we've been dreading or not to chip away at that pile of performance reviews: that's the reward.

But clearly, procrastination can have serious consequences. One of its most vexing conundrums is that while it's rewarding in the (very) short term, procrastination always results in greater anxiety. Who hasn't experienced the mounting dread and stress of putting off something that needs to be done? Simply completing the task eliminates all the anxiety and dread of avoiding it—and not procrastinating precludes the dread and worry in the first place. (Not to mention the stress, the lost sleep, and the anxiety of those last-minute sessions of cramming or staying up all night to get something across the finish line.)

Procrastination is so common, however, that there is an abundance of effective techniques to prevent and break this bad habit. One of the most helpful is to divide a task into small, manageable pieces and then reward yourself each time you hit one of your mini-deliverables. (Just make sure your rewards are healthy ones!) I begin every day by planning my entire workday down to half-hour increments. When I can see the work ahead laid out in bite-size chunks, it eliminates the anxiety of uncertainty by giving me a clear road map of the day, and it creates lots of mini-deliverables that I can enjoy the reward of meeting. Don't underestimate how great it feels to make progress and get another thing done. If you're a person who's motivated by crossing items off a to-do list or rewarding yourself when you meet a goal—totally legit forms of extrinsic motivation—this technique works like a charm.

Avoidance

Avoidance behaviors are any actions we engage in to escape from stress-ful situations or difficult thoughts and feelings. Avoidance is a mal-adaptive coping mechanism. Classic examples are neglecting to pay bills, canceling phone calls or meetings, or declining to speak up or give presentations. People have been known to turn down promotions, or even change or quit jobs, in order to avoid stressful situations. The writer Ashley C. Ford, who we met in chapter 6, has said that fear ruled her life for years, and that the procrastination, self-sabotage, and negative self-talk her anxiety engendered prevented her from pursuing her dreams. But through therapy, supportive relationships, and a commit-ment to getting better, she learned to manage her anxiety and stop avoiding. Her self-talk, she said, changed from "I'm anxious, so I can't" to "You're anxious, and you *feel* like you can't. But try and see. Just try and see." The shift, she said, has done wonders for her.[4]

An interesting subset of avoidance behaviors is the practice of safety behaviors. Safety behaviors (or safeties, as I call them) are anything you do that you *think* will keep you from getting anxious or overwhelmed by panic. Some safeties allow us to move forward in spite of anxiety (keeping a single Xanax pill in your wallet if you're a fearful flyer, for example), and some rob us of the opportunity to learn that the fearful situation doesn't represent the threat to our safety and survival that we think it does. For example, if someone has a fear of being bitten by a dog and responds by avoiding dogs entirely, they never get the oppor-tunity to learn that most dogs are friendly—or to learn the difference between friendly and unfriendly dogs.

Take a minute to think about where you use safety behaviors. For example, a common safety behavior for people with social anxiety is to arrive late to gatherings and leave early. I have definitely done this! Does this behavior cause me to miss out on valuable opportunities? Yes, some-times. I could challenge myself to arrive on time and stay till the end, just to see how it feels.

Consider whether your safeties are helping you meet challenges or are worth trying to cut. Many anxiety treatment modalities will have people rank their anxious situations from least to most difficult, and then with the support of their therapist, gradually expose themselves to the situations while dropping the safety behavior. Over time, you learn that the situations you thought unsafe aren't as threatening as you feared, and that you can successfully deal with them without the safety behavior.

Making impulsive decisions

While some leaders react to anxiety by agonizing over a decision and putting it off, others do just the opposite and make hasty decisions. It can be an enormous relief to move the needle on a project, get something off your plate, or delegate it to someone else. But, of course, the very definition of an impulsive act is one that's carried out immediately, with no forethought and little or no regard for the consequences.

It's easy to imagine the harm that can result from impulsive decisions in the workplace, especially when they occur often. Further, the higher up the chain of the command they occur, the more widespread the effect. I want to make clear, however, that I'm not talking about *quick* decisions—the ability to make decisions on the fly or to cue quick pivots in the midst of the fray is a highly valued leadership skill. Here I'm referring specifically to impulsive decisions that are triggered by anxiety and that result in negative consequences.

For example, anxiety about money can often trigger impulsive decisions. When we're triggered, our anxious mind wants to fix things. But as we know, anxiety can be an unreliable narrator. I'll never forget when financial expert Buffie Purselle relayed on my podcast the story of two clients who received a letter from the tax authority that said they owed $50,000. Purselle explained, "They panicked and they didn't call me. They didn't email me. Instead, they cashed in their 401(k) to pay this debt. It was that reactionary impulse of, 'I just don't even wanna deal with this. I want this scary thing to go away. I'm not going to put forth a plan. . . . I'm just gonna make it go away.'"

When Purselle next saw the couple, they gave her the letter. Turns out, they didn't owe the tax authority anything. The letter was merely an assessment questioning if they owed the money. I could see myself doing something similar, because bad financial news or tax letters often make me so anxious that I'll do almost anything to make the anxiety go away (even temporarily).

Impulsivity can coexist with an anxious achiever's need to plan and prepare. It can coexist with worry and rumination. In the moment, anxiety can impair our ability to make smart decisions because it interrupts executive functions such as attention, focus, and working memory.[5] It can cause us to focus on the wrong things, distort the facts, or rush to conclusions. Ideally, we could postpone critical decisions until we're in a better frame of mind, but we all know that's not always possible.

That's why it's important to deliberately set yourself up to make good decisions—especially during anxious times. Start by acknowledging that your emotions can make you an unreliable narrator and that you will likely be prone to negative thoughts. For example, you may be prepping for a speech, and the last time you spoke, you felt like you bombed. You may even have a long-held belief that you're a terrible public speaker because a middle school recitation drew jeers. Ask yourself, Am I being objective enough? If you're not sure, investigate whether your memory is correct, perhaps by asking a colleague for feedback.

Ultimately, every leader should develop a team of "real talk" peers, people you can consult who will give you their unvarnished opinions. A unilateral, impulsive decision made in the midst of anxious times is almost guaranteed to result in negative consequences, but if you have a trusted team already in place, you can consult with them and still make quick but thoughtful, informed decisions. You can serve this role for others, too. One of the more fascinating aspects of anxiety is that you can often provide clarity and insight to others even if you're an unreliable narrator of your own experience.

If scary financial news is tempting you to act impulsively, Purselle suggests practicing "financial mindfulness." This often boils down to something deceptively simple: waiting to act. When you're triggered by money anxiety, acknowledge your anxiety, try to name the stressor, and tell yourself: "It's OK. I'm not going to react right now. I'm going to forgive myself for whatever the blunder was, because I'm human. And it's fine." Sit in the moment and accept that "this is what I have to deal with, and that's OK. I'm going to figure it out." Wait. Give yourself a day or two. Doing nothing when you're triggered is really hard. But you need to give yourself the time and space to acknowledge, step back, and gather wise counsel.

Spending money you don't have

Throughout my twenties and into my thirties, I engaged in the bad habit of spending money on things I wanted but didn't need. Buying something always made me feel better in the moment, but my debt steadily crept up—and my anxiety with it. Couple that with my long-standing fear of going broke, and I reacted by avoiding money management entirely.

It was only after my interview with financial therapist Amanda Clayman while researching my first book that I realized I had to grow out of one money attitude and into another. I began to examine where my attitudes about money and my spending habits originated, and, not surprisingly, the roots lay in my childhood. Like many people, I grew up as a child of divorce, and my parents used money as a weapon against each other. Caught in the middle, I learned to weaponize money as well—in my teens I'd run up my father's credit card to, frankly, get revenge. Later still, when I had my own credit cards, I replicated that same pattern of spending in order to soothe an emotional hurt.

But when I realized that this bad habit and my near-constant worry about going broke stemmed more from old wounds than from my current financial situation, I was finally able to proactively manage my small business for growth, after years of avoiding it and fearing business debt while piling up credit card bills in my personal life. I broke a damaging pattern and replaced it with a healthy pattern of proactive money management.

Substance use

Substance use is yet another common response to anxiety, and it can be one of the most devastating, especially when it escalates to abuse and addiction. Board-certified addiction psychiatrist Zev Schuman-Olivier helped me understand the relationship between substance use, addiction, and anxiety.

One way to understand addiction, he said, is as a desperate search for control when things feel uncontrollable. The activator (Schulman-Olivier suggested to me in our interview that I replace the word "trigger" with "activator") can be anything that makes you feel out of control—the economy, your job, your social life, your emotions, your bodily sensations or processes, an experience of loss, a global pandemic, a personal or professional setback—and the response is to look for something reliable to make yourself feel better. "And nothing is more reliable, at least in the short term, for helping you feel good than substances," Schuman-Olivier said.

He explained the fundamental tragedy of our impulse for short-term relief: "Unfortunately, what happens is, whenever we try to get in control in uncontrollable circumstances; whenever we try to get certainty when there is, in fact, uncertainty; whenever we try to stop things from changing when, in fact, everything is changing, we generally just set ourselves up for a bigger fall later—for more uncertainty, for more change, and, ultimately, for less control."

Schuman-Olivier's approach to addiction involves mindfulness meditation, awareness techniques, and abundant self-compassion. Part of mindfulness, he explained, is starting to recognize the ubiquity of uncertainty, and the ubiquity of our lack of control over things changing. "To the extent that we can turn *towards* that, that we can welcome in uncertainty and change or relate to it differently, with less fear and more acceptance and warmth . . . the less scary it becomes and the less we start to panic in response to those moments," he said.

Disruptive communication

This is a bit of a catchall category, encompassing rude and unprofessional behavior at work such as interrupting, hijacking a meeting, gossiping, and oversharing. While those certainly can't always be attributed to anxiety, the culprit behind much of this office bad behavior is an anxiety trigger.

Leadership expert Steve Cuss says that leadership anxiety can often take the form of interrupting and trying to have the last word. He even specifically cites mansplaining—an old phenomenon with a modern name—as an anxiety response. "You think you need to tell people what to do, and you actually think you're being helpful," he said. "But [mansplaining] is actually just . . . quelling a need that you have, because the woman you just interrupted and spoke over and explained something to . . . actually didn't need you to do that, and nor did the [other] people in the room."

According to Cuss, mansplaining comes from the need to have an answer. And *that* is rooted in an experience that will be familiar to many anxious achievers and that isn't restricted to gender: the need to look like the smartest person in the room.

It will take a little detective work to know which particular anxiety is triggering your response. Is interrupting quelling a need to be acknowledged, a fear that you won't be seen or heard? Is hijacking a meeting your way to control a situation that feels out of control? Is gossiping at the office driven by a fear of exclusion? Is oversharing due to a habit of speaking impulsively when you're nervous, or an anxious need to fit in? As always, mindfulness and honest self-awareness can help reveal what's behind these common forms of unproductive workplace behavior.

Overwork

This one is so tough, because despite overwhelming evidence that overwork is bad for our health and, ultimately, bad for the bottom line, our culture highly values and rewards it. When I was in a corporate setting, workers who put in excessive hours were prized for their "deep commitment" and habit of going "above and beyond." These days there's additional pressure to be on Slack at all hours. Even if someone isn't actively engaged in work, they must *appear* to be working and be available at a moment's notice.

But I think there's a special relationship between the anxious achiever and overwork. Let's face it, this is our jam. In a Venn diagram of overachieving and overwork, there would be almost total overlap.

Many successful leaders react to stress by working harder, holding themselves and others to an impossibly high standard, or trying to control things that are out of their control. For them, it's hard to imagine not stressing and fussing over every project detail, not taking responsibility for everything, or not always giving it their all. "People respond to anxiety by trying to be more perfect and more in control," clinical psychologist Alice Boyes told me. "They not only have a plan B but plans C, D, and E." In the United States we think of overwork as a "good work ethic," but it and perfectionism are often anxiety tells that only cause further anxiety—in yourself or others.

Overwork can even become addictive, as it was for Jason Kander. Anxious achievers tend to put their feelings of anxiety and depression into overworking, and there may be no more socially acceptable form of avoiding your emotions. Not only does overwork soothe our anxiety, but we're rewarded for it in the form of positive feedback, promotions, salary increases, and new roles.

But chronic overwork has been associated with everything from higher rates of heart disease, obesity, and diabetes to insomnia, depression, heavy drinking, and even suicide. And in a terrible irony, research tells us that overwork does not result in higher productivity or better performance. Overworkers tend to be sicker, unhappier, and less productive, and they report more absenteeism. They can actually end up costing companies more in the long run.[6]

Breaking Free of Destructive Habits

So, armed with knowledge of our triggers, responses, and unhealthy reactions, and maybe even some insight into the themes driving our anxiety, what's the anxious achiever to do? How can we break free of our destructive habits and replace them with habits that help us thrive? In short, how do we get better?

One approach that resonates particularly well with busy leaders is to think of anxiety as a habit that can be replaced.

Judson Brewer is a neuroscientist and an expert in the science of addiction, habit change, and mindfulness. Dr. Jud, as he's known, told me how we can use the built-in feedback loop of habit formation to break free of an unhealthy habit.

Habits, whether good or bad, are formed in a three-step process, Dr. Jud explained: trigger, behavior, reward. Often the trigger is an unpleasant thought or emotion, which prompts us to carry out some sort of behavior in order to gain the reward of distracting ourselves from the trigger. "When something is unpleasant, our brain says, 'Ooh, that's unpleasant. Let's make that go [away] as quickly as possible,'" Dr. Jud told me. Take the example of uncertainty. "When uncertainty abounds, we get anxious and start scratching that itch that says, '*Do* something,'" he writes.[7] That something could be any number of behaviors—stress eating, scrolling social media, exercising, drinking, binge-watching Netflix, overworking—and the reward is that we don't feel the uncertainty while we're engaged in the behavior. The process looks like this:

Trigger: Uncertainty

Behavior: Eat a cookie

Reward: Avoidance/distraction from uncertainty

The brain has now connected distraction from uncertainty (the reward) with eating (the behavior), and the more you engage in the behavior to obtain the reward, the more you reinforce this neural connection.

Very importantly, notice that it's not the *trigger* that drives the creation of the habit—it's the *reward* that does so. "That's why it's called reward-based learning," Dr. Jud said. "If something's rewarding, we're going to repeat it. If it's not rewarding, we're going to stop doing it."

The problem is that the reward's effect doesn't last, and to experience it again you must repeat the behavior. The result is that the brain gets stuck in what Dr. Jud calls an anxiety habit loop, which reinforces itself. And when the reward begins to deliver adverse consequences and we continue to engage in it anyway, what was once a maladaptive habit has now become an addiction.

It's easy to see this dynamic at play in the habitual mental responses that anxiety causes, such as worrying or rumination: the endless loop of "what if" and "if only," or our to-do list on repeat. You may wonder how worry or rumination delivers a reward. The answer goes back to our deeply ingrained desire to avoid negative and unpleasant experiences, which the brain interprets as threats. In this case, when we get anxious and the brain says, "Do something!" the resulting behavior is worry. Worrying distracts us from the original anxiety trigger, and it feels a hell of a lot better than doing nothing. That's the reward the brain is looking for. Worrying and ruminating let us feel like we have some control over a situation, or that we're problem-solving and planning.

In reality, Dr. Jud said, when we're in a state of worry, our focus narrows, our creativity diminishes, and the planning function of our brains is compromised. If we do happen to come up with a solution to a problem while we're in this fretful state, the brain mistakes correlation for causation. In other words, it assumes that the worry produced the solution, when in fact it was just a coincidence.

Why do we act out our anxieties in habitual manners that are bad for us? According to another habit expert, Charles Duhigg, our brain "hates tension." Anxiety makes us tense and so does worrying, and so our brain searches for *any* kind of tension relief. In the workplace, we often act out anxiety through overworking, micromanaging, or spending endless hours in search of perfection on a proposal or a report . . . all to avoid the tension of anxieties.

Remember, though, that leaning into what your anxiety is trying to tell you is hugely valuable. Anxiety is data.

Now, if even the thought of moving toward your anxiety makes you anxious, Dr. Jud has some reassuring news for you. We all have an innate capacity—what he calls a superpower—for breaking bad habits and overcoming anxiety. That capacity is curiosity.

"Curiosity can help us in a number of ways, and it can even help us start to see when we're in a rut of perfectionism, for example, or worrying," Dr. Jud said. "We can ask ourselves right in that moment: What feels better, worrying or being curious about mapping out this habit loop?" For most of us, being open and curious feels way better than feeling anxious and worried. So do we want to perpetuate the anxiety habit loop, or do we want to pause when those anxious feelings arise, and get curious about our own experience?

If you're feeling anxious, get curious and map out your anxiety habit loop:

Trigger: Anxiety

Behavior: Worry

Reward: Avoidance/distraction from anxiety

The next step, Dr. Jud said, is to ask yourself what you're getting from the behavior. Don't stop at an intellectual answer; drop down into your direct experience and get specific about what it feels like, physically and mentally, to be in the grip of worry. For most people, worry is a very unpleasant experience. But it's such an ingrained habit, and we so often mistake it for a state preferable to anxiety, that we may not even realize the truth of our experience if we don't pause to become curious.

"Really, the only way to change a habit is through seeing very, very clearly how rewarding it actually is or isn't," Dr. Jud said. "Our brain can think, 'Oh, worrying is going to help me get things done or it's going to problem-solve.' But if we really look at that closely and say, 'Is that true?'—it's not. It doesn't help us solve problems. What we do know is true is that worry burns us out. It makes us feel more anxious. And so it feeds back and drives anxiety." If we can apply curiosity to our worry, Dr. Jud went on, it can help us see whether we really are getting a reward from our habit of worrying, or if we're doing ourselves a disservice and negatively reinforcing our anxiety.

What is so different and so helpful about Dr. Jud's approach is that anxiety triggers are actually "the least important part of the equation." So rather than waste our time in a futile attempt to avoid or control our triggers, our efforts are better applied to examining the reward part of the anxiety habit loop. When it's time to replace a negative habit with a positive one, make sure the new, healthy habit comes with a reward that provides a similar benefit.

For example, if I want to stop the bad habit of avoiding difficult work tasks, I can plot it out on the habit formation feedback loop and then identify healthy, productive countermeasures:

Unhealthy Habit

> **Trigger:** This task is so complex that I'll never finish it.
>
> **Response:** I can't even think about this yet. (Avoidance)
>
> **Reward:** I don't feel the stress associated with this looming deliverable.

Healthy Habit

> **Trigger:** This task is so complex that I'll never finish it.
>
> **Response:** I'll break the task down into microgoals and complete *one* of them. (Action)
>
> **Reward:** I'll give myself ten minutes in the massage chair.
>
> **Repeat.**

Have fun coming up with ways to reward yourself. The reward can be anything you find meaningful and gratifying—so long as it's positive and it provides a benefit similar to what your bad habit does. And don't forget, it's essential that you repeat the process! That's how you'll establish a new healthy habit. To learn about how to do this in your job, read the "Break a Bad Habit and Make Progress at Work" exercise.

Break a Bad Habit and Make Progress at Work

This exercise is based on Dr. Jud's method of identifying and "unwinding" anxiety habit loops, but we're going to go one step further and see how disrupting an anxiety habit loop can improve our performance at work. I'll give you an example to get started, and you can identify your own anxiety habit loop below.

Step 1: Identify an anxiety habit loop that's compromising your performance.

> **Trigger:** Your boss requests a detailed status update on your team's project.
> **Behavior:** Procrastinate on the work.
> **Reward:** Avoid the anxiety.

Step 2: Examine the behavior with curiosity. You're procrastinating for a reason—what is it? Ask yourself, What is the reward I'm receiving from procrastinating? Is this what I really want to be doing? If I continue to procrastinate, what is the outcome? How does that make me feel in my body? In my mind?

Step 3: Create a new behavior that disrupts the anxiety habit loop and directly addresses the trigger. When you get curious and realize that your procrastination is an anxious response to the stress you feel when your boss asks for an update, you can refresh your habitual response by finding a small, meaningful action to decrease the stress that arose from the trigger.

> **Trigger:** Your boss requests a detailed status update on your team's project.
> **New behavior:** Write one sentence. (Small, meaningful action)
> **New reward:** Feel less anxiety *and* make progress on the report.

If you continue to respond to the trigger with this behavior, you create a new productive habit *and* the report gets done.

Now it's your turn.

Step 1: Identify an anxiety habit loop that's compromising your performance at work.

> **Trigger:** _____
> **Behavior:** _____
> **Reward:** _____

Step 2: Examine the behavior with curiosity. Ask yourself, What is the reward I'm receiving from this behavior? Is this what I really want

(Continued)

Break a Bad Habit and Make Progress at Work

to be doing? If I continue to engage in this behavior, what is the outcome? How does that make me feel in my body? In my mind?

Step 3: Create a new behavior that disrupts the anxiety habit loop and directly addresses the trigger. What is a small, meaningful action that decreases the stress that arose from the trigger and that helps you get your work done?

Trigger: _____

New behavior: _____ (Small, meaningful action)

New reward: Feel less anxiety *and* _____

Mindfulness Is Key

You need to be able to—calmly and with clarity—identify your triggers as well as the unhealthy reactions you want to change. That's where mindfulness comes in.

Mindfulness is the practice of bringing your attention to the present moment, whatever it may be, without judging or interpreting. It's anchoring yourself in what's happening right now by bringing calm awareness to your bodily sensations, thoughts, and emotions. Most of us find that the second we allow ourselves to become still and quiet, our minds seem to fill with a thousand random thoughts. This is what Buddhism practitioners call the monkey mind, which leaps continuously from one thought to the next. For anxious individuals in particular, recollections tend to involve ruminating on past mistakes or regrets, while forward-projecting thoughts consist of fretting over all the ways things could go wrong.

Mindfulness shows us a way through the mental maelstrom. It helps us pause before we react to a bad habit or a safety behavior. You don't need to remain in a state in which your anxiety is revved, your thoughts are scattered, and your focus is fragmented. And the great news is, you don't need to meditate for hours a day to get there, nor do you need to learn an elaborate meditation ritual. "Mindfulness isn't difficult," meditation expert Sharon Salzberg famously observed. "We just need to remember to do it."[8]

Mindfulness can soothe an acute experience of anxiety by calming the fight, flight, or freeze response, but it becomes truly life-changing when you make it a healthy habit and practice it daily. A regular mindfulness practice has been shown to decrease stress, anxiety, and depression; improve the ability to regulate emotions; promote quicker recovery from illness and better health overall; improve focus and lengthen attention span; improve sleep; enhance academic and job performance; and even decrease rates of burnout and turnover at work.[9] Mindfulness is an indispensable element in the anxious achiever's tool kit.

Here's one of my favorite introductory mindfulness exercises. You need nothing more than a few moments to try it out.

1. **Find a comfortable, quiet place to sit.** Set your timer for three minutes, or five if you're feeling ambitious, then settle in and close your eyes.

2. **Take three deep, slow, calming breaths.** I like to breathe in through my nose and then exhale through pursed lips, as if I'm drinking from a straw. This automatically slows down your breathing and activates the parasympathetic nervous system, which signals the brain that all is well.

3. **Bring awareness to your bodily sensations.** Place your back and bottom against the chair and your feet on the floor, with your breath moving through your nostrils and expanding your chest and belly. If there's tension or discomfort, try to relax that area.

4. **Begin to notice your thoughts.** Approach this step with the attitude of a curious, kindly observer: *Oh, there's a thought about x; there's a thought about y.* Regard all of your thoughts without judgment— they're just thoughts. Let them pass by without examining them.

5. **Get back to center.** When you realize you've started to get lost in one of those thoughts, gently bring your awareness back to a bodily sensation you're feeling right now. Take a deep, recentering breath and gently bring awareness back to your thoughts.

6. **Repeat this process until your time is up.** Close with a moment of gratitude for yourself—you took time out of a busy day and did this!

7. **Practice, practice, practice.** Set a time to practice again and follow through.

Now that you've got the basics, you can try out the following two mindfulness techniques. The first helps you gain and maintain mental equilibrium in any anxious situation, but many people have used it to help get through the tough moments of breaking bad habits. The second helps you break the destructive habits you're leaning on to cope with workplace anxiety and replace them with more positive ones.

Dropping anchor

For really tough moments of anxiety, when you need relief quickly, there's a great grounding exercise I use called dropping anchor, developed by Russ Harris.[10] The name comes from the image of dropping an anchor in the midst of an emotional storm. The storm is whatever difficult, overwhelming experience you're going through. When you drop anchor, you're acknowledging that you're flooded emotionally and physically, but you're anchoring deep in your present physical experience. The anchor is anything in the present moment that can help you stay grounded. Anchoring into the sensation of your feet on the ground, for instance, tells your nervous system that you're physically safe and quiets the amygdala, the brain's built-in threat detector. Anchoring helps you realize that your feelings come from your emotions within, not from an external physical threat. Here's one way it can look:

1. **Start by acknowledging that you're having a difficult moment.** Silently say to yourself, "I'm really, really keyed up right now,

and this is hard." Approach yourself with kindness, and without judgment. You are observing and truthfully acknowledging that at this moment, you're in a bad place. You don't need to assess *why* you're there—just acknowledge that you are, and that it's really tough.

2. **Next, ground yourself in the here and now.** Physical sensations work particularly well, so press your feet into the floor, press your back against your chair, press your fingertips together, stretch your arms up high, or wiggle your toes—whatever action is available to you.

3. **Notice that there's a lot of difficulty in this moment . . .** but there's also a body around this emotional pain, a body you can move and control—a body that is *safe*. Now, look around the room and identify five sights. Get quiet and identify five sounds. Notice five things you're doing right now (for example, breathing, noticing, listening, sitting, and wiggling your toes in your shoes).

4. **Notice that in addition to the sights and sounds and actions, there are also painful feelings here.** Then, return once again to noticing your physical sensations.

5. **Repeat the process.** Acknowledge the painful feelings and then notice the physical sensations until you feel grounded, less swept away by the emotional storm, and more engaged in the present.

The aim of dropping anchor is not to distract you from painful feelings, but to help you be present and regain control. The exercise doesn't make the storm disappear—it holds you steady until the storm passes. Practiced enough, it will show you that you are not at the mercy of any emotional storm—you can be resilient through difficult moments.

Habit stacking

Developed by habit expert B. J. Fogg and dubbed "habit stacking" by habit researcher James Clear, this exercise is one of the most effective ways to build a new positive habit. It works by pairing the desired habit with a habit you already have. The basic formula is very simple:

After (or before) [current habit], I will [new habit].

Examples

- After I brush my teeth at night, I will silence my phone.

- Before I respond to a cryptic email, I will do sixty seconds of belly breathing.

Once you get the hang of the basic technique, you can incorporate more complex forms of behavior or take on new habits you find more challenging, using "when" language as needed:

- After I drink my morning coffee, I will spend ten minutes writing my daily to-do list.

- Before every team meeting, I will spend two minutes meditating.

- When I feel the urge to stress eat, I will drink a glass of water.

- When I become aware of the urge to interrupt, I will place my hands in my lap and silently count to thirty.

Habit stacking works best when your cue is very specific and when you can enact your response immediately. So instead of trying to form vague new habits such as "be less distracted" or "incorporate more mindfulness," come up with a specific cue and an action you can take right away: "When the all-hands meeting begins, I will disable phone notifications." "When I log off for the day, I will tidy my workspace."

Getting Unstuck

Taking an honest look at our unhelpful responses to anxiety is hard work. It's scary. It requires us to acknowledge things we may not like about ourselves and would rather ignore. And if we want to get better, it requires us to face our anxiety triggers as well as our unproductive coping mechanisms, and to learn to release the bad habits we lean on and replace them with healthy responses. This can feel very vulnerable, even threatening: it's difficult to give up the things we've come to lean on.

But take heart, anxious achievers. Relinquishing your bad habits opens up room for healthy habits that will propel you forward and move you toward your values and goals, rather than staying stuck where you are. And the fact that we *can* learn to manage our anxious responses is enormously liberating, even thrilling. It returns to us some of the control we lose when our habits take over and become unmanageable. It gives us our power back. It enables us to fully understand ourselves as the unique leaders we are and to perform at our highest level, with the greatest happiness.

8

Perfectionism

In 2018 I had a panic attack while beginning a book lecture at my local public library. I stood at the lectern and became unable to breathe. Nauseous, I felt as if I were about to faint. As it became obvious that I couldn't speak, someone in the audience yelled, "I think we should call 911—she needs an ambulance." I knew, though, that this was a panic attack. I wasn't physically ill. My perfectionism had frozen me, and terrified the poor audience.

When I had the chance to unpack things a little, I realized that the pressure to deliver in my hometown was too great. These were people I might even know, and they'd given up an evening of their time to see me, who would surely disappoint them. It was the first solo talk I'd given for my book, and I felt my prepared material wasn't good enough.

A bit later, as I started to explore why I felt so compelled to deliver an entirely special experience (after all, it was a free event at a small-town public library on a Monday night, not the Super Bowl halftime show), I thought of many events in my past. My botched run as school president my senior year. The graduate school course where the professor excoriated me in front of three hundred students. The other graduate school course where I said something careless in front of two hundred students. The job where I was embarrassed in front of my peers by a cruel boss and accused of "half-assing" an important task, and was then passed over for promotion.

But mostly, I thought about my childhood. Growing up in the 1980s, my sister and I were brought to many adult dinner parties, and we were trained at an early age to entertain grown-ups, while also always deferring to them. By age eight I could sparkle at a table, discussing books and current events; I'd also help with the dishes. "Isn't she something," adults would remark. And I was. I was special, until I became an awkward teenager whose parents' messy divorce meant no more dinners and instead a lot of shaming for being six-foot-two and large. My vain and narcissistic father frankly didn't want me sitting with him at dinner anymore. I didn't feel like I was worth very much to my parents, but it didn't stop me from trying.

Many anxious achievers use perfectionism as a tool to avoid uncomfortable feelings of shame and criticism, and they push themselves to the point of overwork in an effort to achieve impossible standards of perfection. If this is you, ask yourself: Is it possible that your commitment to your work is less about your craft and more about fear?

Perfectionists are never satisfied. They may overwork in fear of the final product being flawed. They may avoid a task altogether, because the stakes feel too high. They may look back after a task is done and be unable to find anything positive in their performance. People with perfectionism pursue self-imposed high standards in one or more areas of their life. Here's the important part: they base their self-worth on their ability to achieve these high standards.

Perfectionism is complicated, because it can be very seductive to think of yourself as a perfectionist. The dominant cultural story is that greatness seems to require it. The best in their fields are so often extolled for their "flawless" performances and "exceptional" output, or we marvel over their determination to accept no less than the best. And honestly, who wouldn't want these things? So we rave over creators who exhibit an obsessive attention to detail or drive themselves to the point of mental and physical exhaustion in their relentless pursuit of perfection. Like so many tricks of the anxious, adopting perfectionism is socially sanctioned and can garner you praise and promotions. But perfectionism is not the pursuit of excellence; it's anxiety. It's crucial to understand what your constant pursuit of outperformance is costing you.

And let's not kid ourselves: It always comes at a price. A meta-analysis that examined data from over fifty-seven thousand people found that high levels of perfectionism correlated with depression, anxiety, eating disorders, self-harm, and OCD.[1] A few weeks after my fiasco at the public library, I was invited to present at the prestigious Talks at Google speaker series. Still smarting and full of doubt, I insisted that a Google staffer interview me instead. For four years I couldn't give keynote speeches, and I didn't even try. I simply couldn't imagine I could offer anyone their money's worth if it was just me and the stage (or screen). Talk about avoidance! My reluctance to give speeches cost me in lost speaker fees and invaluable networking opportunities, until I figured out how to over-come my anxiety.

Even so, when I do commit to a speech, my perfectionism makes preparing agony and post-event reviews misery. The speech takes over my life, and I become obsessed with making it right. After the speech, I worry that I wasted people's time and that they regret inviting me. I'd rather disappear entirely than put out a less-than-perfect product. This applies to cooking Thanksgiving dinner as much as it does to writing something, so the journey to creation is fraught and miserable. And sometimes, it just doesn't happen. I lose out on opportunities to share, to reach people, and to earn money, because I'm afraid I can't deliver a perfect experience.

Clearly, it's vitally important to unmask the fallacies of perfectionism. Thomas Greenspon, an expert on the topic and a recovering perfec-tionist himself, told me that while most perfectionists are conscientious, hard-working, and talented, "if perfectionism could be eliminated completely, none of these personal qualities would change and a great burden would be lifted." In other words, if your perfectionism some-how vanished, you'd still be a conscientious, hard-working, and talented achiever, *but without the attendant anxiety.* "Like an airplane wing, perfec-tionism has a leading and a trailing edge," Greenspon said. "The lead-ing edge is all of the desires to do well, the persistence, the conscientious effort, and the other characteristics of those for whom great success is a goal. The trailing edge is the intense anxiety and all of the attendant behaviors that result from fear of failure. If you let go of the anxiety around perfection, you won't be less skilled or successful. You'll just lose the trailing effect of the anxiety."

Stop and let yourself imagine that possibility. Can you picture a life in which you achieve at the same high levels you do now, but without all the anxiety, stress, and angst that go hand in hand with perfectionism? How about the possibility of achieving even more and living a more joyful, fulfilling life? Without all the anxiety and negative outcomes that come from holding yourself to a standard that's literally impossible to reach, you might just unlock your creativity and let loose your drive—and your joy—in an entirely new way.

The Roots of Perfectionism

"Perfectionism is a symptom of something," Greenspon told me. "It's not the disease." At its core, perfectionism is about anxiety: you're afraid of failing or afraid that making a mistake means that there's something wrong with you. "Perfectionism is more than pushing yourself to do your best to achieve a goal; it's a reflection of an inner self mired in anxiety."[2]

According to Greenspon, the most highly successful people are actually *less* likely to be perfectionistic, because perfectionism can leave you overwhelmed with doubt and indecision and make it difficult to bring any task to a conclusion. In some cases, perfectionism leads to a profoundly discouraged state of withdrawal and underachievement. In other cases, the inability to meet unrealistic standards can drive the perfectionist to overwork and burnout as they attempt to attain the sense of self-worth that eludes them, or assuage the underlying anxiety that they're not acceptable as they are. Both under- and overachievers share at the core of their perfectionism anxiety and lack of self-esteem.

According to renowned perfectionism researchers Paul Hewitt, Gordon Flett, and Samuel Mikail, "The central focus of most perfectionists is on the need to perfect the self and to correct or hide aspects of themselves they see as imperfect."[3] I would replace "imperfect" with "lacking" or "failed." What's driving your perfectionism? Is it about proving your worth to others? Is it about avoiding feelings of shame or judgment? While you may be trying to impress a boss who seems judgmental, oftentimes we're proving ourselves to our parents, who may or may not still be present in our lives, or to an internalized critic we've learned to hear above all others.

Perfectionism is brittle, not flexible. It's not about growth or getting better. It's about holding on for dear life and throwing yourself at something to avoid bad feelings. It has much in common with defensive pessimism. Defensive pessimism is a thought pattern of wishing bad events away: *If I only worry hard enough, I won't get fired.* Perfectionism is a sister mindset: *If I only work hard enough, bad things won't happen.* We work hard enough to be perfect (whatever "perfect" means to us) to prove we're worthy, good, enough, or in control.

Entrepreneur and startup cofounder Sehreen Noor Ali faced a moment of reckoning when she realized her older daughter was becoming a perfectionist just like she was. The light bulb moment arrived when her daughter spilled a glass of water and panicked over the reaction she anticipated. "She was petrified of me," Noor Ali laments. "I saw how she felt the need to be perfect for everyone, the way that I feel the need to be perfect for everyone." But together, with the help of a therapist, the family course-corrected. "We have made such huge, huge strides, and to be honest, I'm pretty damn proud," Noor Ali says. "We've woven a culture of mistake-making into the family, and now my four-year-old says, 'We all make mistakes! We all make mistakes!' I also am moving into more radical acceptance of many things, and have cut down the [negative] self-talk so drastically. It wasn't helping me and in fact led to self-sabotage."

It may not have been your parents who ingrained the need for perfection into you. It could have been a coach, a teacher, a mentor, or a boss. When you experience perfectionistic thinking, the same characters may show up, feeding you the same messages.

Breaking the Habit of Perfectionism

Like a lot of anxiety, perfectionism can become a comfortable habit. If we've been leaning into it since childhood, maintaining the self-talk that powers our perfectionism feels like a superstition or an indispensable ritual. As Noor Ali says, "Our self-talk becomes like an old friend that maybe should've been ditched a while ago."

Anxiety is a habit, and it's a refuge in a way—it's a companion. For example, if you're anxious about flying, you become convinced somehow that your anxiety is what's keeping the plane in the air. So you're not about to give that up. For perfectionists, the self-talk says, "If you just work hard enough, you cannot fail."

How does one begin to let this old friend go? It starts with isolating and hearing your negative self-talk. The piece of ourselves that was always expected to be the best, to be special, can indignantly excoriate the piece that might not be so excellent. "How *dare* you be less than perfect?" self says to self. "When we judge and attack ourselves, we are taking on the role of criticizer and criticized," self-compassion expert Kristin Neff says.[4] And so the cycle continues.

Once you are conscious of how your perfectionist self actually talks to your real self, though, the drive of perfectionism begins to lose its gloss. You can begin to separate a healthy striving for excellence from endless striving for unrealistic expectations.

Perfectionism is a habit learned over decades. "There is a great deal at stake emotionally for which perfectionism is a defense," Greenspon said. "Overcoming perfectionism is a recovery process." Your perfectionism, your old friend, won't go away overnight, and exercises alone won't assuage it. So my goal here is to help get you on the road to recovery by suggesting three new ways of thinking.

Find the motivation

Like breaking any unhealthy habit, it helps to feel really motivated before you start to tackle your perfectionism. I find this question really helpful: What are you missing out on because you're scared to be less than perfect?

Before you go into more negative self-talk ("If I weren't such a perfectionist, I'd be nicer and more people would like me and I wouldn't be a lonely loser"), try to narrow down the options.

For example, my fear of being shamed for public speaking held me back from applying for a TED talk. For years I'd made fun of TED to anyone who'd listen. I even wrote an article about how overrated TED talks are. But in truth, I desperately wanted to give one, because I knew they lend credibility to speakers and authors and help you get to the next level in a speaking career. Voilà, there was my motivation. I also realized that if I was going to be a perfectionist, I'd never reach that level, so I applied to seven various TED and TEDx talks. I got rejected from all of them. It hurt, but frankly, I wasn't ashamed. It felt like a badge of honor; it became a punch line for me.

And then one day I got an email from the TED team asking me to do a talk. Turns out they had seen my submissions and enjoyed them, even though they passed on them at the time. If I hadn't found the motivation to "ditch that old friend," as Noor Ali put it, I would've missed my chance to land a coveted TED spot, which opened a lot of doors for me.

So what's *your* motivation? What are you missing out on because you're afraid to be less than perfect? Identify and name that experience, and you've found your motivation.

Isolate your inner critic

You wouldn't be a perfectionist without the thought traps that keep you there. Many perfectionists have common barbs we like to fling at ourselves. Our inner critics know exactly which buttons to push. Here are some examples of the perfectionistic self-talk I've heard on heavy rotation:

- **Mind reading:** If I don't give it 110 percent, my boss will find someone who does. They'll just fire me.

- **Mind reading:** My parents gave up a lot to send me to excellent schools and prepare me for a successful career. I can't let them down.

- **Labeling:** The typo in my article wasn't a careless error. It happened because I'm lazy and didn't spend enough time proofreading.

- **Labeling:** I can't be mediocre. It's not who I am.

- **Avoidance:** I'm never going to be able to write a good book, so I'm not even going to try.

- **Labeling:** Laura is popular and perfect, and she got promoted before me. If I had more followers on LinkedIn and dressed better, I'd be a director too.

- **Catastrophizing:** I don't deserve what I have. I'd better work harder if I want to keep it.

- **Should statements:** If I don't run at lunch today, I'm going to get out of shape . . . so I should go, even though my knee hurts.

What voice speaks those lines in your head? Is it a specific person? Is it you? Can you take a moment to notice the next time you automatically chime in with a justification for your actions?

Notice the words you tend to use over and over again—about yourself and about others. Some perfectionists gain the reputation of being harsh taskmasters. It comes from the inner critic saying, "If I have to be perfect and you are under my watch, you'd better be perfect too."

How do you feel when your inner critic takes over? What emotions precede it? For example, you might notice that you tend to feel anxious right before your inner critic tells you to pull an all-nighter on a presentation. What's making you anxious? What could help calm the anxiety in the moment?

Another common perfectionist thought trap is people-pleasing. Have you caught yourself bending over backward to help someone who really didn't need the help? Perhaps your inner critic is demanding you make everyone happy at your own expense. Next time it tells you to clean up the conference table after a lunch meeting for the millionth time when it isn't really your job in the first place, tell it to be quiet!

For me, finding perspective begins with noticing and then calming the negative self-talk. Notice when you're being critical. What are your default self-talk phrases? What triggers them?

Once you begin to notice the themes and commonalities in your self-criticisms, maybe you can address them head-on. An easy way to start: Address yourself in the third person, out loud. Here's where practicing self-compassion comes in, and it's a wonderful skill to learn.

Self-compassion means being kind to yourself in a deliberate way, instead of relying on self-criticism. Sometimes I call it the "sweetheart method." My former therapist Wilma told me it would help if I called myself "sweetheart" when I was addressing my inner critic. So sometimes I'll now say aloud to myself, "Now, sweetheart, you're not lazy because you decided not to write that blog post. You're being strategic. Your time is valuable and you don't need to work for free when you are busy with paying work." Honestly, it helps.

If it's just too difficult to be kind to yourself right now, I understand. There's another way to calm your negative self-talk. And you'll love it, because it involves a little self-criticism.

I say this with love, but being stuck in our heads, ruminating and focusing on our flaws all the time, is very self-centered. This method for calming your negative self-talk speaks directly to that inherent narcissism. Once again I have Wilma to thank. One day when I was anxious and frazzled about bombing something, Wilma said, "Why do you have to be so special at everything? Whoever told you that?" I looked at her and said, "I've always been special, since I was three years old." To which Wilma replied, "Well, who says?"

Who says, indeed? Where did I get the belief that I must be special and outstanding at *everything*? Anxiety expert Alice Boyes notes that this narcissism is self-protective. "You end up believing, 'The only way I've succeeded in life or the only way I'm being accepted and loved . . . is by being excellent, by overdoing everything,'" she explains. But that's another thought trap of perfectionism. The truth is that "not being the best at everything isn't a threat to you. It isn't a threat to you getting what you want out of life." Besides, she continues,

> There's nothing fun about a life in which you are the best at everything that you do. . . . Not only is it not possible to always be the star, but it's also just not desirable, either. You really want to be surrounding yourself with people who are better than you at some other things. You don't want to be attempting to be good at everything, because you want to be good at the things that are really important and meaningful to you.

Sometimes when I'm stressing about a looming failure on my horizon, I'll just tell myself, "What makes you so special? Why can't you do B− or C+ work occasionally?" Or even, "Why can't you do bad work or have a bad day like everyone else?" Reminding myself that I'm no more special than anyone else is not self-denigrating, and it isn't a way to let myself off the hook and not give my best effort. It's an act of self-compassion, and a way to gently but effectively expose and address the underlying narcissistic tendencies that power perfectionism.

There's another upside to not being "special," one that's easy to miss: being ordinary means you're not alone. As Boyes said, we can't be the star 100 percent of the time—and who would want to? It can be a lonely and exhausting place. The truth is, we all have our strengths and our struggles; we're all really, really good at some things and on a journey to improve at other things. The trick is to regard our limits with compassion and to share our proficiencies with grace.

Locate external perspectives

As for all those unrealistic standards, whose are those, anyway? It may be that over the years, what was planted by your parents or an influential figure from your childhood or young adulthood has been absorbed into your own self. When I actually sat down with my mom and asked her about her high expectations of me as a child, she was shocked. She believes I was just born this way. Whoever is correct, it doesn't really matter.

If there is someone close enough to you who knows your perfection-ist tendencies, ask them what they think of your standards. Ask them how they would feel if you really screwed something up. Greenspon calls this an "act of intimacy." Maybe you'll discover that it's just not that big a deal to them, and that they've never expected you to work every night until 10 p.m. When you can get external perspectives from people you trust and calm your inner critic, you can begin to reorient yourself to a more authentic view of others' perceptions and expecta-tions, and develop a new, kinder self-understanding.

You can also turn to external perspectives to help with specific prob-lems your perfectionism is causing or exacerbating. When I gained more understanding about how my anxiety was impeding my speak-ing career and found the motivation to get better at public speaking, I hired an adviser to help me. Because I knew my perfectionistic ten-dencies would cloud my judgment and never let me feel really done with a speech, I essentially outsourced that task to a trusted person who could offer a more objective, external perspective. If they thought the speech was good, they must be right! In the end, I was able to offer myself as a keynote speaker because I couldn't let my impossible standards block me anymore.

Finally, if you don't have access to a trusted adviser, try externaliz-ing your self-talk. This is a powerful technique and only takes seconds. When you find yourself subsumed in negative self-talk, simply reframe it as if you're addressing another person. It works best when that person is a loved one or someone you hold in high esteem. Can you even imag-ine uttering to your child, partner, or mentor some of the things you say to yourself? Of course not. This exercise quickly reveals how harm-ful our negative self-talk can be.

When you're a perfectionist, it's so helpful to gain insight from others' perspectives. This might help you ease your perfectionistic habits. Say you know that you may spend too long on your first draft of a presen-tation. Have you ever thought about saying to a trusted colleague, "This is who I am. I have a tendency to prepare for too long, and after I've spent twelve hours on it, I need you to come in and say, 'You know what, I'm taking it from here.'"

Are there ways to communicate in a professional setting that help your coworkers understand you better? "You know me, I'm the kind of person who's going to put everything into this and I'll be up until midnight doing this work. So that's just who I am, and I want you to know about that." If you're capable of saying that to a coworker, then you're already taking the first step toward standing outside of yourself and saying, "Hey, do I really need to be this way? And by the way, where did I get the idea that I do need to be this way? How did that come to be?" Questioning these assumptions begins to loosen their grip on you and leads you into deeper self-awareness.

There may also be a reckoning moment where you acknowledge that your way is not the best way and that, indeed, others might do your work better. Greenspon remembers surrendering some of his own perfectionism:

> When my publisher asked me to write my first book, I wrote
> a really academic first chapter. She gave it back to me and it
> had all these red ink comments . . . and I'm saying, 'Yeah,
> but, and yeah, but, and yeah, but . . .' I couldn't hear her.
> [She] finally ended up saying to me something along the lines
> of, 'OK, here's the deal. You have wonderful ideas that I hope
> we can publish, but if you ever hope these ideas will see the
> light of day, you're going to need to get used to the idea of
> the editorial process.' It was a major launching point in my
> own process of recovery.

Overcoming All-or-Nothing Thinking

Overwork is a throughline for most perfectionists. It's how we try to become perfect. Overwork can feel like an insurance policy against failure: "If only I work hard enough on this presentation, the client will have to buy my product." In fact, the client will do what's best for the client, no matter how perfect your pitch.

All-or-nothing thinking is a common perfectionist's tactic. We think, *Either I'm the best, or it's over for me.* Luckily, you can begin to tame an all-or-nothing mindset by setting some simple rules, called heuristics. In psychology, heuristics are mental shortcuts that allow you to solve problems and reach efficient decisions. They aim to bypass ruminating, curb overwork, and take stress out of decision-making.

Chronic overachievers can manage perfectionism and overwork while still feeling confident they're doing their best once they set up the right guidelines. If you create parameters around projects and set "enough" goals and deadlines, anxious leaders like you can create boundaries that help manage perfectionism while still delivering excellent results.

The easiest way to start is by creating time limits. Imagine you have to prepare a twenty-slide presentation for a client. It may be that your normal instinct is to clear your calendar of every extra item so you have the next five nights and the weekend to work on the slides. But maybe that's not necessary.

Based on your experience, you know you need an hour per slide. And you'll need extra time for designing and proofreading the presentation. That's twenty-five hours total. Can you take two hours out of each workday, three hours from the next few evenings, plus Saturday morning? Give yourself Friday and Sunday completely off. You can build in wiggle room. The idea is to institute the external parameter of containing the work time so you don't go crazy prepping a presentation that really doesn't need the extra time.

Appropriate effort or "enough" goals

Hopefully, in managing your time and using heuristics, you will begin to enjoy the process of creating, of bringing something into being, rather than becoming focused exclusively on the outcome. You can also dare yourself to set "enough" goals and practice using only appropriate effort, rather than going all out and putting in extra effort.

Appropriate effort is the opposite of our culture's expectation to always go above and beyond and always do our very best. Instead, it's doing something well but removing undue emotional investment in the outcome. Buddhism teacher Sally Kempton writes that appropriate

effort is any effort that doesn't involve struggle. For Kempton, the secret
of acting with appropriate effort is to ask herself, "If this were the last
act of my life, how would I want to do it?"[5]

How can you bring appropriate effort into your life? Practice being
a C+ student. I know that statement made some of you gasp, but just
hear me out.

- **Not every project demands your best work.** What if you gave
  only 79 percent? What if your next report doesn't have prose
  that rises to the level of greatness? The key is to acknowledge
  the outcome. Will what you do be good enough for your boss?
  Will what you achieve be good enough for you? The answer to
  both is, almost surely.

- **Compromise is a healthy practice.** Zoom out and focus on the
  big picture. What's worth your best, and what just isn't? The big
  goals are worth it all. But there's a lot that's worth compromising on along the way.

- **Think about some happy accidents.** Was there ever a time when
  a meeting was canceled or a deadline was extended, and you
  magically struck upon an idea or a solution that you'd been
  striving for? When the mind is free, creativity tends to happen.
  Remember that the next time you're inclined to overwork and
  imagine brain space literally opening up as you decide to stop
  for the night.

- **Practice on something outside of work.** You could use exercise
  as a stand-in for setting limits on work time. Science shows we
  need only a certain amount of cardio and strength training
  every week to achieve our goals. If you normally exercise for an
  hour a day, cut it to forty minutes. See what happens. Is the
  process less stressful? Do you dread the gym less?

You can learn to accept less achievement. You can use the So What?
exercise to help you. But here's a heads-up: if you've been conditioned

to achieve, as most of us have, this will make you feel like a failure for a short while.

But *only* for a short while. You may just find that what you gain— more calm, easeful workdays, more unimpeded time and headspace— is worth what you'll lose in so much anxious striving. And is that such a loss anyway? Of course not. Know that it's OK to do some things less well in order to have the complete and healthy life you want.

The So What? Exercise

The So What? exercise is known in CBT as the downward arrow technique. I call it So What? in honor of professor and psychologist Angela Neal-Barnett, who inspired me to answer my inner critic with a loving, "So what?"

The idea here is to help your brain "restructure" automatic negative thoughts by identifying the fears underlying your perfectionistic tendencies. The technique quickly uncovers basic core beliefs we hold about ourselves. Once the core beliefs are revealed, it becomes easier to ask: Is this true? Is it probable that the worst actually will happen?

It's fun for catastrophists and worriers too. Think about a recent time you were perfectionistic. What would have happened if you'd lowered your standards or made a mistake? Let's use my fear of public speaking as an example.

Initial worry (in your inner critic's voice):

If I agree to give a keynote, I'll disappoint the audience.

OK, let's say that happens. So what? (Or, then what?)

They'll resent me for wasting their time.

OK, let's say that happens. So what? (Or, then what?)

They'll say bad things about me or post it on social media.

(continued)

The So What? Exercise

So what?

I'll read a negative review and be really upset. I'll feel so ashamed.

Then what?

No one will want to hire me again to give a talk.

Then what?

I'll be ashamed and feel like a failure at something I really care about doing well. After all, I should be a good speaker—it's part of being a successful business author.

Once you identify the core beliefs driving your perfectionistic tendencies, the therapeutic work begins. As this exercise reveals, much of my perfectionism is driven by a fear of being ashamed. It's colored by many shoulds as well. A successful business author *should* give lots of keynote speeches, even if it makes her anxious. I need to delve deep into these core beliefs and understand why they hold such power over me.

At the same time, I can acknowledge that the likelihood my talk will be so bad that someone would sludge me on social media is slim, and that perhaps my worries, even though they *feel* real to me, are unrealistic.

It's Never Too Late to Have a Happy Childhood

As with so many anxiety-related issues, the road to managing perfectionism helps you start to believe that you are OK as you are. This is the challenge and the promise. Part of the work may be accepting and cherishing your perfectionistic tendencies. After all, who else would care as much as you do?

Part of the work may be accepting that perfection, by definition, is unattainable. Excellence, however, is not. And guess what? Excellence demands mistakes. Muscles need to tear a little to get stronger. I'll never forget when I read tennis legend Andre Agassi's memoir. We think of him, of course, as one of the greats: he won eight Grand Slam tournaments. But he lost way more matches than he won. He had entire years where he lost most of his matches. He was mocked in professional tennis and repeatedly flirted with disaster. But when he lost, he trained in a new way, to build new skills and muscles. He overcame shame and accepted who he was. The pursuit of excellence demands that we grow, and it guarantees that we mess up along the way. This is a profoundly liberating truth for the perfectionist.

When you believe in investing in self-improvement and honest self-reflection, you're agreeing to let yourself be lovable and good, mistakes and all. And the best way to do that is to be connected with somebody who honestly and authentically believes in you. This can be a trained professional. But sometimes that person can be you. When your inner critic is really insistent and has been with you for as long as you can remember, it can be hard to believe that you can learn to calm that critical voice and become your own best cheerleader. If it helps, you can even lean on your perfectionistic tendencies to overcome your habit of perfectionism!

I'm still learning to let go of my perfectionism and become my own self-advocate, and this may very well be a lifelong endeavor. As Thomas Greenspon reminds us, "There aren't any magic solutions to this any more than you can say to a person who is chemically addicted, 'Well, why don't you just go out and stop drinking? You don't have to open the bottle—just say no!'" This work takes time and commitment, and it takes self-compassion and kindness.

But I can tell you, it is entirely worth it. Remember startup consultant Andy Johns from chapter 3, who'd been involved in eight unicorn companies? Johns experienced a lot of trauma in his early life. He says,

> When I was struggling as a child, feeling sad and depressed
> and having panic attacks and a low level of constant anxiety,
> I actually turned to performance and achievement as a drug
> of sorts.

I got every blue ribbon or every trophy, or I hit home runs, or I got straight As or whatever it was that made me feel good, because I didn't always feel good. But when I did those things, I felt good and I felt lovable. My brain, as a kid, came to internalize the collection of messages around me, in conjunction with the messages that society gives, that if I achieved, I was lovable. And if I wasn't achieving, I wasn't inherently lovable for who I was.

So my story as an adult has basically been about achieving at the highest level that I could imagine for myself, but then eventually waking up to realize that seeking external validation through achievement needed to stop, because it was a sign of not feeling inherently lovable for who I was.

After Johns did a tremendous amount of therapy and work on himself, he was able to step back from his "relentless drive to just keep doing more." Johns freely admits he felt a great tension between achievement and self-love. He had to learn to love himself minus the achievement. It was worth it, he says.

What a gift, to be able to do what we like and what brings us joy, and not care as much if other people think it's good! As we grow up and understand where our motivations come from, we can learn to believe that our worth is a given—not dependent upon what we produce or on the quality of our work. And we can choose the work we must do to prove ourselves in our careers, what we can do simply to make ourselves happy.

9

Control

Around the beginning of the pandemic, we were all scrambling. It was one of the most volatile, anxiety-provoking times I can recall.

I called my friend Sarah to check in on her and see how business was going. She told me that her company was in an uproar—the CEO had pretty much disappeared. The numbers did not look good, and the CEO had holed up in his office to make detailed projections of all aspects of the business. His team felt unsettled by his absence—even though they knew he was working really, really hard—especially at a time when they needed reassuring and visible leadership.

I can sympathize with this CEO. The deep dive into worst-case-scenario planning gave him a sense of control in the midst of a frightening situation, and number-crunching can be a source of calm for a data person. He was making his team anxious because he was mindlessly acting out his anxiety and trying to gain some control over an unprecedented situation.

Why does control feel so good to an anxious leader, or anyone, for that matter? Anxious people seek control as a way of protecting themselves from the bad outcomes we imagine. It's driven by the hope that if only we can take the wheel for a while, the thing we fear most won't happen.

This is very similar to the way we've seen worry and rumination work. We know that our brains hate uncertainty and react to it like it's a threat, and that worrying lets us feel like we're actually doing something productive about the uncertainty. Clinical psychologist Christine Runyan points out that sometimes this strategy seems to work: We temporarily avoid the dreaded potential outcome, so worrying becomes a tactic that we repeat. We begin to believe that if we just worry about it enough, it won't happen.

The same thing occurs with control. If we clamp down and try to stay on top of every little thing, and then the feared outcome doesn't occur, our attempts to control the future appear to be working. It's easy to see how seeking control can become a habit for so many of us.

But let me just go ahead and rip the Band-Aid off: we actually have very little control over anything.

This is a hard reality to accept, but since every psychologist, meditation teacher, and wise elder has said it's true, let's at least entertain the idea. We live in an unpredictable world, and sometimes even our most careful planning or our most inspired catastrophizing can't account for what comes down the pike. (If that sounds too scary, just remember that, all things considered, we're just as likely to be surprised by happy outcomes!)

And there's a very important corollary: we still need *some* sense of control. Abundant research tells us that one of the most psychologically harmful experiences is the absence of agency. We need to have at least some power over our lives and our environments; we need to be able to make choices that affect our outcomes. At work, the happiest, most productive workers are the ones who have a sense of autonomy and the agency to make decisions that affect their tasks, output, and schedules.

So, where's the healthy balance between throwing up our hands and letting events unfold as they may, and slipping into anxiety and inflexibility?

Objectively speaking, anxiety expert David Barlow explains, it's true that we simply don't have as much control over events in our lives as we think we do—or certainly, as much as we'd like. But when we function well and have no more than moderate anxiety, he says, we're able to maintain "an illusion of control," which is "a very healthy state of mind." The difference between people with no more than moderate anxiety and people with severe anxiety is optimism, Barlow says. The former group is able to believe that although anything *could* happen, most of the time things will be just fine, and even if something goes wrong, they'll be able to deal with it."

Contrast this state of mind with that of a severely anxious person, whose threat appraisal system is constantly firing and who constantly expects everything to go wrong. Or the anxious leader who responds to a loss of control in an unhealthy, unproductive manner. They may overcorrect and become even more controlling, which can show up at work as micromanaging, having a "my way or the highway" attitude, or acting in a go-it-alone manner. Others can become paralyzed and try to avoid or ignore the anxiety-provoking situation, essentially giving up any measure of control they did have.

None of these reactions is sustainable. It seems that, as with anxiety, there's a Goldilocks point for control: not too much, not too little. And luckily, we can learn to be more optimistic through therapy and other practice.

Why Can't We Let Our Guard Down?

If you're one of those leaders who feels like you can't let your guard down, you're in good company. You may not even *want* to, and I get that. Staying on top of every detail can give you a sense of control when the unexpected happens, when your anxiety is high, or when you're just dealing with the everyday stressors of work.

But it's one thing to be vigilant and another to feel like you have to constantly monitor your environment for threats or plan for the worst. If you're always mentally preparing for an uncertain and scary future, anticipatory anxiety is taking over. Anticipatory anxiety means you are "fearful for an extended period of time about an imagined future situation you see as an unpredictable threat."[1] In uncertain or triggering situations, you may feel that what lies ahead is dangerous or irreparable, and so your brain rushes to prepare for the bad event. Unfortunately, the way your brain usually prepares is to feel more anxiety. Sometimes an excessive need for control comes from anxiety itself. Anxiety triggers experiences from your past and tells you "Don't ever let your guard down" and "It's all up to you." Our efforts to control things are attempts to manage our anxiety, and anxiety, ironically, is an attempt to control our environments so thoroughly that nothing bad can happen.

Anxious people can also experience hypervigilance, a state of extreme, excessive awareness that undermines your quality of life. While psychologists don't consider hypervigilance a disorder per se, it's one of the defining features of PTSD, and it commonly affects those of us who have clinical anxiety.

Where does hypervigilance come from? One source, of course, is trauma. Bessel van der Kolk, who's dedicated his career to understanding how people adapt to and heal from traumatic experiences, explains that trauma leaves us with "a fear-driven brain." When we experience trauma, our threat appraisal system becomes hypersensitive, leading us to see threats where others do not. Trauma also damages the filtering system that helps us distinguish between what's relevant and what we can dismiss. So we may get hung up and hyperfocus on things that other people would ignore or wouldn't even notice.[2]

Another source of hypervigilance is something we discussed in chapter 4: unresolved childhood hurts. Even if you don't have a history of trauma, we all experience negative events in childhood, and they occur at such a formative time that they can have lasting effects. The child who grows up in a violent or unpredictable home learns to do whatever it takes to feel safe—and anxiety can feel like a very effective strategy. So can overfunctioning, and the anxious child may learn to execute and take over tasks to feel better. Whatever the reason, anticipatory anxiety and the craving for control are attempts to feel safe. They arise, quite logically, when our world feels out of control.

If you've ever worked with an anxious, controlling person, you know how difficult this can be. And yet a lot of these individuals are extremely successful. In fact, many people take on leadership roles precisely because of a desire to be in control, and some leaders even credit aspects of their anxiety with their success. It all goes back to what *Atlantic* national editor Scott Stossel told me—an associated good trait comes with every negative anxiety trait. The question is, Can we learn to draw upon our painful experiences for good use?

Leadership coach Jerry Colonna gave me one such example. Colonna and his six siblings grew up in a tough neighborhood with an alcoholic father and a mother who suffered from mental illness. "There was violence in the household and violence outside," he says. In this unstable, unpredictable environment, Colonna developed a type of vigilance that enabled him to predict his parents' moods based on the slightest bit of data. The sound of his father's footsteps in the hallway as he came home from work, for example, could reveal if it was going to be a good evening or a bad evening. Colonna was always planning ahead for the uncertain future.

As an adult, he was able to apply this scrupulous attention to detail and hyperawareness to mastering industries he knew nothing about, and to being aware of details and trends that others missed. He became one of the early pioneers in technology startup investing. He also became a skilled reporter and leadership coach, and credits much of his success in these arenas to the "hyperawareness of the other's sense of being" that he'd developed as a child. Hyperawareness, Colonna told me, "actually served me really, really well, because I would often hear things that the person I was interviewing wasn't even hearing. I could play that back in a question. It's a superpower because all of a sudden, I could step into an empathetic stance. Instead of me being the interviewee and you being the interviewer, we get to have an emotionally intimate conversation. We get to be human beings together because I notice." This is an excellent example of how growing up hyperattuned to other people can be used as a superpower later in life.

The challenge comes when your focus on others becomes so extreme and so draining that you leave no room for yourself. Or when you get so preoccupied with taking care of others and making sure they're happy that you both overstep and neglect to preserve any boundaries. It's also easy to avoid conflict and just do everything yourself, or to blame yourself for a difficult situation rather than risk disappointing the other.

One of the first steps Colonna takes when coaching clients who grapple with anxiety is to help them appreciate these responses as "the wonderful survival strategy" they were. What they learned in childhood kept them safe—it worked! But the next step is to examine the present situation. "Does one really need to worry about whether or not you're safe?" Colonna says. "Is the threat that you once experienced as a child still present? Chances are the *programming* is still present, but the threats are different. The quickest way to understand that the threat has changed is that the amount of power that we have as adults is vastly different than the power we had as children."

This is a lesson that I keep coming back to. Our childhood selves did not have the power or the control to leave or change a dangerous or unpredictable situation. We were dependent on the adults in our lives, even if they weren't dependable and we felt like we had to read their minds and meet their needs. But now, life is different. We have choice, we have agency, and we have a greater measure of control over our environments. Now we can act in wiser, more productive ways—even if we still feel afraid sometimes.

Your Need for Control at Work

So much of the "bad behavior" we see at work—the urge to dominate, to interrupt, to control, to micromanage, to discount or quash differing opinions—is caused by fear, which often operates beneath our conscious awareness. Let's look at some of the most common ways our fear-driven need for control manifests at work. In the next section we'll turn to ways we can relax our grip on control by addressing the fear beneath it.

My way or else

We've probably all worked with a boss who was a controlling leader, giving directions and expecting people to execute on them—at once and down to the smallest detail. Staff members are reluctant or sometimes downright terrified to give the leader feedback or confront them, fearing the boss will react with defensiveness, impatience, or hostility. In this top-down hierarchy, there is no room for discussion, fresh ideas, or differing opinions, because the leader's way is law.

As bad as this sounds, the my-way-or-else leader is not uncommon. Not all of them act like Miranda Priestly, the legendary mean boss from the movie *The Devil Wears Prada*. Often the controlling behavior is more subtle: making passive-aggressive comments, shutting down discussions, being tactless, talking over people, or having unrealistic expectations of team members. This is the boss who needs to be in control of conversations, workflows, deliverables, and processes. There is no working *with* this kind of boss; their need for control ensures that it's a matter of working *for*.

It's tough to work for this kind of leader—and, I admit, really tough to have any kind of sympathy for them. But peek beneath the hood, and I guarantee you'll find deep-seated fears that are driving their iron will. This kind of boss fears losing control more than anything, and when their sense of control is threatened, they react badly.

If you recognize yourself in this type of leader, congrats on being honest and self-aware. But now take a cue from Bowen family systems thinking and consider, How is your behavior affecting the entire team? Leaders who are reacting to their fears by trying to control their environments create stressful conditions that don't enable employees to do their best work. Being controlling undermines employees' autonomy, lowers job satisfaction, and stifles innovation. In the long run, it harms the bottom line. Not surprisingly, turnover under this type of leadership can be rampant.

Only I can fix it

An overly self-reliant stance can be so tempting to the anxious leader—it's yet another means to try to remain in control. In this case, leaders don't give orders and do everything themselves. They don't delegate, trusting only themselves to come through on key deliverables. Things get done, sure, but these leaders spend all their time overworking in order to feel safe, and are often exhausted. The risk of burnout is high.

Sometimes the only-I-can-fix-it leader is motivated by arrogance. But guess what's beneath a lot of arrogant behavior? Feelings of insecurity. We pretend we know it all to mask our fear, or try to overcompensate for it. According to Bowen theory, only-I-can-fix-it leadership is a classic example of overfunctioning. In response to their own fears, these leaders turn to the quickest means to alleviate anxiety, which is swooping in and problem-solving rather than trusting their teams to perform.

The effects of only-I-can-fix-it leadership are low employee autonomy, low motivation and engagement (why bother when you know the job will be done for you, or you won't even be given the opportunity to try?), low job satisfaction, and employees feeling they don't have a stake in the work product or the organization's mission.

Micromanaging

Micromanaging is one of the most common tactics leaders rely on to maintain control. Another form of overfunctioning, micromanaging can look like getting too involved in the details, becoming overly involved in monitoring others' work, and overcommunicating with or checking in on employees.

Colonna thinks that micromanaging is anxiety married to perfectionism. "When I work [as a coach] in an organization, if I see micromanagement as a predominant cultural attribute, chances are there's a tremendous amount of fear," he says.

All of this rings true to me. And importantly, it correctly locates the source of the anxiety with the individual leader—it's not coming from the team. However, teams are usually abundantly capable and don't need managers checking in on them every few hours in order to perform well. That worry is the leaders' own anxiety speaking.

Practice Releasing Control—and Calming Your Anxiety

"I think that the most hypervigilant, micromanaging, perfectionist people make themselves feel awful." That's another thing Colonna said to me, and I think he's right.

Wouldn't it be great for both you and your team if you could relax just a bit, release your grip a little, learn to sit back, and let your team perform and grow and flourish? Leading doesn't have to feel bad, nor be draining. Here are some strategies that can help you calm your fears and grow into being a leader who collaborates, motivates, and inspires.

Adopt a practice mindset

A lifetime of anxious planning won't change overnight. Those of us who worry all the time may have built faith that it's our anxiety that keeps bad things from happening, and that belief is hard to let go of.

But correlation doesn't equal causation. Worrying your way to where you are may *feel* true, but who's to say that if you subtracted all the anxiety and worry and obsessive control, your indelible excellence wouldn't shine through anyway?

The truth is, letting go of longtime habits feels scary, so you need to approach this with a practice mindset. "Hey, I'm new to this," you can tell yourself. "I won't immediately be great at it—I'll need lots of practice."

It's OK to take baby steps in order to let go of your need to control. For example: resist the temptation to check up on your people for one hour. (And if that was easy, make it two.) Practice enduring some uncomfortable feelings, rather than jumping in immediately to mediate a conflict. Rather than automatically doing everything yourself, delegate low-stakes tasks. Work your way up to giving team members greater and greater responsibility.

Practice open awareness

Renowned meditation teacher Sharon Salzberg describes open awareness as "our ability to observe conditions as they are without feeling the need to change them." The fruit of such an approach to life, Salzberg says, is acceptance, and acceptance leads to the end of conflict, which leads to clarity of purpose and vision, which in turn leads to skillful action. Open awareness helps us give colleagues the benefit of the doubt, endows us with patience, and gives us a more amenable attitude toward criticism and suggestions.

If you're the kind of person who has relied on yourself to fix things your whole life, the practice of open awareness may feel impossibly hard. Salzberg acknowledges that it "may sound passive to our action-oriented ears." And yet, she says, the capacity to rest comfortably in the present moment with all its imperfections is "the foundation of all true happiness."[3]

An attitude of open awareness leads us to a very different type of leadership, one that is the opposite of controlling, being overbearing, and micromanaging—that of surrender. What are we surrendering, exactly? The need for self-centered control.

"Thus viewed, the purpose of leadership in any domain is not to shine the spotlight on oneself, but on others," Salzberg writes. Leaders can then "help to create an environment where workers feel valued rather than dominated, encouraged rather than held back. Surrender allows a leader to get out of his or her own way and focus instead on unlocking the potential of those whom they serve—the employees who need leadership to thrive." Moving from being self-focused to being mindful of the big picture, Salzberg tells us, allows us to grow as individuals, do a better job, deepen our relationships with colleagues, and remain open to change and flexible in our expectations.[4]

Just remember that this, too, is a practice, one that we'll need to cultivate over time. There's a reason adept mindfulness practitioners meditate every day—they have to keep up the practice.

Practice loving-kindness meditation

One of the best ways to practice and develop open awareness is an ancient form of meditation called *metta*, or loving-kindness meditation. It's an active form of meditation that focuses on sending goodwill to all, including yourself. (It also happens to be great for lowering acute anxiety and cultivating self-compassion.) In its simplest form, all it takes is you saying these words, aloud or mentally, slowly and sincerely, repeating them for a set time or until you feel calmer and less constricted:

May I be free from harm. May I be strong and healthy. May I be happy. May I live a life filled with ease.

If you wish, you can then extend goodwill toward a person for whom you are grateful, a neutral person, a person with whom you struggle, and, finally, to all beings.

"When you say those wishes sincerely, every element of the practice is a relief," Salzberg writes. "The phrases channel the energy instead of allowing it to proliferate. As you do this, you are back in charge and you can feel the body relaxing as the space around your anxiety opens up and releases. When you release control, you are free to choose how to react rather than being inhibited by frightening conjectures."[5]

Seek clarity and structure

If you feel the need to control things because remote work, your new boss, or your new hire is making you anxious, seek clarity. We get anxious when things are unclear, uncertain, or ambiguous. As productivity expert Bob Pozen says, "The first and most important thing is to establish success metrics for your team." Success metrics are the key to everything because they "force the clarification of goals and better communication," and once they're in place, there's no need for micromanaging because the employee has a clear mandate. The manager can then leave the employee to do their work and follow up with periodic check-ins.

What's great about this approach is that it reduces anxiety for the entire team. Everyone knows what's expected of them and when, and employees are given autonomy while the manager remains in a leadership role—there to guide, strategize, and facilitate, rather than dive in and fix things.

You can also use structure to relieve your anxiety and lay out clear plans for scheduling, deadlines, and longer-term career goals. I start each day by planning it out in half-hour blocks, and I know plenty of leaders who use elaborate color-coding systems to delineate their time for work, family, community involvement, exercise, and leisure. Especially if you're the type of person who loves being organized and making lists, a detailed plan can help you avoid being gripped by anxiety and make you more able to calm controlling behavior.

Try noting and naming

Before diving into our emotions and acting on them, pause to note and name your emotions. This will take a little practice. So the next time you feel a rush to control or fix something, pause and turn inward. What emotions are driving this automatic response? Name them gently, without judgment: "Oh, it's fear. Oh, it's anger."

Research has shown that when we identify and name difficult emotions, we're less likely to experience a stress reaction. Pausing brings some emotional freedom: instead of overly identifying with the difficult emotion ("I am afraid"), we can recognize that we're *having* the emotion ("I'm experiencing fear right now"), which gives us more choice in how to respond.[6]

Salzberg says there are three benefits to the practice of naming, which she describes as naming the thought or feeling arising in the present moment: (1) It creates a calm interior space where we aren't reacting to the thought or feeling. (2) It provides a kind of instant feedback system. If we find that we're reacting with resentment, self-blame, or self-criticism, we now have the chance to return to a state of open awareness. For example, rather than "There I go again with the anger!" try "Yep, this is what's happening right now." (3) Noting reminds us that all feelings are transient. You may feel anger or fear in *this* moment, but feelings aren't forever; they always pass.[7]

Hand over the reins

Sometimes you'll just have to hand over the reins to your team—even when you feel afraid to do so—by stepping out of a process you'd usually control or delegating a work product you would usually manage, for example. Once again, this is a practice, and you can start small and work your way up if you need to. Chances are, you may be pleasantly surprised by what your team is capable of when you let them spread their wings.

Amelia Burke-Garcia, a digital health communicator and researcher who's led nationwide public health campaigns, spoke to me about how she and her team were managing a federally funded multimedia campaign about the Covid-19 pandemic. She noted how her management style in this crisis differed from the one she used ten years ago, when she was leading the Centers for Disease Control and Prevention's national influenza vaccination campaign. Both were high-stakes and high-pressure situations, but back then, as a less experienced leader, Burke-Garcia confessed to being "much more of a micromanager and constantly worried about being able to deliver and achieve." She acted out her anxieties by checking in too frequently, even though she had no concerns about her team's capability. "It was a reflection of my own worries and concerns," she said. Her challenge, like every leader's, was "finding that balance between being attentive and supportive and allowing [the team] to operate independently and trust that they're doing a good job."

Since then, Burke-Garcia has worked intentionally to avoid micromanaging. She said,

> I've come to a place of recognizing that I need to give people space to be their own person. I think that there's this balance between mentoring people to be the best that they possibly can, but then also letting them be their own people, with their own ways of communicating and saying and writing and doing things. I may not agree with every part of that, but that's OK. So it's an interesting dynamic of seeing the benefits of all of the hard work that was put in early on to mentor and grow staff, but then also knowing when to take a step back and let people go out on their own.

Setting Boundaries Helps You Control What You Can

One of the ways to control what we actually *can* control is to protect our boundaries and set limits. Boundaries are crucial. Once you understand yours, they're like a magic ingredient—one you didn't even know you were missing until you wound up anxious, feeling like your work life is out of control, and headed toward burnout.

Before we can start setting boundaries, let's learn what boundaries are (and aren't). Because so many of us have become accustomed to working without healthy boundaries, I asked an expert for a refresher.

"A general working definition of a boundary would be a guideline that we set or create for ourselves to identify what feels permissible or what feels safe as we operate in life," says Rebecca Harley, a psychologist and Harvard Medical School assistant professor of psychology. If we're on the inside of that boundary, Harley adds, we feel confident that we're going to be OK and that we can function at our best. It's when we're chronically on the outside of the boundary that problems arise.

This is why it's so important for leaders to understand their boundaries and those of their teams, especially in times of anxiety. When we know our boundaries, we can set limits. "The notion of a limit is like the line that you want to try to observe, being careful not to cross," Harley says. "It's what you are or aren't willing to do, or what you are or aren't willing to tolerate."

A prime example is work hours. Especially as it's become all too easy for work to encroach upon family or leisure time, it's crucial that we know our boundaries around how much we're willing to work and when we're willing to put in those hours. Harley advises identifying that boundary, communicating it to your manager and teammates, and then setting a limit to make sure the boundary is preserved. An example from her own life is leaving her phone downstairs after a certain time. This boundary keeps her safe from overwork and from spending too much time online, and the limit that preserves the boundary is literally placing her phone a floor away, where she can't reflexively reach for it.

Boundaries can be about anything we need to safeguard our person, time, energy, and minds. Some are more tangible, such as my need for a certain amount of personal space, or your need for your work area to be organized in a certain way. Others are intangible, such as the boundaries we set to protect our time, energy, emotions, or mental health.

You can set boundaries around the amount of sleep you require, the amount of interaction you have with a difficult coworker (or *how* you interact with them), or the amount of time you'll allow yourself to revise a report. Really, a boundary can constitute anything that you need to safeguard your physical, mental, and emotional health and to help you function at your best.

Roxane Gay is a bestselling author and the contributing opinion writer for the Work Friend column in the *New York Times*, where she writes about the everyday problems that arise at work and how our workplaces contribute to our general happiness, or lack thereof. A great many of the questions she receives from readers illustrate that so much of the conflict we experience at work comes about as a result of us disrespecting each other's boundaries. I asked Gay how she would explain boundaries to a reader seeking her advice and how they could know when theirs are being crossed.

"I would tell someone, think about what would make you comfortable in a situation and what would make you uncomfortable," she said. "And that's where your boundary is—that moment where you go from comfort to discomfort. It doesn't have to be anything more than discomfort. Your initial boundaries are, 'I don't care for that.'"

I love her answer's simplicity, and that it underscores that boundaries are different for each person. Your extraverted colleague may relish and draw energy from dropping into your office for an ad hoc brainstorming session, but others could experience this as a violation of a physical and mental boundary. Where is your discomfort? What sparks the response, "I don't care for that"? That's where your boundary is.

Gay frequently receives requests for advice about how to enforce healthy boundaries. The most common examples, she said, concern overwork and work bleeding into late nights and weekends. "I'm not talking about your typical, 'Let's everybody pitch in because we're on a deadline,'" she said. "I'm talking about consistent overwork, consistent seventy- or eighty-hour work weeks. It's just unreasonable." So many people, she said, are subjected to overwork because they believe their job "is predicated on that kind of sacrifice." The sad truth is, they're right. Too many work cultures routinely cross healthy boundaries when it comes to work expectations; it now happens so frequently that many of us have come to accept it as the norm.

Thankfully, we have voices like Gay's. "It's OK to just say, 'You know what? My workday ends at six. I don't work on Saturdays and Sundays. I don't check email on the weekends. I don't check email after five,'" she said. Gay notes that she, too, must be intentional about maintaining her boundaries. This applies even when, like Gay, you have a lot of people depending on you and eagerly waiting for you to deliver. "I refuse to believe that there's anything that happens at . . . 7:30 or 8 p.m. that cannot wait until the next morning," she said. "It can!" What's more, the "false senses of urgency" that characterize so much of our work culture are our own creation. "And they're wrong," she said. "They're not necessary."

Gay acknowledges that it can be easier to maintain your boundaries once you're more senior, and that we live in a culture that encourages a lack of boundaries. Yet identifying and preserving them is absolutely worth the effort it takes. And sometimes that work begins with knowing your self-worth and value.

"The reality is that sometimes you need to believe you deserve to have boundaries," she said, adding that you have a *right* to boundaries— you don't need to tolerate whatever people bring to your door. "It's not 'mean' to stand up for yourself. If your employment boat can be rocked by a very reasonable boundary, then it's probably time to start looking for another job."

Play detective to figure out your boundaries

Maybe you already know exactly what your boundaries are. Or maybe, like so many of us, you've had your boundaries ignored for so long that you're not clear on where your needs begin and others' demands end. Our boundaries often become blurred little by little, without us even noticing, until it feels totally normal to sleep with your smartphone and respond to work messages at all hours, or to forgo family commitments and show your face at Zoom meetings even when you have nothing to contribute. And especially with anxious achievers, it's so easy to get caught up in the grind of perfectionism, people-pleasing, and producing that we forget how to pay attention to what we're actually feeling. Whatever the reason, we all need to take some time to figure out our emotions and experiences—to identify, in Gay's words, the moment we go from comfort to discomfort.

Often a spike in anxiety or another difficult emotional state is the telltale sign that a boundary has been crossed. "Little flare-ups of anxiety are signals we can actually decide to tune into," Rebecca Harley told me. How does one do this? By playing detective.

"You don't necessarily have to go searching," Harley said. "It's just about trying to turn your attention inward . . . tuning in to whatever's there in the present." In other words, mindfulness. "That's really what we're talking about here, is just paying attention, ideally in a curious and not judgmental way, to just observe and describe whatever your internal experience is in that moment," she said. When you take on that role of detective—*Hmm, let's just see what we find here*—you approach yourself with less fear and less judgment. And that is key. "Rarely have I ever seen judgment do anything other than shut us down." (For more on figuring out your boundaries, read the "Identify Your Boundaries and Limits" exercise.)

Let's say your boss asks you for an update on the memo you've been working on, and you snap at her. Both of you are surprised by your reaction—her request was perfectly routine and not even delivered with any urgency. Now you're embarrassed and must apologize, and you feel rushed to finish up, which is hard to do because you can't stop replaying this moment in your head and beating yourself up for it.

But what if you took five minutes to play detective and go on a little fact-finding mission? Maybe you tune in and discover an unpleasant mix of anxiety, anger, and irritation. *Great, now we have something to work with!* your detective self thinks. What's behind these difficult feelings? Well, as it happens, this morning the office oversharer dropped by and unloaded on you while you were drafting the memo. They're more senior, so you felt you didn't have any choice but to stop what you were doing and listen. They droned on and on as your Slack notifications accumulated and your anxiety and irritation escalated. Once the person

Identify Your Boundaries and Limits

Here's another exercise to help identify your boundaries. Tune in and consider, What needs safeguarding? A good way to begin is to complete these two sentences:

• I don't feel safe when . . .

• My work performance is compromised when . . .

Use the information this exercise yields to identify a boundary and a limit you can set to make sure your boundary isn't crossed. Here are some examples:

I don't feel safe when . . . my coworker asks for my advice on personal matters.

What needs safeguarding: my emotional energy, the separation between my professional and personal lives

Boundary: I will not engage in discussions of my coworker's personal life at work.

finally moved on, you managed to get back to work, but just half an hour later your boss called—and you reacted automatically.

This is an easy example, as it doesn't take a lot of tuning in to see that the office oversharer violated your physical and mental boundaries. They were in your space and you didn't want them there, and they displayed no regard for your time, energy, or responsibilities. But now consider: if this is what happened on a single occasion, what would happen if your boundaries were chronically disrespected? The cumulative effect can result in deep frustration, lower productivity, and eventually burnout.

Limit(s): I'll tell my coworker that I don't feel comfortable dispensing advice, and that I need to stay focused on work while I'm at the office.

My work performance is compromised when . . . I say yes to too many things.

What needs safeguarding: my time, my physical and mental energy

Boundary: I will say no more often. Or, I will say yes to myself more often.

Limit(s): I will not say yes to a new work request until I've vetted it with a trusted adviser and we both agree it's a good idea. Or, I will dedicate evenings after 7 p.m. to my personal enrichment and turn off all work-related notifications.

Granted, it's not always possible to get exactly what you need. You may not have the luxury of finding three ninety-minute uninterrupted blocks in your calendar, or you may not have the option of saying no to incoming requests. In cases like these, talk to your manager and see if you can find a creative compromise. You never know until you ask.

Sometimes, though, our boundaries aren't as easy to identify. What if you're in a job that you like, but you feel increasingly exhausted and less motivated? Playing detective can work here too. For example, you tune in and get curious about those feelings, and you discover that the numerous sales events you're attending are draining your energy—this just doesn't mesh well with your introverted nature. Your boundary has to do with time, and even more so with energy. How many networking events can you handle before you begin to feel the discomfort that signals a healthy boundary is being crossed? (Remember: discomfort can feel like anxiety, irritation, exhaustion, cynicism, or other difficult internal states.) Based on that information, set your limit: *I will do no more than two networking events per month.* Or, *I require x amount of time between networking events to recharge and be my best.*

And based on *that* information, talk to your manager. Share your honest assessment about what's not working and what you need to deliver your best performance. If you have ideas for how to make that happen, all the better. Maybe networking responsibilities can be rotated among team members. Maybe some events can be virtual. Strategizing with your boss in this way not only helps to clearly communicate and preserve your boundaries, it also demonstrates your leadership abilities and your investment in the organization's mission.

• • •

At the center of our psyches are a few common fears, and the fear of losing control is one of them. It drives us to do many things to protect ourselves, some of them quite irrational—which is so very understandable. The prospect of losing control *is* frightening. As ever, the key is to pause and bring awareness to the situation, and to not act impulsively out of the anxiety that we feel about losing control.

Approach this endeavor with as much self-compassion as you can. Facing deep-seated fears requires us to take an honest look at what scares us most, and to take on some practices and attitudes that make us feel vulnerable. It means we try a different stance: acceptance rather than resistance, self-compassion rather than self-blame, gentleness rather than force. Ultimately, accepting the inevitability of letting go of control is the only thing that can release us from the anxiety controlling our everyday lives.

10

Feedback, Criticism, and Impostor Syndrome

Feedback—and its harsher cousin, criticism—can be very difficult to hear, even if you don't struggle with anxiety. But anxious people tend to be especially fearful of being judged, and when factors like perfectionism, people-pleasing, and overfunctioning come into play, failing to live up to some ideal can trigger deep feelings of fear and shame. And when impostor syndrome is involved, even gentle criticism and helpful feedback can seem like public confirmation of what we suspected all along—we're phonies who don't deserve our success.

Lots of anxious achievers fear criticism and feedback, mostly because we fear shame. It doesn't matter how "helpful" the feedback is or how gently it's delivered—I fixate on the negative and feel like everything's my fault. I have two go-to reactions to negative feedback, neither of which is mature or productive. I might blow up and start to "throw bombs," as a couples therapist once put it, or I might go silent and retreat.

But the thing is, criticism and feedback are part of work life, and avoidance is not a good strategy. Knowing what you need to improve is healthy and necessary, and when you have a boss, a coach, or a mentor who will help you identify those areas and show you how to get better, it's a true gift. Everyone is going to give and receive feedback throughout a career, and you can't lead if you can't handle it.

Fortunately, learning to receive feedback is a skill—something we can practice and get better at. Likewise, *giving* useful feedback is an essential business skill we can learn. And because anxiety can deepen our empathy, anxious achievers who really struggle with receiving criticism, or who are deeply hampered by impostor syndrome, are— ironically—often the best at offering compassionate, actionable feedback and at spotting and supporting a team member struggling with impostor feelings.

Effective, Honest Check-Ins

Poppy Jaman, who runs the UK's City Mental Health Alliance and who we met in chapter 7, has an ultra-simple way for managers to help ease the anxiety burden for employees before providing feedback: have regular one-on-ones with your direct reports—and begin every meeting by asking how they are. "There's no point in us discussing your projects, your targets, and the business objectives if you are not in . . . a good place," Jaman says.

She's absolutely right. Someone can't focus on what their boss is saying when anxiety has taken the reins—and demonstrating consistent, genuine concern for employees establishes trust and shows that they're valued and that their needs are heard. This lowers the anxiety all around, and removes a lot of the dread anxious employees can feel before feedback sessions.

But here's the thing: when you ask, you need to be present for the answer. It's easy to be skeptical about the value of a check-in; a colleague noted to me that his boss would ask all the right check-in questions . . . while also checking her phone and email constantly, and even interrupting the check-ins to respond to things. If you are going to check in with direct reports or colleagues, center yourself first. Are you ready to listen, or will your own leadership anxiety get in the way of your colleague's answer? Check-ins are best when they are frequent and don't feel like a big deal. When a check-in feels like an unusual occasion, anxiety can spike.

When done right, a good, frequent check-in builds trust. Jaman's simple, effective practice was so successful that it became standard operating procedure at her organization, as well as at several law firms and corporations she advises. Considering how isolating depression and anxiety can be, it's little wonder that a genuine check-in can make such a difference.

The Ongoing Need for Feedback

I hate to break it to you, but you may need to seek out critical feedback more often as you become more successful. Research has found that the more experience and power a manager holds, the less accurate their assessments of their leadership effectiveness are, and the more likely they are to overestimate their skills and abilities.

Why does this happen? Researchers have two hypotheses. First, senior leaders simply have fewer people above them who can provide candid feedback. Second, the more power a leader holds, the less comfortable people are giving them feedback, for fear it will hurt their own careers. Business professor James O'Toole adds that as a leader's power grows, their willingness to listen shrinks, either because they think they know more than their employees or because they fear that seeking feedback will come at a cost—usually, that they'll be seen as weak.[1]

Ironically, it's the leaders who seek out and are willing to accept critical feedback that tend to be the most effective. In a study of more than fifty-one thousand participants, leaders who were rated as being "very poor at asking for and acting on feedback" were also rated as poor in their overall effectiveness. Those rated highest in asking for and acting on feedback, meanwhile, were also rated highest in effectiveness. Why does feedback make us better leaders, while avoiding it makes us less effective? According to these researchers, "leaders who resist feedback make changes based on their internal assumptions (which are often wrong), or they don't make any changes at all."[2]

This conclusion caught my eye. What's another group whose internal assumptions are often wrong? People with unmanaged anxiety and depression.

Now, obviously, not everyone who's wrong about an assumption has anxiety or depression. Still, there's a connection to consider. The voice of unmanaged anxiety and depression is notoriously unreliable. It will tell us that we shouldn't take a risk, that we're not fit to be leaders, that we should stay small and safe and quiet, that we're frauds who will be found out any minute, that there's no point in improving or even trying.

These are all examples of negative self-talk, or, to borrow from the language of the study, they're *wrong internal assumptions*. To use my preferred language, it's a bunch of garbage that anxiety pumps out. Sure, in some sense anxiety is trying to keep you out of the line of fire, but unmanaged anxiety constantly misjudges the level of threat. It can't help itself. So don't let it prevent you from seeking the very feedback that has the potential to catapult you to the next level, and don't let it bamboozle you into inaction.

Anxiety expert Alice Boyes offers a few ways to make seeking and accepting feedback a little easier. The first concerns who is delivering it. "It's a lot easier to get constructive feedback from someone who thinks you're talented and who thinks you're a competent human," she says. Someone, in other words, who trusts in your talents and competencies, and in whose opinions and observations *you* trust. If your manager doesn't fit the bill, you'll still have to hear their feedback and deal with it. All the more reason to find people who *do* fit the bill, whether that's an executive coach, a trusted coworker, or a colleague in your industry.

Next, consider the format that works best for you. For example, "it's a lot easier not to be defensive if you're getting feedback in a form that's written rather than being given it on the spot," Boyes says. This way, you won't need to respond immediately, and you can have time to digest the feedback privately. Is a formal sit-down with your boss too anxiety-provoking? See if it's possible to speak on the phone. Another option is to adjust the amount of feedback you're receiving. If you're soliciting post-event feedback via a survey or online rating system, for instance, you can limit the number of respondents. "Instead of getting 100 people to do a survey, I might get five people and then digest that first," Boyes says. "Or is an hourlong meeting with your manager too much? See if you can divide it into two half-hour sessions."

Also, Boyes says, remember that sometimes feedback is simply not that helpful. "Think about the fact that even from someone who's a really useful feedback-giver, it may be that only 80 percent of it is on point," she says. "Recognize that you don't need to accept every point of feedback—you can disagree or prioritize."

Anxiety and Impostor Syndrome

The *impostor syndrome* (also known as *impostor phenomenon*, the preferred term in academic circles), was first identified in the 1970s by psychologists and researchers Pauline Rose Clance and Suzanne Imes. They studied more than 150 highly successful women who were known for their superior achievements but who nonetheless were beset with "impostor feelings." "Despite their earned degrees, scholastic honors, high achievement on standardized tests, praise and professional recognition from colleagues and respected authorities, these women do not experience an internal sense of success," the researchers observed. "[They] maintain a strong belief that they are not intelligent; in fact, they are convinced that they have fooled anyone who thinks otherwise."

The participants in this study attributed their success to luck, effort (rather than inherent ability), or error (someone mistakenly selecting them for a job or accolade). In what I imagine to be a tone of equal parts frustration and sorrow, Clance and Imes concluded that "these women find innumerable means of negating any external evidence that contradicts their belief that they are, in reality, unintelligent."[3]

Commenting on this study, impostor syndrome experts Lisa and Richard Orbé-Austin say the women "used hard work and diligence as a cover-up for their perceived inadequacy." The women engaged in a cycle that can be seen in figure 10-1.

FIGURE 10-1

The impostor cycle

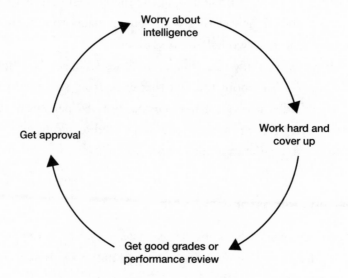

Worry about intelligence

Work hard and cover up

Get good grades or performance review

Get approval

Source: Lisa and Richard Orbé-Austin, *Own Your Greatness* (Berkeley, CA: Ulysses Press, 2020).

Receiving praise resulted in temporarily feeling good, but once the good feelings subsided, the women returned to worrying about their intelligence or ability to perform. "Within this cycle, there is no internalization of the successful experience," the Orbé-Austins note. "The accomplishment isn't accepted as part of their identity or attributed much value, so the next time they perform, it's as if the previous accomplishments never existed. Thus, the cycle begins again."[4]

Impostor syndrome is not just experienced by women; men feel it too. Some of the signs that you may be struggling with impostor syndrome include:

- You engage in the impostor cycle seen in figure 10-1.

- You deny your ability and attribute your success to luck, mistake, overwork, or a relationship.

- You discount praise and feel guilty about success.

- You fear failing and being discovered as a fraud.

- You do not feel intelligent (even though tests or performance indicate you are).

- You have anxiety, self-esteem issues, depression, and frustration from internal standards.

- You struggle with perfectionism.

- You overestimate others and underestimate yourself.

- You do not experience an internal feeling of success.

- You overwork or self-sabotage to cover feelings of inadequacy.

- You fear that you won't live up to expectations.

- You set very challenging goals for yourself and feel disappointed when you fall short.

- You are an overachiever.

- You sabotage your success.

There are varying definitions of impostor syndrome, in part because it is not a recognized psychiatric illness. Its core components, however, are captured in the American Psychological Association's description: "The situation in which highly accomplished, successful individuals paradoxically believe they are frauds who ultimately will fail and be unmasked as incompetent."

Though it seems counterintuitive at first glance, many anxious leaders experience *more* impostor syndrome as they grow in their careers and become more successful. Every promotion, accolade, achievement, or career move gives them a fresh opportunity to doubt themselves. This happens because with impostor syndrome we're unable to internalize and own our successes.

Jeannette Kaplun, an award-winning journalist and influencer, has over twenty years of experience on TV, radio, and in building digital media companies. In 1999 she cofounded Todobebé, a resource network for moms from Spanish-speaking countries, and in 2012 she launched Hispana Global, a bilingual platform for Hispanic women, where she is currently the CEO. "The problem with anxiety is that it's associated so closely with impostor syndrome," she told me. "You feel that you don't know anything that you're doing, and you start doubting yourself. If you start asking too many people for advice, then you get very confused, and you can actually become very scattered, and that's never good when you're building a business."

I think a lot of anxious people can relate to this. When impostor syndrome makes us doubt our competence or confidence, it's understandable that we start trying to "borrow" them from others by seeking their approval, advice, and assurance. While others' input (and feedback!) is certainly appropriate at times, what Kaplun is rightly pinpointing is that when impostor syndrome and doubt sneak in and send us scurrying to solicit the opinions of others, we can lose our way in the midst of all that advice.

So how do we recenter and find our way back to our gut instinct, our vision? How do we remind ourselves, "Hey, wait a minute—I got myself here in the first place! I know what to do."

First, Kaplun said, you need to learn to recognize your symptoms of anxiety. You need to know how anxiety *begins* to manifest for you, so you can deal with it before it takes over your mind and your emotions. Kaplun's healthy coping mechanisms are breathing exercises, writing down what she's feeling (a great way of externalizing anxiety), and establishing priorities and a daily schedule so she won't become overwhelmed.

As for impostor syndrome, you tell yourself the truth. You remind yourself that "there's a reason why you've achieved what you've achieved," she said. "There's a reason why you're doing it and connecting with people in a way that others are not. . . . Go back to what you know, what you have done. The effect that you're having on other people might help you center yourself and realize, 'You know what? I need to go with my gut.'"

Behavioral scientist and consultant Tanya Tarr suggests personifying the voice of your impostor syndrome, which she calls her "inner saboteur." Interestingly, she distinguishes the inner saboteur from the inner critic, because, she says, helpful criticism has its place. The inner saboteur, on the other hand, "is trying to kill your motivation." Personifying that voice helps you realize who is actually saying those things, where that voice comes from (usually a critical person from your past), and, most importantly, distinguishes that voice from your own. When you can identify the voice of your inner saboteur, Tarr says, name that person "and tell them to shut the hell up."

Like Kaplun, Tarr recommends that you take stock of your achievements and remind yourself of your accomplishments. "The counterbalance to impostor syndrome is authentic confidence and authentic pride," she told me. If, like a lot of anxious people, you find it difficult to identify your achievements or you shy away from it for fear of being egotistical, Tarr offers three practical solutions.

First, ask people. Find people you trust from your professional or personal life who can provide an objective view, and ask them to help you identify things you've done well.

Second, maintain that clips file. This is a standard practice in journalism; it's simply a collection of your published articles. So what's your version of a clips file? Photographers and artists and designers maintain portfolios; others keep an updated list of accomplishments in their CVs; others showcase their favorite work on their websites. I have a Google Drive folder with my favorite examples of my work. Whatever it is, this is objective evidence of your accomplishments.

Third, keep every email that contains positive feedback. Any time you start to doubt yourself, go back to your emails and you'll find a collection of external validation, complete with time stamps.

What If My Impostor Syndrome Isn't Even about Me?

Numerous commentators have pointed out that impostor syndrome may arise more from the systems we work in than from us. Writers and workplace equity experts Ruchika Tulshyan and Jodi-Ann Burey note that the predominant concept of impostor syndrome "puts the blame on individuals" and "took a fairly universal feeling of discomfort, second-guessing, and mild anxiety in the workplace and pathologized it, especially for women." The conventional view of impostor syndrome implies that *workers* must be fixed, rather than fixing the places where we work.[5]

Though not everyone who has experienced discrimination or oppression in the workplace also experiences impostor syndrome, there is some evidence that underrepresented employees, such as women and people of color, can be especially vulnerable to workplace-induced impostor feelings. Tulshyan and Burey point out that when impostor syndrome was first studied, researchers did not take into account the impact of systemic racism, classism, xenophobia, and other biases. But we now know, they say, that self-doubt and the feeling of not belonging in white- and male-dominated workplaces can be even more pronounced for women of color, due to the implicit or explicit messages they receive. The result is that the normal, natural feelings of uncertainty and self-doubt "become magnified by chronic battles with systemic bias and racism" for women of color.[6]

Lisa Orbé-Austin points out that while toxic and discriminatory workplaces can trigger impostor syndrome, the research shows that its origins usually lie in childhood experiences and familial dynamics that led individuals to not prioritize themselves. For example, if you grew up in a household where meeting everyone else's needs was your focus, investing in your own needs and internalizing your own accomplishments will feel foreign.[7] That said, Orbé-Austin agrees that toxic and discriminatory workplaces can make impostor syndrome more difficult to overcome. For example, workplaces or even entire systems of oppression may cause them to think, "Maybe you got here because of a diversity program. Maybe you're not good enough."[8]

Whether your impostor feelings can be traced all the way back to childhood or to a negative experience later in life, it's clear that certain environments trigger them, exacerbate them, and make them more difficult to overcome. Kevin Cokley, one of the world's leading experts on the impostor phenomenon, says that stressful and competitive environments "always become incubators for impostor feelings."[9] Tulshyan and Burey note that impostor syndrome "is especially prevalent in biased, toxic cultures that value individualism and overwork," and Orbé-Austin emphasizes the need to counter such workplace cultures, as these organizations actually *benefit* from maintaining impostor syndrome in their employees.[10] Why? Because employees struggling with impostor feelings work harder and look for approval from external sources—including their managers, who, consciously or unconsciously, are part of the toxic culture of the organization.[11]

Hilary is the senior director of marketing and communications for an oncology association. (Her name has been changed and the name of her firm has been withheld by request.) I got in touch with her after she sent me this extraordinary message on LinkedIn: "Impostor syndrome is what keeps me at my current job. I'm understaffed, overworked, and so beyond burnt out. I've been promoted three times in seven years yet I'm unsure about leaving and finding something better because I think I'm going to be found out as a total fraud. I can't be the only one, but it feels like it sometimes!"

Hilary's is a textbook case of impostor syndrome. Notice that she's been promoted three times in seven years—she's now a senior director— yet she still fears that a future employer will discover that she doesn't know what she's doing. What's more, she, like many who struggle with impostor feelings, chronically overworks—and just as Orbé-Austin cautioned, her organization is more than happy to let her. Because of staff turnover and vacant positions, Hilary has been juggling four different roles and more than fifty work projects. When she checked with payroll about how much she worked in 2021, she discovered that she'd put in at least 450 hours of overtime.

As Hilary and I chatted, it became clear that her organization itself suffers from a bit of impostor syndrome. It's not the premier medical society in the field, which is a source of collective anxiety and shame, and this makes Hilary's job in communications and marketing extra tough. "I hate to say it, but it's like being in a bad relationship," she said. "Sometimes you forget what normal is. It takes getting out of that situation to really have clarity and see how other people are living, because I'm sure that not everybody's life is like this. But you get so caught up in your own life, in the day-to-day, and just surviving."

Hilary's organization is clearly dysfunctional, and she's been in it so long that she has internalized the dysfunction. She knows she needs to leave, but her impostor syndrome keeps her stuck—and her organization is reaping the benefits.

When Impostor Syndrome Fuels Ambition

Researchers have identified two overarching responses to impostor syndrome. One is the path of procrastination, which is a kind of self-sabotaging response to feelings of fraudulence. Worried they won't succeed, these workers put off tasks until the last minute, and when they do succeed, they discount it as undeserved or a stroke of luck. The other is the path of overpreparation. These are the workers who overachieve, overwork, and overfunction.

Cokley has described how his own impostor feelings spur him toward overpreparation.[12] Even though he has studied the topic for many years, published studies in eminent journals, and given talks on the impostor phenomenon "dozens, and dozens, and dozens" of times, he approaches each talk as if he's never given one before, spending many hours preparing. "I never want people to hear me and think, 'He does not know what he's talking about,' so I really overprepare!" he confessed.[13] Overpreparers go the extra mile on every task, even if it's a subject or a process that, like Cokley, they know like the back of their hand.

Both paths can compromise well-being, and as we saw with Hilary, the path of overpreparation can lead to exhaustion and burnout. But there's no question that overpreparers tend to be very successful and highly valued by their teams and organizations.

I identify with this group. Like so many anxious achievers, my fear of being found out as incompetent or undeserving fuels my ambition as well as my tendency to overachieve, overwork, and chase after the unattainable goal of perfection. The original title of my podcast was *Anxious Ambition*, and I honestly don't think I could untangle those two words.

Sometimes I wonder, If I weren't so anxious, would I be ambitious at all? Or would I just be able to *be*? Would I be able to stop and enjoy things and not constantly worry about what's around the next corner? Would I be able to feel OK—oh, miracle of miracles—*just as I am*?

What I realize now is that my ambition has always been about anxiety and has also become a bad habit. In other words, I'm engaging in the impostor cycle: anxiety turns to worrying and feeling impostor syndrome, and those feelings are channeled into action in the form of overworking and overachieving. Then I get rewarded for the action, so I figure, *Well, this must be working for me in some way.* And I continue.

Social media entrepreneur Jyl Johnson Pattee reached out to me when she saw a LinkedIn post I did on impostor syndrome. Her story is fascinating because her longtime struggle with "Mr. Impostor Syndrome," as she refers to it, has fueled her ambition and her drive to create a successful business.

Pattee says impostor syndrome has been with her throughout her career, but it reached a fever pitch in the late 2000s, after the Great Recession of 2008 threw a wrench into her plans. At that time, Pattee had left her corporate job just nine months prior to be a stay-at-home parent to two young children—and then her husband was laid off in April 2009. With "no savings and no backup plan," and her husband suffering severe depression after being unable to find a job, Pattee felt it was up to her to keep the family afloat. She'd been hosting live events on Twitter "just as a way to get my extrovert fix," and her husband suggested she try to sell sponsorships for the events.

Pattee's response? "Yeah, right! I had been an instructional designer and project manager at FranklinCovey, working in soft-skills training for nearly ten years," she said. "What did I know about sales? Furthermore, who would I sell to? What would I say? What would I promise? Tracking tools weren't even on the market yet. How would I prove the results?"

But Pattee turned out to be great at sales, and she entered the market at just the right time: she landed a few clients right away, and within two months she had a full-blown influencer marketing agency. "We literally could not keep up with business," she said. "And I didn't even have a website! . . . So even though I still had this impostor syndrome, I didn't even have time to give it the space."

As the business became established and demand remained high, Pattee's impostor feelings returned. "I would attribute all my success to luck . . . and I would never take the credit," she said. "I woke up every day, wondering if that would be the day people would realize I had no prior PR or digital media experience—that I was literally making everything up as I was going. In other words, that I was a phony." To others, she appeared "super confident," even to the point that some found her intimidating. "But how on earth could they feel [this] way about someone who was clearly faking it till she made it every second of every day?" Pattee said. "One plus one did not equal two!"

Any time she had a spare moment, Pattee told me, terror would overtake her. But that terror was one of the things that kept her going. I think this happens a lot, especially when we don't come from wealth and we feel that everything depends on us, or when we're anxious by nature. In both cases the cost of mistakes feels astronomically high, so we push and push and push ourselves to keep going.

Even today, with an established business and decades of accomplishments behind her, Pattee still struggles with impostor syndrome. Recently, as she was working with a consultant to update her résumé, she "couldn't believe" what the résumé was reflecting back to her. "I could suddenly see how Mr. Impostor Syndrome lied to me," she said. "The proof was on the paper. I had actually accomplished a thing or two—or more! It was a big wake-up call for me about the power we give our thoughts and beliefs."

Though her fear of being "found out" and losing her business had fueled much of her drive to succeed, it came with a cost. "The thing that is so damaging about giving in to Mr. Impostor Syndrome is when you actually believe it," she said. "You feel small, unqualified, and terrified. I lived in terror for years, waiting for the other shoe to drop, thinking we'd end up on the street, homeless. It was a very real possibility to me based on the 'fact' that I was not who people thought I was."

Pattee perfectly describes the experience of so many anxious achievers. No matter how many years of experience we have, how many accolades we've earned, or how much money we've made, we still grapple with the feeling that our success has somehow come to us mistakenly, and that at any moment it can all be taken from us. That terror can drive achievement, but we need guardrails and healthy coping mechanisms to make sure it does not come at too high a cost.

For Pattee, the healthy counterforce to the terror that Mr. Impostor Syndrome inspired in her was resilience and grit, which she considers her superpowers. "Embracing all the parts of yourself is empowering," she said. "Putting myself out there even in the midst of my terror helped me keep Mr. Impostor Syndrome at bay and actually hit some desired results."

Dealing with Fear by Defusing

The brightest and best and most successful among us will still occasionally receive negative feedback that's hard to hear. We make mistakes, don't hit sales goals, fall short of targets, misread and mismanage situations. That's just life—it happens. And it's clear that a sizable number of extremely successful people will continue to grapple with impostor feelings no matter how high their stars rise. So how do we manage our anxiety around feedback so that we don't avoid this crucial element of leadership, and how do we manage our impostor feelings such that our performance isn't impaired and we don't drive ourselves to exhaustion in an effort to prove our worth?

Granted, that's a pretty tall order, and I'm the first to admit I still have a long way to go. But I've found that acceptance and commitment therapy, or ACT, provides a powerful framework for managing even my biggest anxious feelings and most damning negative self-talk, including my fear of feedback and my impostor feelings, both of which run deep. ACT teaches us not to become *fused* with our anxious feelings and negative thoughts, and instead to *defuse* and get some distance from them. From a state of defusion, we can:

- Look at thoughts from an external, observing point of view

- Notice thoughts rather than becoming caught up in them

- Let thoughts come and go rather than holding on to them and letting them dictate our actions[14]

This is one of the things that's so revolutionary about ACT: instead of trying to change, eliminate, fight, or resist our difficult thoughts and feelings, we work on changing how we *relate* to them.

One of the first things to realize is that thoughts are just thoughts— ephemeral, passing, ever shifting. Once we begin to see that, we realize that we don't have to place so much stock in our thoughts and negative self-talk. We don't have to believe their content, let our behavior be dictated by them, or let them hijack our mood and self-confidence. ACT, as you can see, does not place much value on thoughts—which is one of the reasons I like it so much!

Russ Harris, one of the world's experts on ACT, says that earlier in his life, his own impostor syndrome would show up any time he made a mistake, no matter how trivial, and it would take the form of this thought: "I'm incompetent."

"I would get very upset, believing that thought was the absolute truth," he writes. This is a perfect illustration of the ACT concept of fusion: facts don't matter when you're fused with a thought. Harris notes that sometimes he'd try to argue with the "I'm incompetent" thought by pointing out that everyone makes mistakes, that no mistake he'd ever made was serious, and that he still did his job very well. At other times he'd review a list of his accomplishments, or remind himself of positive feedback he'd received. He even tried countering his negative self-talk by repeating positive affirmations about his abilities.

Nothing worked until he learned to defuse his thoughts. He realized that the "I'm incompetent" story was just a mental reaction that showed up automatically, no different from the thousands of other thoughts passing through his mind throughout the day. Thoughts are not a problem, he said, as long as we see them for what they are: just a few words that pop into your head.[15]

If you find that you're fused with some negative thoughts around feedback, criticism, or being revealed as a fraud, try one of Harris's defusion techniques. The idea is that we can unhook from or defuse our

negative thoughts that keep us stuck if we learn to take them less seriously. Here are four of the most well-known ACT techniques:

Use the "I'm a banana" trick

Identify the negative thought that tends to hook you repeatedly—for
example, "I'm incompetent"—and replace it with "I'm a banana." How
does that make you feel? Silly? You bet. But does "I'm a banana" carry
as much truth as "I'm incompetent"? Yep! And do your impostor feelings start to lose their sting after the 100th time you've replaced "I'm
incompetent" with "I'm a banana"? Most likely.

Sing your negative thought

To the tune of the "Happy Birthday" song, sing your negative thought,
either in your mind or aloud. It's the same mechanism at work: "I'm
such an idiot" is painful and can undermine action . . . until you sing it
in a silly way.

Give it a character

Repeat your negative thought in the voice of a cartoon character, a
movie star, or a character from your favorite TV show or meme. Want
to quickly defang your fears of not belonging? Repeat "You don't belong
here!" to yourself in the voice of a Monty Python character. Or use the
trick we learned from Andrew Sotomayor in chapter 5 of hearing negative thoughts as chipmunks. "You'll never belong!" loses its bite after
you hear it a few dozen times in the voice of Alvin the chipmunk.

Use visual effects on your thought

Type your negative thought on your computer in big, bold font: "I'm a
loser." Now play around with the text: Increase the font size, change it
to all caps, render it in the most ludicrous font you can find, give the
letters rainbow colors, use highlights. Make the text jump up and down,

wiggle, or dance (or just imagine this happening); make (or imagine) a disco ball bounce across each word. Once again, you're dialing up the ridiculous factor, which immediately makes you take your thought less seriously.

Harris says that as silly as these exercises are, they're powerful, because they help you unhook from your negative thoughts and see them for what they are: just words and pictures in your mind. Then you have a lot more choice about how you respond to them.[16]

If you can defuse your negative, limiting thoughts, you can detach from this negative inner experience and reduce its influence on your behavior. You don't have to fight the thoughts or feel bad about having them. You simply accept that they're there, and then gently, with self-compassion, set about changing how you relate to them.

And then get on with your life.

11

Social Anxiety

Arvind Rajan was unpacking in his Phoenix hotel room. The technology CEO had just flown cross-country to mix and mingle with peers at a weekend-long industry conference. But as he got ready for the opening cocktail mixer, anxiety gripped him. He made it to the event, but quickly became overwhelmed and left after ten minutes. Rajan simply couldn't face the prospect of making small talk with all those people for two days. So he repacked his suitcase, sprinted to the airport, and flew home to Washington, DC. He was too ashamed to bill the trip to his company, so he paid the expenses out of pocket.

Years later, Rajan was able to laugh about this incident, but his fear of meeting and mingling with people he didn't know was no minor thing. On the contrary, it made him less effective in an essential aspect of his job, which was to build and maintain a broad network of key people in his industry. Over the next several years he forced himself to attend networking events, and outwardly he was very successful. But situations that required him to move through a room and make small talk left him with extreme anxiety, sweaty palms, and the feeling that he was failing as a leader. It wasn't until he understood and accepted his social anxiety, and mastered other ways to connect and build his professional network, that his internal discomfort diminished and he began to flourish both internally and externally as a leader.

I'm sure many of you understand Rajan's impulsive reaction to his fears—and his resulting shame. I too have let social anxiety turn me around from doing what I needed to do, and those incidents have caused me embarrassment and shame. But, fortunately, Rajan and I are not alone. There are many, many ambitious people who struggle with social anxiety—including famous people whose jobs require them to be in the spotlight.

Kevin Love, the five-time National Basketball Association All-Star, helped the Cleveland Cavaliers reach four straight NBA Finals, including a 2016 title, and he also happens to be an Olympic gold medalist. Love has candidly discussed his struggles with depression and social anxiety. Clearly, mental illness hasn't stopped him from reaching the pinnacles of success, but at times it has impacted his performance and, behind the scenes, left him miserable. He suffered a highly publicized panic attack on the court in 2017, and has said that at his lowest point, his social anxiety was so bad that he couldn't leave his bedroom.

Love spoke to me about the incongruity of being not only a famous person who struggles with social anxiety but also a star athlete who's expected to be invincible. "As an athlete, we're looked at as superheroes," he said. "I know that from growing up and having these superstars in my eyes like Charles Barkley or Shaquille O'Neal, or even before that with Larry Bird and Magic Johnson and Michael Jordan . . . these guys are indestructible. Nothing can hurt them."

Before he was with the Cavaliers, Love was the star player for the Minnesota Timberwolves. But his anxiety was so bad that he was never able to enjoy the city or even go outside much. "I had my little pockets where I would go, I had a couple of restaurants, and then I would just be basically shutting [myself] in my apartment or in my room by myself," he said.

For a long time, Love tried to achieve his way out of depression, and his identity and self-worth were dependent on his performance. Now he's accepted that anxiety and depression will always be with him, and through therapy, medication, and openly sharing his struggles, he's learned how to support his mental health and remain competitive. "Being unapologetically myself and walking into a room and just being me at all times—that is so freeing," he said. "You're just yourself. And you learn to love yourself more."

Pernicious leadership myths and stereotypes insist that leaders never feel socially anxious, but of course that's not true. It is true, however, that social anxiety can be strange and difficult to understand. It makes no sense that many leaders can stand up in front of thousands and deliver a killer keynote address, but want to hide in the bathroom rather than mingle with a few people afterward. Some leaders may feel fine pitching to a boardroom of strangers, yet be paralyzed when talking to their staff. Others may relish office parties and networking events, but panic if you put them on a stage.

As with all anxieties, the experience varies from person to person, and it's critical to understand why certain people and professional situations trigger your social anxiety. Chances are, you can't entirely avoid these people and situations—nor should you. But as Rajan and Love have shown us, you can learn to manage your social anxiety and perform at the top of your game.

Social Anxiety, Introversion, and Shyness

The Anxiety and Depression Association of America says the defining feature of social anxiety disorder, also known as social phobia, is "intense anxiety or fear of being judged, negatively evaluated, or rejected in a social or performance situation." People with social anxiety fear being perceived as unintelligent, awkward, incompetent, or uninteresting. They also fear *appearing* afraid or awkward, so their outward signs of anxiety—such as sweating, shaking, blushing, losing their train of thought, or having a tremor in their voice—cause them deep distress. All of this discomfort leads many people to avoid social situations altogether, and if those situations are unavoidable, they engage in various coping mechanisms to get by, some quite unhealthy.

Ellen Hendriksen is the author of *How to Be Yourself: Quiet Your Inner Critic and Rise Above Social Anxiety* and a clinical psychologist at Boston

University's Center for Anxiety and Related Disorders. "Social anxiety, fundamentally, is this belief that there is something wrong with you," she told me. "And that, unless we conceal and hide that perceived fatal flaw, we will be revealed, and everybody will judge and reject us."

That perception, Hendriksen explained, could be based on a mistaken assumption, or it could be due to a negative experience, usually from childhood, such as being bullied or having overly critical parents. Wherever it comes from, she said, we develop the belief "that we are stupid, or awkward, or nobody wants us here, or [we're] a loser, or any of these terrible things that our brains just latch on to and hold on to for years and decades." And then we work very, very hard to hide that perception. "I want to emphasize that word *perception*," Hendriksen said, "because in social anxiety, whatever the reveal is, it's fundamentally not true." There it is again, that unreliable narrator voice of anxiety.

It's important to distinguish here between social anxiety, introversion, and shyness. The words are sometimes used interchangeably, and they do share some characteristics, but they are not the same things. To begin with, social anxiety disorder is a diagnosable mental health condition, while introversion and shyness are personality traits. The *Diagnostic and Statistical Manual of Mental Disorders* tells us that social anxiety disorder is marked by persistent, marked fear about certain social situations (because you believe you'll be negatively judged or publicly embarrassed); fear or anxiety that is out of proportion to the situation; fear, anxiety, or resulting avoidance that interferes with your functioning; and fear, anxiety, or avoidance that cannot be attributed to another cause.[1] Introversion, meanwhile, has to do with social *energy*. It describes people who engage in alone time because they enjoy it and need it to recharge after they've been in group situations. For introverts, solitude is a necessity, whereas for people with social anxiety, it's an act of self-protection and a means of avoidance. Shyness, on the other hand, has to do with the fear of social judgment, and can manifest in many of the same ways as social anxiety—embarrassment, blushing, sweating, or worry about how you're being perceived, for instance. The main difference is in the severity of the fear, how much the fear impacts your functioning or quality of life, and the degree to which you're avoiding things.[2]

Why are these distinctions so important? To begin with, you need to know what you're dealing with in order to get the right kind of help. Social anxiety disorder can be debilitating and can go untreated if you chalk up your discomfort to extreme shyness or introversion. Moreover, you need to know yourself—your strengths and vulnerabilities, what sort of work you're cut out for and what just isn't a good fit—if you want to achieve excellence.

As we've seen with anxiety in general, there are strengths and skills that people with social anxiety are particularly good at. "Social anxiety is a package deal," Hendriksen told me. "It comes bundled with some . . . really awesome traits [such as] conscientiousness, increased empathy, [and the] ability to listen." Conscientiousness is especially valuable in the workplace. It's "being responsible, being dutiful, being thorough—everything a boss would want in an employee," she said. "So folks with social anxiety are often superstar employees. They get stuff done, they do it well." We also have keen intuition, appropriate caution (a look-before-you-leap mentality), and a highly attuned social radar. Though our social antennae are too sensitive, as Hendriksen put it, they make us really good at reading a room. Research shows that people with both diagnosable social anxiety disorder and subclinical social anxiety exhibit a higher degree of "empathic accuracy," or the ability to read cues telegraphed by the words, emotions, and body language of another person.[3]

The challenge, though, is that we socially anxious people have a radar that can be *too* attuned to social cues and details, especially if they are negative or can be interpreted as such. While it's great that no detail escapes us, being persistently afraid of others' disapproval or of public rejection means our interpretations of details isn't always reliable. The frown on another's face may actually have nothing to do with us.

Great leaders are good at reading a room and sensing others' cues, but they also know when to take social cues personally and when to pause and get curious about what's motivating other people. They don't assume that others' actions are always about them. *Why was my boss so curt this morning, when I know she's really happy with my performance?* Well, something could be stressful at home, or maybe she just had an

206 A Leader's Tool Kit for Managing Anxiety at Work

interaction with someone who was curt with *her*. Whatever it is, it likely has nothing to do with you at all.

So, how do you keep all the empathy and ditch the sense of rejection? Through good treatment and practice! Now let's learn how we can rethink the leader's role as a performer.

The Roots of Leadership as Performance

The strangeness of social anxiety—how it can manifest in contradictory ways in the same person—is what the Australian comedian Jordan Raskopoulos calls a "shy loud." I just love this coinage, which she introduced during her TEDx talk after hearing it from a socially anxious friend. "I am *only* confident onstage," she explained. "If you see me afterwards, or in the street, you will see me as a timid, mumbly wreck who's probably lost for words." Social situations such as chatting with people she doesn't know, checking her email, and talking on the phone terrify her. The paradox of deeply anxious yet high-functioning people like herself, she said, is that in a public role they seem self-assured and outgoing and fun, but in conversation they can't make eye contact and can't hold up their end of the conversation, so they can come across as rude, aloof, or arrogant. But the truth is quite different: "I . . . actually care about the thoughts and the feelings and opinions of people so much that I'm often stunned into silence," Raskopoulos says.

That's the lousy irony of operating in a culture that values smooth, spontaneous, extroverted social interactions over softer, slower, thoughtful ones. Susan Cain, author of *Quiet: The Power of Introverts*, and her "quiet revolution" must be credited with bringing the value of introverts and their unique gifts for leadership to the fore, but we still have a ways to go. Thankfully, the old model of the aggressive alpha who commands the room is giving way to more collaborative, nuanced forms of leadership—but the myth that a leader must be an outgoing people person or charismatic socializer lingers.

Does a leader really need to be a people person above all? Is an outgoing personality a nonnegotiable requirement for being effective?

Absolutely not! I think that somewhere along the way, the idea of being a leader became conflated with the idea of being a performer.

We need to remember that a leader's primary role is not to entertain an audience. It is to communicate effectively with their team.

Being a good communicator is different from being an orator or performer. It's also different from being entertaining or charming. The communication skills required for leadership involve being able to articulate ideas and instructions in a way that people can understand and that leaves them motivated. These skills demand that you listen deeply, process information, and then respond. Of course, it's important that, at some level, the people you work with like talking to you. But again, this takes a different skill set than being able to charm them.

All of this is not to say that there aren't public performance *aspects* to leadership. But let's put this in perspective. Most of us won't be making a living as professional speakers or be routinely addressing audiences. What happens far more often is that we must address boards, teams, and clients, and the requisite skill set there is about effective communication, not entertainment. Considering the relatively small number of times we're called upon to enthrall an audience—a keynote or even a short speech at the holiday office party—many of us worry too much about our public speaking skills.

So what if we could deemphasize the public performance aspects of leadership, and instead focus on the need for effective communication? Whether you're socially anxious or not, reframing your role as a *communicator* more than a *performer* removes so much pressure, and it opens up room for many different kinds of leadership—and many different kinds of leaders.

And practically speaking, it means you devote more of your mental energy and your time to honing your communication skills than to fretting about the (false) need to be entertaining. Here's one of the best-kept secrets about the communication difficulties that come with social anxiety: they're a solvable problem.

For example, if making small talk triggers your social anxiety, you can listen instead—just ask people lots of questions. Many people love to talk about themselves and their work, and being the prompter of conversation, rather than the one carrying it, takes the focus off of you and gives you the chance to gather information. If leading meetings gives you anxiety, you will need to practice your public speaking so you are as clear and effective as possible. Structure your meetings so you can be at your best. Assign speaking roles to teammates or provide lots of visuals for people to focus on, so they're not focusing on you.

Is Social Anxiety Getting in Your Way?

Ask yourself: Am I avoiding opportunities that could really benefit me? Am I denying myself the chance to try something I think I'd really like? Am I allowing myself to be passed over—for a job, a promotion, a chance to speak at a meeting? Am I feeling lonely and depressed because I'm so isolated? If so, is my fear of social situations or of being judged a factor?

If you answered yes to any of these questions, let me assure you that you're in good company. Hendriksen points out that social anxiety is the third most common psychological disorder, right after depression and alcoholism.[4] Interestingly, Stefan Hofmann, one of the foremost experts on cognitive behavioral therapy and social anxiety, says that social anxiety per se is not the problem. "Once you start avoiding, once this thing is starting to interfere with your life, then it becomes a problem," he told me. The fear itself, as bad as it feels, is not your primary obstacle. It's the resulting avoidance behavior, your response to the fear, that disrupts life and jeopardizes relationships, performance, and happiness.

Avoidance can occur in two ways.

Overt avoidance is when we bypass the anxiety-provoking situation altogether. In social anxiety, that could mean we stay home, or we stay silent, or we even quit a job or refuse to take part in anything requiring a public role.

With *covert avoidance*, we do show up but don't fully participate. As Hendriksen explains, "Perhaps we keep our lives really close to the vest. We don't talk about ourselves, or maybe we just run into the meeting right when it begins and then leave right when it ends, so we don't have to mingle and do small talk." Other examples include avoiding eye contact, speaking very softly, speaking very quickly (so the interaction will end sooner), or even wearing plain clothes so you won't call attention to yourself. These sorts of safety behaviors are also known as *partial avoidance*, and they keep anxiety at bay by limiting our exposure to the anxiety trigger. They decrease anxiety temporarily but prolong it in the long term, because they teach you that you're only safe in social situations if you engage in those behaviors.

Psychotherapist Carolyn Glass points out, however, that there is another type of safety behavior that's actually helpful, precisely because it helps us *not* avoid. Having Lorazepam in your wallet and ready to use in a pinch, for example, can be a great way to calm both anticipatory and present-moment anxiety. The key is that you're still engaging in the activity that triggers your anxiety, not avoiding it. Your safety behavior, in other words, is enabling you to continue moving toward your goal.

On the other hand, Hendriksen explains, total "avoidance maintains the anxiety because we never get to learn that the worst-case scenario that we imagined doesn't always happen, and that, really, we can handle some of these blips and bloops that occur when we interact with our fellow humans." In a nutshell, that captures the trap of anxiety. We don't do the thing we're afraid of—because, obviously, who wants to feel afraid? But the avoidance only reinforces the fear, and every time we avoid, the fear gets a little bigger and becomes a little more entrenched.

The best way to get over the fear is to expose ourselves to it little by little, which will indeed give us the opportunity to see that we are capable of handling the "blips and bloops" that happen during normal social interaction. If we avoid it altogether, we deprive ourselves of that chance, and we risk becoming lonely, depressed, and inhibited in our professional growth and development.

Interrupting the cycle of avoidance and anxiety doesn't mean, however, that you throw yourself into the deep end of the pool—which may be a tempting prospect for overachievers. Exposure therapy is most effective when you gradually work up to doing the thing that frightens you, and under the guidance of a caring professional. If we expose our-selves to the anxiety trigger too soon and experience a setback—a panic attack or public embarrassment, for instance—it's too easy to feel like we've failed, which reinforces the fear.

Communications expert Lee Bonvissuto used to suffered from debil-itating social anxiety, as well as what she describes as "very fun breath-based anxiety," which left her feeling like her heart was going to pound out of her chest, gasping for air and fearing for her life. "It was so debil-itating for so many years that I would check myself into the emergency room, convinced that I was having a heart attack," she says. But when she decided she was ready to get better, she ran toward her fear—literally.

"I knew [running] was going to simulate a panic attack, [so] I would go running, and I would welcome [those feelings]," she says. "I would feel my heart beating out of my chest, I would practice speaking through it, and I would say, 'You're not dying.'" She did that enough times that she became comfortable with the feelings of a pounding heart and los-ing her breath, and she began to trust the idea that she could make it through. Today she's a public speaking coach!

Ground Yourself in Your Values

One of the core observations of acceptance and commitment therapy, or ACT, is that when we're acting in ways that aren't aligned with our deepest values, we experience negative psychological repercussions such as anxiety, depression, lack of self-esteem, and less effective decision-making.[5] So it's worth considering if your social anxiety stems from a misalignment between your actions and your values. Maybe the reason you're so socially anxious is you feel the need to be someone you're not. Maybe you feel the need to perform in a way that doesn't feel authen-tic. Or maybe you took on a project or even a career in an effort to live up to someone else's expectations, rather than your own.

Because so much of social anxiety is driven by shame and the fear of being exposed as flawed in some fundamental way, one of the most effective places to start working on lessening your social anxiety is to separate your expectations and desires from other people's expectations and desires. To do that, you'll need to be clear on your values.

In the ACT framework, values are defined as "what is most important, deep in your heart; what sort of person you want to be; what is significant and meaningful to you; and what you want to stand for in this life."[6] It's this kind of deep self-knowledge that's necessary to set goals that are truly important to you and the work you want to do, and to carry out what ACT calls *committed action* to achieve those goals. When your actions are aligned with your values, there's no guarantee that your feelings of anxiety will vanish, especially if you're anxious by nature. But alignment prevents the creation of further anxiety. And if your goal means that you must feel some anxiety for a short time, it's your values, your deeply held beliefs, that will get you through it. (For more on knowing your values, read the "Identify and Anchor in Your Core Values" exercise.)

Becoming clear on your values is also necessary to take on one of the biggest challenges we face as we grow into leadership: to stand strong on our own. Especially when we fear displeasing others and being judged negatively, this is easier said than done. But becoming your own self—a *differentiated self*, in the language of Bowen theory—allows you to stay steady in the midst of changing events, uncomfortable feelings, and untrue, anxiety-fueled thoughts that steal our confidence ("They don't think I belong here" or "They're going to laugh at me"). Building a differentiated self that's grounded in your deeply held values helps to turn down the volume on social anxiety, because you can more easily see the truth and resist being swayed by the way you imagine people are reacting to you.

According to Kathleen Smith, an expert in Bowen theory, the part of the self that changes according to who's in the room and how you perceive that people are reacting to you—in other words, the part that is negotiable and isn't operating out of your core values and beliefs—is called the *pseudo self*. When the pseudo self is in charge, we often try to lower anxiety, Smith writes, by seeking out one of the four As: attention, assurance, approval, and agreement.[7] Anxious people may be especially susceptible to relying on external validation to build themselves

Identify and Anchor in Your Core Values

If you're plagued by doubt and are having trouble connecting with yourself and your core values, take some time to define a few things:

- What is most important to me, regardless of the job I'm in now?

- What sort of person do I want to be in this life?

- What do I stand for?

- What are some examples of good work that I've done?

- How do I know when I've done good work?

Now, review each of your answers and ask: Is this really and truly *my* core belief, or am I borrowing some of these beliefs and values from others? See if you can distinguish between what you truly desire and hold dear, and what's filtering in based on your perception of what other people want and expect. (Hint: You can use the four As to guide you. Ask yourself, Where are my core beliefs based upon what I think will gain attention, give me assurance, garner approval, or generate agreement?)

When we're anchored in our core values and beliefs, we can find self-worth within ourselves. We can more easily see reality, rather than guessing what everyone is thinking. Here's what it could look like:

- It's not true that they don't think I belong—that's just my social anxiety speaking.

- So what if they don't think I belong? *I* know I belong here.

- Will they really laugh at me? In all likelihood, no.

- So what if they do laugh at me? I'll survive.

- So what if I give a speech that isn't my best? I'll do better next time.

- So what if people noticed me sweating and blushing?

- My content and slides were great, and that's what the audience came for.

up—a behavior known in Bowen theory as *borrowing self.* If you have social anxiety and are convinced that others are judging you harshly, you can see the conundrum that borrowing self and depending on others' validation presents!

Further, if your confidence and your sense of calm come from other people, there's no guarantee those feelings will last. If someone seems to enjoy talking to you or claps after your speech, you feel OK. If the article with your quote is positive and no one says anything mean on Twitter, you're good. But what happens when you don't get the praise you expected or wanted? What happens when the attention wanes? When you make a mistake? When you fail?

Leadership requires that you are able to trust yourself and believe not only in the quality of your decisions but in the quality of your work and your leadership—especially when things go wrong. Occasional setbacks and mistakes won't take you down, because you know who you are and what you're capable of. Being anchored in your beliefs means you can take a leap, and you can fail and won't suffer too greatly for it. It means you can rely on yourself to evaluate the merits of your work, and not board the roller-coaster ride that can come when you rely on other people's reactions. "We let so much of our self-worth be dependent on variables outside our control," Smith writes.[8]

Social Anxiety Triggers, and Managing Your Reactions

There are many moments along a career path that could trigger anxiety for anyone. Who doesn't have butterflies before an interview, a big presentation, or a negotiation? But for the leader with social anxiety, such moments can feel completely overwhelming or even unachievable.

Here's the good news: every challenging social situation can be overcome if you expose yourself to it little by little. This diminishes the fear and builds your confidence each time. What you're doing, at root, is practicing.

We tend to think people are born knowing how to give a speech or close a sale, but that's simply not true. Many of the leadership skills we associate with successful people are just that: skills learned over time. So why do we hamper ourselves with unreasonable expectations? The truth is, all of us need to practice these skills, and those of us with social anxiety, who can expect to encounter a further degree of difficulty, will simply need to practice more.

And that, my socially anxious friends, is indeed good news, because it means we can practice our way through even our most difficult fears. So take heart. You can do this.

Networking

Even if we're not actively searching for a job or trying to recruit new talent, we need to remain active in our fields, collaborate with colleagues in our industries, and stay on top of the latest developments. All of that requires some level of networking.

If you're prone to social anxiety, though, networking can feel like an invitation to feel bad about yourself. The whole enterprise comes laden with shoulds: *I should be putting myself out there, I should be more interesting, I shouldn't find this so difficult, I shouldn't spend so much time hiding in the bathroom or yearning for this conference to be over or worrying about what others are thinking about me.* It's ironic that when you have social anxiety, networking—which is all about connecting with others—can turn into an entirely self-focused event.

Career expert, keynote speaker, and *New York Times* bestselling author Lindsey Pollak has advised thousands of people on how to manage career transitions and growth—and she's a fellow anxious achiever who has lived with anxiety her whole life. When I asked for her advice on how socially anxious people can successfully navigate a networking event, her response was wonderfully refreshing. "The headline, I would say, is, 'You have to be who you are,'" she said. "If you have social anxiety and perhaps you're introverted, I don't think it will serve anyone's best interest, or have a positive outcome, if you try to walk into a ballroom at a conference and tell a joke to a group of twenty people. I just think that's a recipe for disaster, discomfort, and lack of success." Instead, she said, go in with the mindset that you're going to be unapologetically *you*—your true, authentic self. If you're not a gregarious extrovert, so what? "I don't want to work in a place or network with people who are not OK with who I really am," Pollak said.

Next, lower your expectations. This may feel counterintuitive to overachievers, but it's far healthier—and more realistic—to accept that it's not all going to be perfect. As Pollak explained, "If you walk into that conference and say, 'My goal is to talk to three people, and probably two of those interactions are not going to be great, so if one goes well, I'm ahead,'" it removes so much pressure. And if your interaction with the person you really wanted to talk to is mediocre, or if you miss them entirely, it's perfectly acceptable to follow up with them later. "Send them a really well-crafted email afterward," Pollak suggested. "Say, 'I'm so sorry, I didn't get a chance to catch up with you at that event. Loved your speech, would love to set up a fifteen-minute Zoom call.'"

If the thought of going alone is overwhelming, you don't have to. "I often recommend that introverts and people with anxiety bring a friend," Pollak said. People with social anxiety tend to interpret social interactions negatively or feel that they're being judged when they're not, so "bringing a 'wing person' is a really good strategy."

During the event, do whatever you can to get out of your head. In cognitive behavioral therapy this is called *maintaining an external focus*. You can't trust the unreliable narrator voice of anxiety, so don't listen to it! Instead, shift your attention to anything external: the people you're with, the nice room, the lovely snacks or wine. When people speak to you, give them your full attention. And if it falls to you to speak first, my friend Allison Shapira, who is a speech coach, says all you have to say is, "What brings you here?" That's it! You don't need to craft a prize-winning speech or overthink it.

Neuroscientist and anxiety expert Wendy Suzuki says that empathy and compassion can be a buffer against social anxiety. Look around the room—chances are, most of the people there are experiencing some degree of anxiety or nervousness too, and you know what that feels like. So can you flip your social anxiety into compassion for them? This is a great way to take the focus off of yourself and place it on something external, and to extend kindness to others at the same time. "It is actually possible to build your social muscle and use it to boost your connections, and your anxiety is giving you clues to what icebreakers and lifelines other people might be grateful for you to extend," Suzuki says.[9]

Finally, as much as you can, minimize your negative assumptions. We know that trying to guess what other people are thinking is futile, and that anxiety will automatically focus on and exaggerate the negative. If you've been talking to someone and suddenly they excuse themself, don't assume it's because you're boring and unimportant. It's a networking event! The whole point is to talk with many different people. Realize that you can't understand another person's motivations or read their mind—and then move on.

Interviewing

For the socially anxious individual, interviewing can spark all-or-nothing thinking, catastrophic imaginings, and existential dread about your future. And this is just the anticipatory anxiety! Once you get to the interview, you're anxious about the impression you're making, and then afterward you may find yourself ruminating on every tiny thing that you fear went wrong (an example of what the social anxiety community on Reddit calls "cringe attacks").

Often it's the anticipatory anxiety that's the worst part. The sad irony of anticipatory anxiety, of course, is that the thing you're dreading is almost never as bad as the anxiety-fueled fantasies you've created . . . not to mention that this "pregame" anxiety lasts far longer than the dreaded event. Anticipatory anxiety steals valuable time and makes you feel defeated. It makes you question yourself and undermines your confidence—right when you need it most, in the case of interviewing. As if all that isn't bad enough, the anxious catastrophizing and "worrying ahead" just breed more anxiety—they're self-perpetuating.

Clinical psychologist Jenny Taitz says we can use the strategy of "opposite action" to break the cycle of anticipatory anxiety. Instead of worrying ahead, identify ways you can *cope* ahead. You can think of coping ahead as "productive worry," Taitz explains.

One coping-ahead strategy I've used is to practice the beginning of my interview so many times that muscle memory can take over, because I know those first few minutes will be when my anxiety is highest and I'll be at the greatest risk of losing my train of thought or blurting out something I later regret. Maybe you'll practice how you're going to greet your interviewer, the elevator speech that describes your company or background, or how you'll explain your latest accomplishment, the reason you feel passionate about this position, or your unique qualifications for the job. Knowing I have something ready to say relieves a great deal of pressure. Once the ice is broken and the interview is off and running, I can relax and let the conversation flow naturally.

Another way to practice coping ahead, Taitz says, is to be realistic about how your social anxiety will likely manifest in the midst of the interview. As she explains, "Realize that in the moment I'm going to think, *I don't sound as good, I don't look as good, I'm not as interesting as these other people. Do I belong? My impostor syndrome isn't really a syndrome, it's real.* Taking this view will keep you from being surprised when those difficult thoughts and feelings arise, so you can call them out for what they actually are—anxious feelings, not true statements about yourself. Then you can quickly shift your focus away from your internal monologue and back to the interview. This is good advice generally: bring all of your attention to the interviewer. Listening and focusing on another person takes the spotlight off of you, and gives no oxygen to your negative self-talk.

Next, not only should you not expect to turn in a "perfect" performance during an interview, Taitz says, but you should embrace your imperfections. "The research supports this," she explains. "People who have social blunders are more endearing than people who are perfect—those people are more intimidating." Similar studies have shown that people who commit occasional *faux pas* are more likable. "That's human, that's so endearing," Taitz says. "So that's actually one of the tips that I have for people: love your *faux pas*. Love that you made a mistake, own it. . . . People love people who show up and listen and are present."

In a similar vein, Lindsey Pollak says that if it feels right for you, you can straightforwardly disclose your anxiety. "Walk up and say, 'I'm a little nervous, or a little socially awkward, or I'm a little introverted,'" she says. "Sometimes that takes the tension away. It prepares the other person, and it gets you over it."

Managing conflict

Conflict and difficult emotions like anger can be extra scary if you're socially anxious. You may worry that if you show anger or disapproval, you will get frozen out or a colleague will reject you or punish you. You may feel that you must always be likable or unobjectionable, and that showing anger or displeasure will harm your reputation. Let's face it, conflict is just plain hard. It's especially hard at work, where being effective depends on smooth relations among teams and colleagues.

But, of course, conflict will sometimes arise in any group, and learning to manage it is a crucial business skill. And we know that, like any anxiety-inducing experience, the situation will only worsen if we avoid it.

Here, too, you can practice managing your anxiety in baby steps and gradually work your way up to high-stakes situations. Conflict and workplace dynamics expert Amy Gallo calls this "practicing conflict in more contained spaces." Having a conflict with your boss or an aggressive person is really scary, so she recommends you don't start practicing there. "Are there relationships in which you feel safe, where your social anxiety isn't a big factor, that you can try out some conflict resolution skills or try out being more direct?" she asks. A conflict-averse friend of hers, for example, practiced with her friends by finding small, low-stakes ways to assert herself. "Like being direct about not wanting to go to that restaurant for dinner, or being direct about when was a better time for her to have a phone call," Gallo says. This way you gain the experiential knowledge that you can do this and see that your worst fears didn't come to pass. You didn't fall apart, your friends still like you, they still want to have dinner with you.

Next, be on the lookout for people who are good at negotiating conflict, and model your behavior on theirs. "How do they advocate for themselves?" Gallo says. "How do they handle things when things get heated? What do they say when someone disagrees with them? How do they bring a group back to consensus after things get tense?"

You can even try to emulate that role model's behavior when you go into a situation where you know there will be conflict. Picture yourself as someone who isn't afraid of conflict, Gallo suggests, and think, *I'm going to be that person in this conversation.*

Then in the midst of the conversation, stay rigorously focused on the goal. We're all hardwired to be liked, and if we have social anxiety, we're probably preoccupied with wanting the encounter to end. "But ultimately, you want to be driven by what you really need and what's the best way to get that," Gallo says. If you're going to come away from the conversation with something you really want—the raise you deserve, a way to get a project over the finish line, a clear path to the promotion you've been eyeing—the momentary anxiety you'll feel will pale in comparison and will be so worth it.

Finally, I asked Gallo what to do if a conflict situation becomes too intense or if, like me, someone has been in situations where they cried or froze. How do you stay in the moment or power through when you've reached the end of your reserves?

"Truthfully, my best advice is *don't* power through," Gallo said. "We often assume that the conversation has to be resolved right then. But if your emotions take over in that situation and you cry or you shut down, or even start yelling . . . that conversation isn't going to go well. My best advice there is to just say, 'I'm crying, I'm not ready for this conversation. I need to come back to it.'" Take a break, maybe by going for a walk around the block or even sleeping on it and coming back to it the next day. "Especially if you're negotiating something that's high-stakes, accept that it's going to take several conversations and you will make mistakes along the way," Gallo said.

So cut yourself some slack, and give yourself the gift of taking some time to regroup. "Go back [and] get resourced," Gallo said. "Talk to your trusted colleague, your trusted friend. Get a good night's sleep. Talk to your therapist, whatever you need to do, and then return. . . .

It's OK to go back and say, 'I'm not happy with where we ended up. I'd like to readdress that,' or 'I'm not happy with the dynamic between us. I think we need to approach this conversation a different way.'"

I think this is good advice all around: give yourself the time you need to become more comfortable. With social anxiety, even a low-stakes event like suggesting a different restaurant can *feel* like a big conflict, a huge threat. So congratulate yourself for doing the hard work of facing big fears.

Negotiating

When it comes to negotiating, research has shown that anxious people tend to make weaker first offers, respond more quickly to each move their counterpart makes, and exit negotiations more quickly.[10] Have you ever left money on the table or even refused to negotiate just to avoid anxiety? It makes sense: negotiating is full of uncertainty, and you can't control the outcome. Any hint of impostor syndrome makes it that much harder, as you grapple with feelings that you don't deserve what you're asking for.

Tanya Tarr, a behavioral scientist who specializes in coaching leaders to negotiate effectively, offers this helpful reminder: All of us have some level of social anxiety, and you actually *want* to have some anxiety ahead of a negotiation. Why? Because moderate anxiety is a sign that you care, that you have skin in the game. It helps you focus and gives you energy.

"The way that anxiety or anticipation registers physically in the body is a jolt of adrenaline," Tarr says. "So it actually feels the same when we're anxious or when we're excited about something." The key to keeping our anxiety manageable and being able to enhance our performance is "to safely choose to put yourself in situations where you will feel that [anxiety], but [training] yourself to react in a way that is predictable and strategically advantageous to you." In other words, Tarr says, "Practice. And practice. And practice." Look for small, low-stakes opportunities to ask for what you want, such as a day off, a small change in the schedule, or an improvement to a workflow. You can also role-play a negotiation, Tarr says, but be sure to pick a person you trust who can spark some low-level anxiety, because it needs to feel real.

To help with the troubling physical sensations of anxiety, the answer is counterintuitive: ground yourself in your body. "Find a physical place to focus on to ground yourself before you go into the situation," Tarr says. Once, while waiting to conduct an onstage interview with a political celebrity, she paused to regulate her breathing and bring all of her awareness to the soles of her feet. This grounding technique is a "physical hack" that draws attention and energy away from your anxious mind and brings calm awareness to what's happening in the here and now. Tarr used another grounding technique onstage by concentrating on how she was sitting: bottom all the way to the back of the chair, spine straight. This is a classic technique that experienced meditators use, and that you can bring into the negotiation room.

Finally, always, always do your market research. "You need to have a very clear understanding from a business perspective . . . of the market value of either your skills and abilities or your business and products and services," Tarr says. "Because if you price [according] to the market, there is no reason to feel emotional about that. That is just what the market is demanding." This is a data-driven way to "remove emotion entirely," she explains. In a business setting, "emotions do not drive decisions. Profitability drives decisions." If your impostor syndrome shows up and tries to tell you you're worth less, you can show it the numbers and tell it to shut up.

Becoming a (more) public leader

Being promoted and feted can actually be a miserable and confusing experience for the anxious achiever! Of course you're proud and excited, and in your heart you know you deserve your perch. Yet doubt is always close at hand.

Greater success almost always comes with more time in the spotlight. So how can the socially anxious leader take on—and even get really good at—the aspects of leadership that require them to take on a more public role? If ever there was a time to recenter yourself in your values and beliefs and to lean on yourself, this is it.

Lindsey Pollak has delivered more than two thousand speeches, yet she still gets nervous before each one and afterward often worries she said the wrong thing. "There's an old joke in the public speaking world," she told me. "At a funeral, you'd rather be in the casket than delivering the eulogy. *That's* how much people hate public speaking." She uses that knowledge to her advantage. "I know that most of the people in my audience wouldn't want to be up on that stage and are thrilled not to be on that stage. So if you're in a meeting and you're speaking, I think you can take some comfort in knowing that nobody wants to be there," she said. The audience is on your side from the get-go, in other words—they're thrilled it's you up there and not them!

In the same vein, Pollak reminds us that audiences really want you to succeed—if for no other reason than it's uncomfortable to watch someone struggle. "There is absolutely nothing worse . . . than being in the audience when someone up there is sweating and uncomfortable and nervous and saying 'um' every other word," she said. "So what I try to teach in public speaking classes, and what I try to implement myself, is that the audience really wants you to be good. They're rooting for you because they don't want to go through that experience." I think it's important, too, to remember that there's a reason you're up on that stage. You wouldn't be there if you didn't have something valuable to offer.

Next, Pollak suggests, "look for those smiling faces in the audience. I look for the people who are nodding in appreciation, and I force myself to find those people and overlook the ones who are on their phones or even maybe not paying attention as much. And that is really powerful, to always remember that they're cheering you on."

What if the worst happens? What if we bomb or say the wrong thing? "My biggest fear is that I will misspeak or say something I didn't know was offensive and have my whole career dissolve over it," Pollak admits. In our age of social media, where a thoughtless remark can go viral, this fear is not at all unfounded. If this does happen, she recommends apologizing as quickly as possible. "I have bombed and I'm still here," she said. "I have offended people and I'm still here. I have messed up and I'm still here. If you do that once in a sixty-minute speech, that still means that fifty-nine other minutes were perfectly fine. And so I've gotten through my worst possible fear and it turned out OK. . . . There's some element of learning from bombing that is also really valuable."

This is one of the biggest and most important lessons we learn from facing our fears: What we thought was unbearable is bearable. What anxiety told us we couldn't survive, we not only survive but emerge stronger and wiser from.

Loving Your Socially Anxious Self

Here's the truth: Social anxiety will probably always be with you to some degree. It shouldn't be debilitating or so unmanageable that it stops you from doing the things you'd do if you weren't afraid. But even after years of hard work, your social anxiety may never vanish completely—it may just be part of who you are.

So here's a radical idea: why not embrace it?

I, for one, have wasted too much time wishing that things that seem effortless for other people—talking on the phone or making small talk with strangers, for instance—weren't so difficult for me. But this is who I am, and there are plenty of other skills that *are* effortless—some of which I have precisely because of my social anxiety. Deep, instant empathy, for example.

Here's another truth about social anxiety: You do not need to change your personality or become a gregarious glad-hander to succeed. You are built for achievement and success just as you are. You may have to work harder at the social aspects of leadership, but when has hard work ever dissuaded you from meeting a goal? It could just be that your social anxiety opens up opportunities and avenues to success that are far more impactful—and more exciting!—than anything you could have planned for yourself.

So this is your task. Given your unique combination of life experiences and the particular way your social anxiety manifests, what is the way for *you* to participate boldly and effectively in public life? What do you have to offer that no one else does?

Keeping that end goal in mind can carry you through whatever work you need to do to manage your social anxiety—and learn to leverage it for its unique gifts.

The leaders who have learned to manage their social anxiety and who have earned great success did not get there by denying their fears or neglecting to work on their weaknesses and imperfections. They accepted the reality of their difficult emotions and brought their whole selves—their advantages and disadvantages—to the task of leadership. They truthfully acknowledged how social anxiety was hampering the kind of leader they wanted to be. Then they learned to respond with conscious action that brings them ever closer to being the kind of leader they dream of being.

You can do this too. The world is waiting for you.

CONCLUSION

Find Joy

Being anxious all the time robs you of joy. And the capacity for joy is essential to your leadership (and your life!). Without joy, you can't find hope for the future or tap into a deep well of innovation and creativity. When you're joyful, you want to bring others along with you—and they can see your vision and want to join the journey.

But unmanaged anxiety keeps you stuck in imagining, and then reimagining, a scary future.

I'm talking about the kind of anxiety that is with you day in and out, whispering that danger lies just around the corner. When we're obsessing about danger, how can we possibly let ourselves be free to feel joy, or lead with any kind of effectiveness?

While writing this book, I had the worst mental health crisis I'd experienced in thirteen years. My unraveling really took me and my family aback. For weeks I existed in a state of panic and anxiety. I didn't care about anyone else—I couldn't. I couldn't see beyond my own suffering, which my mental illness magnified a thousandfold. My anxiety caused me great worry and fear about my children, but I didn't spend time with them. I worried constantly about work and my financial future, but I couldn't do even the smallest task. I was stuck in a nightmare loop of thought traps.

I had to take a leave from work. Every single thought I had was scary, and I sobbed through each one. My mind lived in catastrophe, and I was so depressed. It was terrifying: Was this it for me? Was I going to feel this way forever? After so many years of being able to manage through, I suddenly had no hope for the future.

Eventually I began to recover by doubling down on therapies and starting new medications. And I knew I was getting better when I found joy in a really small thing: I made some soup for my friends who'd driven my kids to activities while I was ill. I really took my time making the soup delicious for them, because I wanted to show them my gratitude. Finally, I could focus on something other than myself.

That's the thing about unmanaged anxiety—it can narrow your lens to one subject: you. Anxiety loops keep you stuck inside yourself.

So the question is, How can you get out when you're hurting and everything feels hopeless and scary? How can you take one small step toward freedom and mental health and joy when you feel locked in and overwhelmed?

I have five suggestions.

First, get the treatment you need. This is the first, foundational step on the path to getting better.

Second, try to get out of your head and focus on something outside of yourself.

The truth is, anxiety makes you self-absorbed. You spend so much time fretting over your future, obsessing over what others think of you, fearing criticism and shame, worrying about a bodily sensation that surely means you're dying, and losing sleep over the prospect of losing everything. The obvious and most effective counteraction is to turn your focus outward.

Harvard Business School professor and leadership expert Amy Edmondson told me that she thinks the reason we all yearn for psychological safety in our work and in our daily lives is that we want to contribute to the greater good, or the team, or the company retreat—but we fear being judged. "We want to be unencumbered by what people think about us," she said. "It's such an unhealthy thing to be tied up in knots about—'How do I look?' 'What do people think of me?'—versus the healthier, and I would say more joyful, state of being—'Wow, this is a really interesting project and I'm glad to be part of it, and I feel it matters.' That's what we want. I think we want to make a contribution."

It's OK to start very small. When my depression was at its worst, focusing for just a few moments on *anything* external was a victory—the sound of a bird chirping outside my window, petting the dog, jotting down notes for a LinkedIn post. On other days I tried to imagine a more joyful state of being, or to remember, if only for a few moments, what it was like to be in the flow, contributing something meaningful.

This is where the people in your life are so helpful. Anxiety and depression can be so isolating, and they can severely narrow your focus. "When you're in those very dark places, it takes a lot of trust and a lot of vulnerability to invite people in," Wildfang cofounder and CEO Emma Mcilroy says. But it's critical to do so, because "all you really have is this pinhole view," and you need to get out of your head and rely on your team to help you make good decisions. "Other people can see even 10 percent of a solution that you couldn't," Mcilroy says.

Shopify's Harley Finkelstein, who we met in chapter 2, reaches out for help when he realizes anxiety is causing him to "over-rotate." "I'm incredibly transparent and candid with my team," he says. "I talk my team through these things to say, 'There may be times where you hear me asking questions and you think I'm really in the weeds,' or 'Hey, there are going to be times where I'm going to ask you to do something and you're going to not understand why. And you're going to have to help me figure [it] out.'" He welcomes pushback from his team when they don't agree with a decision, and he relies on them to point out if he's fixated on something that really isn't the big deal that anxiety is telling him it is. I'd love to work for someone like this—wouldn't you?

I know it can be difficult to be this vulnerable with colleagues, but vulnerability is a tremendous leadership skill, and we need more leaders to take a stand and be open about their mental health struggles.

Remember, being open doesn't require taking a big, dramatic action or gathering the team and spilling your guts. You don't have to share details; just sharing the state you're in externalizes your experience, gets you the help you need, and models healthy behavior for others.

In honor of Mental Health Awareness Month, the serial entrepreneur Paul English, who we met in chapter 4, shared his decades-long struggle with bipolar illness with his team at Lola. The overwhelming reaction? Gratitude for his honesty and vulnerability. "Me being open about my own struggles gives people permission to be open about theirs," he said. "I've just found that if you're open with people, they'll lean in and help you. . . . People will follow confidence, but they'll be loyal to vulnerability."

The social psychologist Amy Cuddy says we need leaders who exhibit both vulnerability and strength. "Most leaders today tend to emphasize their strength, competence, and credentials in the workplace, but that is exactly the wrong approach," she writes. "Leaders who project strength before establishing trust run the risk of eliciting fear, and along with it a host of dysfunctional behaviors."[1]

Being vulnerable builds trust and closeness, and nothing establishes trust more effectively than the emotional connection fostered through empathy and shared humanity. Leaders who model strength and vulnerability earn the confidence of their teams and create the environment of psychological safety that employees and organizations need to thrive.

If you're reluctant to reach out to your team, try to frame it in your mind as a performance issue. Think about it: It's in the best interest of everyone—team members, employers, shareholders, clients, customers—for you to succeed. And you simply cannot perform at your best if you don't feel your best. Mcilroy captures this so powerfully. "When I'm happy, I can deliver 150 percent," she says. "When I'm really sad and depressed, I can deliver 70 percent."

Anxiety and depression will tell you that this is it, that you're washed up and have no hope of getting better. They are wrong. Reach out to the trusted people in your life who can tell you the truth. When I was at my lowest, my family and friends offered an objective counterpoint to my negative self-talk and self-defeating thoughts. They reminded me that I've weathered emotional storms in the past and would do so again. Other leaders I know have written themselves notes while they're feeling strong and healthy that say, in effect, "Don't give up. This will pass. You *will* return to _____." Fill in the blank with a description of you at your most joyful and effective.

Which brings me to the third suggestion: as best you can, remind yourself that when you do get through this, you will be a stronger, more resilient leader. I admit that it's hard to believe this, or even care, when you're in the midst of the darkness. But again, you can rely on your support team and your notes from your well self for a dose of truth and hope.

At Mcilroy's lowest point, when she had three days of cash left and her gastrointestinal system was a wreck, she feared she was finished. But she got through it with help from her teammates, doctors, and loved ones, and she emerged a better leader. "I've built tremendous resilience and capacity through this process," she told me. "But as with most people who have built tremendous resilience, it comes from very negative, dark situations. You don't build resilience by being in sunny, happy places all the time. That's literally not what resilience is. To have the ability to handle hard, difficult things, you have to have lived through hard, difficult things."

Leaders who have survived storms know they can steady the ship. When we've been through mental illness and have managed through it, we can embrace life's complexities and lead our people through catastrophes. We can make sure our clients and employees feel seen, heard, acknowledged, and cared for, because we know what that meant for us when we were hurting and needed help the most.

Fourth, tap into the values that have shaped your life and that form the basis of your leadership vision.

Psychotherapist Russ Harris offers these questions to center your values:[2]

- What sort of person do you want to be?

- What sort of personal strengths and qualities do you want to cultivate?

- What do you want to stand for?

- How do you want to behave?

- What work fills you with meaning?

- What can you offer to the people you work with?

- What can you offer to the world?

I always come back to what management strategist Nilofer Merchant calls your "onlyness," a term she coined back in 2011. Onlyness is the spot in the world where only you stand. It's informed by your values, personal history, and perspective. What parts of your history and experience have informed and shaped what you care about today? This includes both the positive and the negative experiences that have made you who you are—don't shy away from the dark parts—and that have led you to care about the issues that capture your attention, inspire you to act, and motivate you to make an impact.

How would you apply your spot in the world—where only you stand—to the visions and hopes you have for the future and what you want to offer the world? Whatever the answer is, remember it. No one can lead like you can.

Fifth, find what brings you joy.

Even making the choice to step out of your comfort zone and be a leader can be a joyful, courageous experience. As a fast-rising star in public radio, Priska Neely was encouraged to start hosting radio shows. It was flattering to be in demand and have her talents recognized, but Neely had misgivings. So she conducted "an audit of what gives me joy," as she puts it. She realized that managing and mentoring journalists behind the scenes brings her more joy than being on the air. "Ultimately, I just feel like I can have a greater impact in helping to train people and validate people and get their stories on the right track, so that there can be more people doing what I've been able to do," she says. Neely is now the managing editor of a public radio collaboration in the Southern United States, building and managing a team.

Conduct an audit of what brings you joy. When do you feel most in flow and effective? What are you doing when you feel your actions hold true significance and you're creating the change you've always wanted to? Along with your values, the things that bring you joy are powerful sources of motivation that can sustain you through difficult times.

Anxiety can mask potential sources of joy—and if we let it go unmanaged, it can steal our joy altogether. Maybe that alone can be your motivation for learning to manage your anxiety. What joy are you missing out on because you're afraid? What are you preventing yourself from trying because you're afraid to be less than perfect? Is it stepping into a bigger role? Having a louder voice, a wider impact, a broader reach?

I happened to interview social media entrepreneur Jyl Johnson Pattee about impostor syndrome when I was at my lowest point, and she said something that really struck a chord with me: "There's too much life to live, too much meaningful service to give, and too much ROI to drive to be held back by impostor syndrome."

She's absolutely right. And the same is true for anxiety, or depression, or bipolar disorder, or OCD, or whatever it is that's holding you back and threatening to steal your joy. There's too much to miss out on—and too much the world will miss from you—to let yourself be sidetracked by your emotional and mental struggles.

I'm better now, thank goodness, but I'm not cured. Dark times probably lie ahead. But relief comes when I take the focus off of myself— my anxiety-ridden, fretful, often frustrating and exhausting self—and shift it to the reasons I push myself so hard. For me, the external reasons are my family above all. Internally, I'm motivated by a deep desire to do good in the world, to give back in some appreciable way, especially when I've been the recipient of so much. So I hang on to the belief that I'll manage through again and that I need to make the most of the good days I have. I need to channel my anxiety for good, and anchor deep within, to the source of my values and my joy. I know what I stand for in life and what being a good person means to me. I know the impact I want to have. I have found so much joy in writing this book and (I hope) in helping you through a dark time of your own.

So, when all is said and done, how do you flourish as a leader without succumbing to the narcissism of anxiety?

You acknowledge the fear, take care of yourself, and then figure out how to keep going. You say yes to help, in all the forms you're fortunate enough to receive. You push through to be there for others, even if you're hollow inside. You lean on your community, just as someday they will lean on you. You feel the horrible feelings and the desire to hide under the covers, but you don't do it—you manage through it instead. You remember that living with anxiety and overcoming its challenges gives you hard-won strength and resilience that you can channel into extraordinary contributions.

You remind yourself of the joys and gifts that anxiety wants to steal from you—and you say, as many times as it takes, "No, that's too high a price to pay."

Then you feel the fear and do your thing anyway.

You lead.

NOTES

Introduction

1. Anxiety and Depression Association of America, "Anxiety Disorders—Facts and Statistics," https://adaa.org/understanding-anxiety/facts-statistics; Saloni Dattani, Hannah Ritchie, and Max Roser, "Mental Health," Our World in Data, last updated August 2021, https://ourworldindata.org/mental-health.

2. Mental Health America, "COVID-19 and Mental Health: A Growing Crisis," 2021, https://www.mhanational.org/research-reports/covid-19-and-mental-health-growing-crisis.

3. Jude Mary Cénat et al., "Prevalence of Symptoms of Depression, Anxiety, Insomnia, Posttraumatic Stress Disorder, and Psychological Distress among Populations Affected by the COVID-19 Pandemic: A Systematic Review and Meta-Analysis," *Psychiatry Research* 295 (2021).

4. Mind Share Partners, "2021 Mental Health at Work Report," 2021, https://www.mindsharepartners.org/mentalhealthatworkreport-2021.

5. Hara Estroff Marano, "Even CEOs Get the Blues," *Psychology Today*, last reviewed June 9, 2016, https://www.psychologytoday.com/us/articles/200303/even-ceos-get-the-blues.

6. Morra Aarons-Mele, "Your Mental Health and Your Work," September 30, 2019, in *The Anxious Achiever*, produced by Mary Dooe, podcast, MP3 audio, 32:11, https://hbr.org/podcast/2019/09/your-mental-health-and-your-work.

Chapter 1

1. It's important to distinguish feeling anxious from experiencing an anxiety disorder. For more, see https://www.healthline.com/health/anxiety/anxiety-vs-anxious.

2. Tené T. Lewis et al., "Self-Reported Experiences of Discrimination and Health: Scientific Advances, Ongoing Controversies, and Emerging Issues," *Annual Review of Clinical Psychology* 11 (2015): 407–440; Yin Paradies, "A Systematic Review of Empirical Research on Self-Reported Racism and Health," *International Journal of Epidemiology* 35, no. 4 (August 2006): 888–901.

3. Jonathan D. Schaefer et al., "Enduring Mental Health: Prevalence and Prediction," *Journal of Abnormal Psychology* 126, no. 2 (2017): 212–224.

4. Rollo May, *The Meaning of Anxiety* (New York: W. W. Norton & Company, 1977).

Chapter 2

1. ScienceDaily, "Being Anxious Could Be Good for You in a Crisis," December 29, 2015, https://www.sciencedaily.com/releases/2015/12/151229070643.htm.

2. Michael A. Freeman et al., "The Prevalence and Co-occurrence of Psychiatric Conditions among Entrepreneurs and Their Families," *Small Business Economics* 53 (2019): 323–342.

3. Mind Share Partners, "2021 Mental Health at Work Report," 2021, https://www.mindsharepartners.org/mentalhealthatworkreport-2021.

4. Alice G. Walton, "Why the Super-Successful Get Depressed," Forbes, January 26, 2015, https://www.forbes.com/sites/alicegwalton/2015/01/26/why-the-super-successful-get-depressed.

5. Donna M. Bush and Rachel N. Lipari, *Substance Use and Substance Use Disorder by Industry*, Substance Abuse and Mental Health Services Administration, April 16, 2015, https://www.samhsa.gov/data/sites/default/files/report_1959/ShortReport-1959.pdf.

6. Stephanie Sarkis, "Senior Executives Are More Likely to Be Psychopaths," Forbes, October 27, 2019, https://www.forbes.com/sites/stephaniesarkis/2019/10/27/senior-executives-are-more-likely-to-be-psychopaths.

7. Wendy Suzuki, *Good Anxiety: Harnessing the Power of the Most Misunderstood Emotion* (New York: Atria Books, 2021), 212.

8. Suzuki, *Good Anxiety*, 124–125.

9. Suzuki, *Good Anxiety*, 105.

10. Morra Aarons-Mele, "Understanding 'Good' Anxiety," April 6, 2022, in *The Anxious Achiever*, podcast, MP3 audio, 38:56, https://www.linkedin.com/pulse/how-channel-good-anxiety-morra-aarons-mele.

11. Suzuki, *Good Anxiety*, 147.

Chapter 3

1. Tasha Eurich, "What Self-Awareness Really Is (and How to Cultivate It)," hbr.org, January 04, 2018, https://hbr.org/2018/01/what-self-awareness-really-is-and-how-to-cultivate-it.

2. Eurich, "What Self-Awareness Really Is."

Chapter 4

1. Center for Disease Control and Prevention, "About the CDC-Kaiser ACE Study," last reviewed April 6, 2021, https://www.cdc.gov/violenceprevention/aces/about.html.

2. Harvard University Center on the Developing Child, "ACEs and Toxic Stress: Frequently Asked Questions," https://developingchild.harvard.edu/resources/aces-and-toxic-stress-frequently-asked-questions; Cynthia L. Harter and John F. R. Harter, "The Link between Adverse Childhood Experiences and Financial Security in Adulthood," *Journal of Family and Economic Issues* (September 2021): 1–11.

3. Jennifer Greif Green et al., "Childhood Adversities and Adult Psychiatric Disorders in the National Comorbidity Survey Replication I: Associations with First Onset of DSM-IV Disorders," *Archives of General Psychiatry* 67, no. 2 (2010): 113–123.

4. Jessica Graham et al., "The Mediating Role of Internalized Racism in the Relationship between Racist Experiences and Anxiety Symptoms in a Black American Sample," *Cultural Diversity and Ethnic Minority Psychology* 22, no. 3 (2016).

5. Akshay Johri and Pooja V. Anand, "Life Satisfaction and Well-Being at the Intersections of Caste and Gender in India," *Psychological Studies* 67 (2022): 317–331.

6. Johri and Anand, "Life Satisfaction."

7. The Bowen Center for the Study of the Family, "Introduction to the Eight Concepts," https://www.thebowencenter.org/introduction-eight-concepts.

8. The Bowen Center for the Study of the Family, "Differentiation of Self," https://www.thebowencenter.org/differentiation-of-self.

9. Bowen Center, "Differentiation of Self."

10. Kathleen Smith, "The Gift of Self-Regulation," kathleensmith.net, May 15, 2019, https://kathleensmith.net/2019/05/15/the-gift-of-self-regulation.

11. Kathleen Smith, "50 Ways You're Overfunctioning for Others (and Don't Even Realize It)," kathleensmith.net, July 7, 2019, https://kathleensmith.net/2019/07/07/50-ways-youre-overfunctioning-for-others-and-dont-even-realize-it.

Chapter 5

1. Matthew Whalley, "Cognitive Distortions: Unhelpful Thinking Habits," Psychology Tools, March 18, 2019, https://www.psychologytools.com/articles/unhelpful-thinking-styles-cognitive-distortions-in-cbt.

2. Anne Lamott, *Bird by Bird: Some Instructions on Writing and Life* (New York: Anchor Books, 1997), 116.

3. Elaine Mead, "What Is Positive Self-Talk (Incl. Examples)," Positive Psychology, September 26, 2019, https://positivepsychology.com/positive-self-talk.

4. Shankar Vedantam, "Being Kind to Yourself," October 11, 2021, in *Hidden Brain*, produced by Hidden Brain Media, podcast, MP3 audio, 51:53, https://stage.hiddenbrain.org/podcast/being-kind-to-yourself.

5. Vedantam, "Being Kind to Yourself."

Chapter 6

1. Matthew Whalley, "Cognitive Distortions: Unhelpful Thinking Habits," Psychology Tools, March 18, 2019, https://www.psychologytools.com/articles/unhelpful-thinking-styles-cognitive-distortions-in-cbt.

2. Whalley, "Cognitive Distortions."

3. David D. Burns, "Secrets of Self-Esteem #2," Feeling Good, January 6, 2014, https://feelinggood.com/2014/01/06/secrets-of-self-esteem-2-negative-and-positive-distortions.

4. David D. Burns originated these concepts in *Feeling Good: The New Mood Therapy* (New York: Harper, 1980) and *The Feeling Good Handbook* (New York: Harper-Collins Publishers, 1989). All quotes from Burns are taken from these two books unless otherwise indicated.

5. Burns, *The Feeling Good Handbook*. For a complete list of thought traps, see University of Pittsburgh School of Social Work, Pennsylvania Child Welfare Resource Center, "Thinking About Thinking," n.d., https://www.pacwrc.pitt.edu/curriculum/313_MngngImpctTrmtcStrss ChldWlfrPrfssnl/hndts/HO15_ThnkngAbtThnkng.pdf.

6. Elizabeth Scott, "How Rumination Differs From Emotional Processing," Verywell Mind, November 12, 2020, https://www.verywellmind.com/repetitive-thoughts-emotional-processing-or-rumination-3144936.

7. Burns, *The Feeling Good Handbook*.

8. Whalley, "Cognitive Distortions."

9. David D. Burns, Feeling Good (blog), n.d., https://feelinggood.com/sunday-hike.

Chapter 7

1. Bessel A. van der Kolk, "The Compulsion to Repeat the Trauma," *Psychiatric Clinics of North America* 12, no. 2 (1989): 389–411.

2. Seth J. Gillihan, "Why It's Easy to Procrastinate—and 7 Ways to Break the Habit," *Psychology Today*, December 12, 2016, https://www.psychologytoday.com/us/blog/think-act-be/201612/why-its-easy-procrastinate-and-7-ways-break-the-habit.

3. Gillihan, "Why It's Easy to Procrastinate."

4. Meena Hart Duerson, "How Ashley C. Ford Changed Her Relationship to Fear and Transformed Her Life," *Today*, March 6, 2020, https://www.today.com/tmrw/writer-ashley-c-ford-overcoming-fear-finding-success-t175404.

5. Xia et al., "Anxious Individuals Are Impulsive Decision-Makers."

6. Will Yakowicz, "Why Employees' Long Hours Can Hurt Your Company's Bottom Line," *Inc.*, August 20, 2015, https://www.inc.com/will-yakowicz/study-finds-long-hours-hurts-company-bottom-line.html.

7. Judson Brewer, *Unwinding Anxiety: New Science Shows How to Break the Cycles of Worry and Fear to Heal Your Mind* (New York: Avery, 2021).

8. Sharon Salzberg, *Real Happiness: A 28-Day Program to Realize the Power of Meditation* (New York: Workman Publishing, 2019), 110.

9. Courtney E. Ackerman, "23 Amazing Health Benefits of Mindfulness for Body and Brain," Positive Psychology, March 6, 2017, https://positivepsychology.com/benefits-of-mindfulness; Matthew Thorpe and Rachael Link, "12 Science-Based Benefits of Meditation," Healthline, updated October 27, 2020, https://www.healthline.com/nutrition/12-benefits-of-meditation.

10. For the exercise itself, see Russ Harris, *The Single Most Powerful Technique for Extreme Fusion* (self-pub., 2016), https://www.actmindfully.com.au/upimages/The_Single_Most_Powerful_Technique_for_Extreme_Fusion_-_Russ_Harris_-_October_2016.pdf.

Chapter 8

1. Karina Limburg et al., "The Relationship between Perfectionism and Psychopathology: A Meta-Analysis," *Journal of Clinical Psychology* 73, no. 10 (October 2017): 1301–1326.
2. Melissa Dahl, "The Alarming New Research on Perfectionism," The Cut, September 30, 2014, https://www.thecut.com/2014/09/alarming-new-research-on-perfectionism.html.
3. Paul L. Hewitt, Gordon L. Flett, and Samuel F. Mikail, *Perfectionism: A Relational Approach to Conceptualization, Assessment, and Treatment* (New York: Guilford Press, 2017), 23.
4. Neff, Kristin. *Self-Compassion: The Proven Power of Being Kind to Yourself.* William Morrow Paperbacks; Reprint edition (June 23, 2015), 27.
5. Joe Perez, "Daily Wisdom: The Secret of Acting with Appropriate Effort," Center for Integral Wisdom, January 3, 2013, https://centerforintegralwisdom.org/daily-wisdom-the -secret-of-acting-with-appropriate-effort.

Chapter 9

1. Dan W. Grupe and Jack B. Nitschke, "Uncertainty and Anticipation in Anxiety: An Integrated Neurobiological and Psychological Perspective," *Nature Reviews Neuroscience* 14 (2013): 488–501.
2. "Bessel van der Kolk, M.D. on 3 Ways PTSD Affects Your Client's Brain," NICABM, January 12, 2018, video, 1:02, https://www.youtube.com/watch?v=DkjTUbWk_C8.
3. Sharon Salzberg, *Real Happiness at Work: Meditations for Accomplishment, Achievement, and Peace* (New York: Workman, 2013).
4. Salzberg, *Real Happiness at Work*, 238.
5. Sharon Salzberg, "What to Do When Anxiety Overwhelms You," On Being, May 2, 2018, https://onbeing.org/blog/sharon-salzberg-what-to-do-when-anxiety-overwhelms-you.
6. Christopher Germer, "A Guided Meditation to Label Difficult Emotions," Mindful, January 23, 2019, https://www.mindful.org/a-guided-meditation-to-label-difficult-emotions.
7. Salzberg, *Real Happiness at Work*.

Chapter 10

1. Tasha Eurich, "What Self-Awareness Really Is (and How to Cultivate It)," hbr.org, January 04, 2018, https://hbr.org/2018/01/what-self-awareness-really-is-and-how-to-cultivate -it.
2. Jack Zenger, "What Is Your Fear of Feedback Costing You?" zengerfolkman.com, September 14, 2021, https://zengerfolkman.com/articles/what-is-your-fear-of-feedback-costing -you.
3. Pauline Rose Clance and Suzanne Imes, "The Imposter Phenomenon in High Achieving Women: Dynamics and Therapeutic Intervention," *Psychotherapy Theory, Research, and Practice* 15, no. 3 (Fall 1978).
4. Lisa Orbé-Austin and Richard Orbé-Austin, "What Is Impostor Syndrome? Learn How to Own Your Greatness," Ulysses Press, April 28, 2020, https://ulyssespress.com/blog/what-is -impostor-syndrome-own-your-greatness.
5. Ruchika Tulshyan and Jodi-Ann Burey, "Stop Telling Women They Have Impostor Syndrome," hbr.org, February 11, 2021, https://hbr.org/2021/02/stop-telling-women-they -have-impostor-syndrome.
6. Tulshyan and Burey, "Stop Telling Women They Have Impostor Syndrome."
7. Lisa Orbé-Austin, "Stop Gaslighting Women When They Say They're Experiencing Impostor Syndrome," LinkedIn, March 8, 2021, https://www.linkedin.com/pulse/stop-gaslighting -women-when-say-theyre-experiencing-orbe-austin-phd.
8. Kim Mills, "Speaking of Psychology: How to Overcome Feeling Like an Impostor, with Lisa Orbé-Austin, PhD, and Kevin Cokley, PhD," July 2021, in *Speaking of Psychology*, produced by Lea Winerman, podcast, MP3 audio, 34:25, https://www.apa.org/news/podcasts/speaking -of-psychology/impostor-syndrome.

9. Shankar Vedantam, "The Psychology of Self-Doubt," December 13, 2021, in *Hidden Brain*, produced by Hidden Brain Media, podcast, MP3 audio, 49:09, https://hiddenbrain.org/podcast/the-psychology-of-self-doubt.

10. Tulshyan and Burey, "Stop Telling Women They Have Impostor Syndrome."

11. Orbé-Austin, "Stop Gaslighting Women."

12. Mills, "Speaking of Psychology."

13. Mills, "Speaking of Psychology."

14. Gabriela Sadurní Rodríguez, "Defusion: How to Detangle from Thoughts & Feelings," The Psychology Group, https://thepsychologygroup.com/defusion.

15. Russ Harris, *The Happiness Trap: How to Stop Struggling and Start Living: A Guide to ACT* (Trumpeter, 2008).

16. Russ Harris, "4 Tips to Help You Unhook from Difficult Thoughts or Feelings," thehappinesstrap.com, August 29, 2019, https://thehappinesstrap.com/unhooking-from-difficult-thoughts-or-feelings.

Chapter 11

1. Substance Abuse and Mental Health Services Administration, "Table 16: DSM-IV to DSM-5 Social Phobia/Social Anxiety Disorder Comparison," in *DSM-5 Changes: Implications for Child Serious Emotional Disturbance* [internet] (Rockville: Substance Abuse and Mental Health Services Administration (US), June 2016), https://www.ncbi.nlm.nih.gov/books/NBK519712/table/ch3.t12.

2. Mind My Peelings, "Introvert, Shyness, and Social Anxiety: What's the Difference?" April 2, 2021, https://www.mindmypeelings.com/blog/introvert-shy-social-anxiety.

3. Karen Auyeung and Lynn E. Alden, "Accurate Empathy, Social Rejection, and Social Anxiety Disorder," *Clinical Psychological Science* 8, no. 2 (2020).

4. Ellen Hendriksen, "The 4 Differences between Introversion and Social Anxiety," quietrev.com, https://quietrev.com/the-4-differences-between-introversion-and-social-anxiety.

5. For a complete list, see Olga Góralewicz, "A Full List of Values for Acceptance and Commitment Therapy (ACT)," Loving Health, February 15, 2021, https://loving.health/en/act-list-of-values.

6. Russell Harris, "Embracing Your Demons: An Overview of Acceptance and Commitment Therapy," *Psychotherapy in Australia* 12, no. 4 (2006): 2–8.

7. Kathleen Smith, *Everything Isn't Terrible: Conquer Your Insecurities, Interrupt Your Anxiety and Finally Calm Down* (New York: Hachette Books, 2019), 27.

8. Smith, *Everything Isn't Terrible*, 28.

9. Wendy Suzuki, *Good Anxiety: Harnessing the Power of the Most Misunderstood Emotion* (New York: Atria Books, 2021), 168.

10. Alison Wood Brooks, "Emotion and the Art of Negotiation," *Harvard Business Review*, December 2015, 56–64.

Conclusion

1. Amy J. C. Cuddy, Matthew Kohut, and John Neffinger, "Connect, Then Lead," *Harvard Business Review*, July–August 2013.

2. Russ Harris, The Happiness Trap, n.d., https://thehappinesstrap.com/upimages/Complete_Worksheets_2014.pdf.

INDEX

ableism, 24

abuse, 69–71

acceptance and commitment therapy (ACT), 197–198, 210, 211

acceptance seeking, 77–78

accomplishments, keeping a record of, 107

ACT. See acceptance and commitment therapy (ACT)

action, 63
  awareness and, 62
  committed, 211
  in the rapid power reclaim method, 73

activating events, 53–56

activators, 130. See also triggers

activist mindset, 41–42

adaptive coping mechanisms, 58–59

adult survivors of a damaged past (ASDPs), 71

adverse childhood experiences (ACEs), 69–71

Agassi, Andre, 161

agency, 63, 71
  control and, 164, 168
  dealing with your past and, 53, 85–86, 168
  knowing your triggers and, 63
  self-talk and, 92–93
  your past and, 86, 92–93

agreement, 211, 213

alignment
  of drive and purpose, 4
  of roles with strengths, 37
  of work with your strengths, 37
  with your values, 210–211

all-or-nothing thinking, 102–103, 118
  finding shades of gray and, 116
  perfectionism and, 156–160

ambition, 17–32
  impostor syndrome and, 194–197
  too much, 36–37

American Psychological Association, 2, 26–27, 189

amygdala, 30

Anand, Pooja V., 70

answers, admitting to not knowing, 8

anticipatory anxiety, 165–166, 216–217

anxiety
  ambition and, 17–32
  anticipatory, 165–166
  avoiding, 7–8
  defanging, 46
  definition of, 27
  disclosing your, 217–218
  diverse types of, 47–48
  fear vs., 2
  feeling and living through, 225–232
  good traits with, 167–168
  irrationality of, 31–32, 47–48
  just enough, 24
  managing, 18, 28, 34–35
  normal vs. problematic, 27–28
  prevalence of worldwide, 2–3
  pros and cons of, 38–42
  recognizing the symptoms of, 190
  reframing, 5–7
  rightsizing, 42–43
  role of, 30–31
  as a signal, 66–68
  sources of, examining, 44
  as a superpower, 11–13
  trait, 2
  triggers and tells, 47–63
  understanding your, 49–53
  unmanaged vs. managed, 3–4

Anxiety and Depression Association of America, 27, 203

anxiety disorders, 27–28
  untreated vs. managed, 34–35

The Anxiety Toolkit (Boyes), 93

The Anxious Achiever podcast, 4, 42, 194

anxious achievers
  self-blame by, 110
  skills/advantages of, 21–22
  thought traps of, 102–112

approval, 77–78, 211, 213

arrogance, 170

assumptions, 185–186
  minimizing negative, 216

assurance, 211, 213

attention, 211, 213
attention training, 42
authenticity, 10
automatic responses, 11, 66–67
  rethinking, 83
  self-differentiation and, 78–80
avoidance, 57, 126–127, 152
  covert, 208–209
  of criticism, 183–184
  overt, 208
  partial, 209
  social anxiety and, 208–210
awareness, 9–11, 25–26
  of automatic responses, 60–62
  group, 76
  hyper-, 167
  mindful, 96
  mindfulness and, 139–140
  of negative self-talk, 90–92
  open, 171–172
  of thought traps, 100
  "why" vs. "what" questions for, 62

balanced thinking, 116–117
Barlow, David, 42, 164–165
Beck, Aaron, 90–91, 101
Being an Inner Ally to Yourself at Work
    exercise, 96
Bernstein, Danny, 62
biases, 24, 70, 192
blaming, 109–110
Bonvissuto, Lee, 210
borrowing self, 213
boundaries
  for control, 175–182
  differentiation of self and, 77–83
  figuring out your, 178–182
  perfectionism and, 157
Bowen, Murray, 75–77, 211, 213
Boyes, Alice, 93, 111, 132, 153–154, 186–187
Brackett, Marc, 53–54, 67
brain
  anticipatory anxiety and, 165–166
  anxiety and, 29–32
  in anxious vs. laid-back people, 34
  control and, 164
  habits, cognitive load and, 122–123
  negative self-talk and, 94
  neuroplasticity in, 32, 39–42, 83
  perfectionism and, 159–160
  tension and, 134
Break a Bad Habit and Make Progress at Work
    exercise, 136–138

Brewer, Judson, 132–135, 136
Buddhism, 138, 157–158
bullies, 77–78
Burey, Jodi-Ann, 192, 193
Burguieres, Philip, 9
Burke-Garcia, Amelia, 175
burnout, 26, 36–37, 194
  mindfulness and, 139
  need for control and, 176, 180
  overfunctioning and, 79
  overly self-reliant leaders and, 169–170
  perfectionism and, 148–149, 159
  prevalence of, 3
Burns, David, 101, 102, 103, 107

Cain, Susan, 206
Calarco, Jessica, 109
calm, 80
career transitions, 214–215
caste systems, 70
catastrophizing, 57, 105–107, 118, 152
  So What? exercise and, 159–160
CBT. *See* cognitive behavioral therapy (CBT)
celebrations, 73
Center for Anxiety and Related Disorders, 42
chameleons, 77–78
change
  anxiety as a signal for, 41–42
  planning for, 82
  thought traps and, 118–119
characters, creating for negative thoughts,
    93–94, 199
check-ins, 184–185
Check Your Reactions exercise, 59, 61
Chesney, Taylor, 118
childhood experiences, 68–75
choice
  creating, 72
  dealing with your past and, 85–86
City Mental Health Alliance, 123–124,
    184–185
Clance, Pauline Rose, 187
clarity, 173–174
Clayman, Amanda, 66–67, 129
Clear, James, 141–142
cognitive behavioral therapy (CBT), 90–91,
    101, 112, 159–160
  maintaining an external focus in, 215
cognitive distortions. *See* thought traps
Cokley, Kevin, 192–193, 194
Colonna, Jerry, 68–69, 71, 73–75, 85, 167–168
  on micromanaging, 170
committed action, 211

communication, 9–10
  disruptive, 130–131
  as a leader's role, 207–208
  public speaking and, 221–223
  thought traps and, 100
  willingness to listen and, 185
comparative shoulds, 109
compassion, 215–216
competence, 48–49
compromise, 158, 168–169
conclusions, jumping to, 104–105
confidence, 79–80, 191
conflict
  managing, 218–220
  self-blame and, 110
  understanding your emotions and, 48
conscientiousness, 43, 97
  perfectionism and, 147–148
control, 23, 163–182
  addiction and, 130
  illusion of, 164–165
  impossibility of complete, 63
  practicing releasing, 170–175
  reality vs., 164
  self-blame and, 110
  setting boundaries for, 175–182
  taking control of anxiety and, 39–42
  why we hang on to, 165–168
  at work, 168–170
coping-ahead strategies, 216–217
coping mechanisms, 32, 58
cortisol, 95
covert avoidance, 208–209
Covid-19 pandemic, 3
  catastrophizing during, 106
  as collective trauma, 77
  control during, 163
  habits during, 122–123
  media campaign on, 175
creativity, 7, 21, 35, 41, 42, 225
  facing your past and, 83
  perfectionism and, 158
  self-awareness and, 61
  understanding your emotions and, 48
  worry and, 134
Cuddy, Amy, 228
culture effects, 23–24
  appropriate effort and, 157–160
  comparative shoulds and, 109
  false urgency and, 178
  impostor syndrome and, 192–194
  labeling and, 103
  leadership as performance, 206–207
  overwork and, 61, 85, 131–132

perfectionism and, 146–147
  self-optimization and, 10
curiosity, 19–20, 134–135
  in examining behavior, 137
Cuss, Steve, 131

David, Susan, 57
decision-making
  impulsive, 127–129
  thought traps and, 100
defanging anxiety, 46
defense mechanisms, 58–59
defensive pessimism, 149
delegation, 23
depression, 2, 147, 227
Diagnostic and Statistical Manual of Mental
    Disorders, 203–204
differentiation of self, 77–83
  based on your values, 211, 213
discomfort, 7–8, 35
  learning to tolerate, 8–9, 40–42
  self-differentiation and, 83–85
disruptive communication, 130–131
downward arrow technique, 159–160
dread, 48
drive, 47–48
dropping anchor, 140–141
Duhigg, Charles, 134

ecological factors, 24
economic inequality, 24
Edmondson, Amy, 113–114, 226–227
effort, appropriate, 157–160
emotional reasoning, 112
emotions
  decision-making and, 127–129
  as information, 67–68
  list of, 57
  negative, 39
  noting and naming, 174
  self-differentiation and, 77–83
  thoughts in determining, 90–91
  understanding your, 48
empathy, 10, 21, 43
  emotional connection through, 228
  social anxiety and, 215–216
English, Paul, 76, 228
entrepreneurship porn, 35–36
Eurich, Tasha, 62
exercise, 58
  appropriate effort in, 158
  thought traps and, 115

exercises
　Being an Inner Ally to Yourself at Work, 96
　Break a Bad Habit and Make Progress at
　　Work, 136–138
　Check Your Reactions, 59, 61
　grounding, 140–141
　habit stacking, 141–142
　Identify and Anchor in Your Core Values, 212
　Identify Your Boundaries and Limits,
　　180–181
　Identify Your Triggers, 56–57
　mindfulness, 139–140
　Questions to Help You Develop a More
　　Differentiated Self, 81–82
　Quick and Easy Body Scan, 50–51
　Rapid Power Reclaim Method, 72–73
　self-compassion break, 96
　So What?, 158–160
　on thought traps, 100
expectations, 211
　lowering your, 215
exposure therapy, 209–210, 213
external focus, 215

facts, balanced thinking to find, 116–117.
　　See also reality
failure parties, 114
family history, 11
　childhood experiences, 68–75
　control and, 166–168
　facing, 62–86
　in learning anxiety, 17–18
　negative self-talk and, 92–93
　negativity bias and, 69–71
　perfectionism and, 146, 149, 160–162
　playing detective with, 52–53
　positive effects from, 72–74
　self-blame and, 110
　thought traps and, 101
　trauma in, 43–45, 166
　workplace as family system and, 75–77
family systems theory, 75–77, 211, 213
fear, 31
　anxiety vs., 2
　changing your response to, 74–75
　childhood experiences and, 74
　of criticism, 183–184
　defusing, 197–200
　exposure therapy and, 209–210
　feeling and acting through, 225–232
　hypervigilance and, 166
　losing control and, 182
　of shame, 113
　wisdom in, 74–75

feedback, 183–200. *See also* trusted advisers
　check-ins for, 184–185
　defusing fear and, 197–200
　format for, 186–187
　giving useful, 184
　in habit formation, 132–136
　learning to receive, 184
　ongoing need for, 185–187
The Feeling Good Handbook (Burns), 102
fight, flight, or freeze response, 139
filtering, 107, 166
Finkelstein, Harley, 43–45, 47–48, 227
Finney, Susan I., 70
Flett, Gordon, 148–149
flexibility, 149
flying, anxiety around, 20
focus, 34, 226
　catastrophizing and, 106–107
　downsides of too much, 36–37
　on the future, 34–35
　maintaining an external, 215
　worry and, 134
Fogg, B. J., 141–142
Ford, Ashley C., 106, 126
Ford Motor Company, 114
fortune telling, 104, 105

Gallo, Amy, 218–220
Gay, Roxanne, 177–178
Gilbert, Paul, 101
Gillihan, Seth, 124–125
Glass, Carolyn, 55, 58, 86, 209
goals, 22
　imagining yourself without anxiety, 29
　perfectionism and, 157–160
goodwill, extending, 172–173
Greenspon, Thomas, 147–148, 155, 156, 161
grounding techniques, 221
guided meditation, 116

habits, 121–143
　avoidance, 126–127
　breaking free from destructive, 132–138
　common unhelpful, 123–132
　disruptive communication, 130–131
　dropping anchor and, 140–141
　getting unstuck from, 142–143
　impulsive decisions, 127–129
　knowing when they aren't helpful, 123
　micromanaging, 123–124
　mindfulness and, 138–142
　overspending, 129
　overwork, 131–132

procrastination, 124–125
    stacking, 141–142
    substance use, 129–130
    why we form, 122–123
handing over the reins, 174–175
happiness, 71
Harley, Rebecca, 49, 176, 179
Harris, Russ, 140, 198, 200, 229–230
Healing at Work (Winchester & Finney), 70
health issues, 62–63
help, asking for, 22
Hendriksen, Ellen, 203–204
Hewitt, Paul, 148–149
Hidden Brain podcast, 94
Hiding in the Bathroom (Aarons-Mele), 19
Hispana Global, 190
Hofmann, Stefan, 208
household dysfunction, 69–71
*How to Be Yourself: Quiet Your Inner Critic and
    Rise Above Social Anxiety* (Hendriksen),
    203–204
humor, 115
hypervigilance, 17, 30
    control and, 166–167
    definition of, 166
    using, 43

IBS, 38
Identify and Anchor in Your Core Values
    exercise, 212
Identify Your Boundaries and Limits exercise,
    180–181
Identify Your Triggers exercise, 56–57
identity, 12
"I'm a banana" trick, 199
Imes, Suzanne, 187
impostor syndrome, 99, 187–191
    ambition and, 194–197
    defusing fear and, 197–199
    joy and, 231
    systems in creating, 191–194
impulsive decisions, 127–129
information, anxiety as, 67–68, 134
infrastructure, 22
inner critic. *See* negative self-talk
inner saboteur, 191
insecurity, 84–85
insight, 63
inspiring others, 12
integration, 73
interviews, 216–218
introversion, 203–206
intuition, 205–206
isolation, 227

Jaman, Poppy, 123–124, 184–185
job satisfaction, 48
Johns, Andy, 48, 161–162
Johri, Akshay, 70
joy, 162, 225, 230–231, 232
judgment, 90, 179
    negativity bias and, 69
    perfectionism and, 149, 155
    self-compassion and, 96
    social anxiety and, 204
jumping to conclusions, 104–105

Kander, Jason, 121–122, 132
Kaplun, Jeannette, 189–190
Kayak, 76
Kempton, Sally, 157–158
Koehn, Nancy, 23

labeling, 103–104, 152
Lamott, Anne, 91
leaders and leadership, 3
    anxiety inherent to, 22–26
    competence and warmth in, 48–49
    differentiation of self and, 78–83
    disruptive communication by, 130–131
    glamorization of problematic behavior and,
        35–36
    introversion and, 206–208
    mental health disorders and, 35–37
    mindsets for new, 7–11
    myths and stereotypes about, 203
    need for control by, 168–170
    need for ongoing feedback and,
        185–187
    overfunctioning and underfunctioning,
        79–80
    the past and, 66
    as performance, 206–208
    public speaking and, 221–223
    risk-taking and, 101–102
    self-awareness and, 61
    social radar and, 205–206
    systems thinking and, 77–83
    thought traps and, 101–102, 112–114
    triggers for, 53–54
    trusting yourself and, 213
    values and, 229–230
leadership styles, 112–114
leveraging your anxiety, 7, 34, 37, 63,
    224
limbic system, 29–30
listening, 185
Lola, 228

Love, Kevin, 202–203
loving-kindness meditation, 172–173

maladaptive coping mechanisms, 58–59
management, 21
    of anxiety, 25–26
    80/20 rule in, 124
    micromanaging and, 84, 123–124
market research, 221
Mastromonaco, Alyssa, 33–35, 38
May, Rollo, 30
Mcilroy, Emma, 227, 228, 229
meditation, 41, 44, 68, 139
    guided, 116
    in habit stacking, 142
    loving-kindness, 172–173
meetings, 17, 54
    avoidance and, 126
    boundaries and, 178
    social anxiety and, 208
    structuring for introverts, 208
    triggers and, 50, 56
mental filtering, 107
mental health
    conditions, 2–3
    conditions, prevalence of, 27, 36–37, 208
    negative self-talk and, 92
    perfectionism and, 147
    range of, 26–29
    shame around, 5–6
    speaking out about, 9
    success and, 35–38
Mental Health America, 3
Mental Health at Work Report, 3
Mental Health First Aid England, 123–124
Merchant, Nilofer, 230
metrics, 173
micromanaging, 84, 123–124, 170
    handing over the reins vs., 174–175
Microsoft, 62
Mikail, Samuel, 148–149
Miller, Jason, 65–66, 67–68
mindful awareness, 96
mindfulness, 130, 138–142
mind reading, 104–105, 151–152
mindset, 7–11
    activist, 41–42
    practice, 171
    thought traps and, 115
Mind Share Partners, 3, 36
mini-deliverables, 125
money
    anxiety about, 127–129
    spending what you don't have, 129

monkey mind, 138
motivation, 17–18, 63
    in breaking habits, 150–151
    control and, 170
Mubarak, Hosni, 33
My Age of Anxiety (Stossel), 29

naming emotions, 174
narcissism, 153–154
Neal-Barnett, Angela, 159–160
Neely, Priska, 230–231
Neff, Kristin, 94–97
negative reinforcement, 125
negative self-talk, 10–11, 89–97
    creating characters for, 93–94
    definition of, 90
    externalizing, 92–94
    finding themes in, 152–153
    internal assumptions and, 186
    mental health and, 92
    negative effects of, 95
    perfectionism and, 150, 151–154
    self-compassion and, 94–97
    social anxiety and, 217
negativity bias, 69–71
neglect, 69–71
negotiations, 218–221
networking, 214–216
neuroplasticity, 32, 39–42, 83
noise anxiety, 67
Noor Ali, Sehreen, 149, 150, 151
noting and naming, 174

Obama, Barack, 33
obsessive compulsive disorder (OCD), 2, 147
onlyness, 230
open awareness, 171–172
opinions, facts vs., 116–117
opportunities, missing, 2, 28, 208–209
    discounting the positive and, 107–108
    perfectionism and, 147
    social anxiety and, 208–209, 220, 223
opposite action strategy, 216–217
optimism, 165
Orbé-Austin, Lisa, 187–188, 192
Orbé-Austin, Richard, 187–188
ordinariness, 154
organizations
    anxiety created by, 23–24
    systems theory on, 75–77
O'Toole, James, 185

overfunctioning, 78, 79–81, 83–85,
194–197
overpreparation, 194–197
overt avoidance, 208
overthinking, 110–112
overwork, 35–37, 121–122, 131–132
perfectionism and, 146
setting boundaries and, 177–178

panic attacks, 17, 145–146
Parra Vera, Andrea, 45–46
partial avoidance, 209
patriarchy, 24
Pattee, Jyl Johnson, 195–197, 231
people-pleasers, 121–122
control needs and, 179, 183
perfectionism and, 152–153
Perel, Esther, 77
perfectionism, 57, 145–162
all-or-nothing thinking and, 156–160
breaking the habit of, 150–156
excellence vs., 160–162
fallacies of, 147–148
goals and, 157–160
perspective and, 154–156
roots of, 148–149
performance
just enough anxiety for, 24
negative self-talk and, 97
success metrics for, 173
understanding your emotions and, 48
personality traits, 2, 42–43
anxiety as, 39
role alignment with, 37
social anxiety and, 223–224
personalization, 109–110
perspective, 153, 154–156
pessimism, 165
defensive, 149
phobias, 48
physical tells, 49–53
planning, 21, 34–35
for change, 82
self-differentiation and, 83–84
polarized thinking, 102–103
Pollak, Lindsey, 214–215, 217–218, 222
post-traumatic stress disorder (PTSD),
121–122, 166
power, 7, 8
abuses and abdications of, 61
giving away, 53
to heal, 75
need for feedback and, 185
organizational structures and, 24

taking back from anxiety, 11–12
of visual effects, 199–200
Pozen, Bob, 173
practice
of loving-kindness meditation, 172–173
mindset for, 171
of open awareness, 171–172
praise, 187–188
preparation, 23
pride, 191
procrastination, 124–125
Procter & Gamble, 45–46
productivity, 34
professional development, 214–215
psychological safety, 113–114, 226–227
public speaking, 221–223
purpose, 18–19, 20
Purselle, Buffie, 127–129

Qualtrics, 36
Questions to Help You Develop a More
Differentiated Self exercise, 81–82
Quick and Easy Body Scan exercise, 50–51
Quiet: The Power of Introverts (Cain), 206–207

racism, 24, 70, 192
Rajan, Arvind, 201–202
Rapid Power Reclaim Method exercise,
72–73
Raskopoulos, Jordan, 206
reactions vs. responses, 78. *See also* responses
reality
control and, 164
impostor syndrome and, 190
negative self-talk vs., 95
social anxiety and, 217
thought traps vs., 103–104
reflection, 8
perfectionism and, 161
self-differentiation and, 81–82
reframing, 109
regrouping, 219–220
relationships, understanding your emotions
and, 48
resilience, 71, 229
responses, 39. *See also* habits
"Am I sure?" question for, 72
automatic, 11
automatic, uncovering, 60–62
awareness of your, 25–26
common unhelpful, 123–132
family systems theory on, 75–77
getting unstuck from, 142–143

responses (*continued*)
  identifying triggers and, 54–55
  identifying your typical, 56–59
  to negative feedback, 183–184
  pausing before, 31–32
  physical tells, 49–53
  to social anxiety, 213–223
  unhelpful, 121–143
  your greatest hits, 56–59
responsibilities
  balancing work/home, 54
  family history and, 73
  overwork and, 132
  personalization/blaming and, 109–110
responsibility
  delegating, 23, 171
  overfunctioners and, 79
  self-compassion and, 97
  underfunctioners and, 79–80
risk-taking, 36–37, 47–48
  thought traps and, 101–102
ruminating, 110–112, 118, 153–154
  control and, 164
Runyan, Christine, 164

safety behaviors, 126–127, 209
Salzberg, Sharon, 139, 171, 172, 173, 174
SAP, 36
saying no, 117, 181
Schuman-Olivier, Zev, 130
self, borrowing, 213
self-aggrandizement, 91
self-blame, 110
self-care, 37, 232
self-compassion, 63, 94–97
  breaks for, 96
  control and, 182
  loving-kindness meditation and, 172–173
  perfectionism and, 150
  self-blame vs., 110
  thought traps and, 115
self-differentiation, 77–83
  developing, 83–86
  grounding yourself in your values and, 211, 213
self-esteem, 79–80
self-knowledge, 9–10, 19–20
  of automatic responses, 60–62
  "why" vs. "what" questions and, 62
  of your triggers and tells, 47–63
self-regulation, 80
self-reliance, 169–170

self-talk
  avoidance and, 126
  awareness of, 90–92
  externalizing, 155
  negative, 10–11, 89–97
  neutral, 91
  perfectionism and, 150, 151–154
  positive, 91
  procrastination and, 124–125
self-worth, 85
shame, 5–6
  fear of, 113
  grounding yourself in your values and, 210–211
  negative self-talk and, 94–95
  perfectionism and, 146
Shopify, 43, 47–48, 227
"should" statements, 108–109, 152
shyness, 203–206
signal anxiety, 67
sleep, 35
Smith, Kathleen, 78–79, 80, 81–82, 84, 211, 213
social anxiety, 10–11, 201–224
  conflict management and, 218–220
  grounding yourself in your values and, 210–213
  interviewing and, 216–218
  introversion, shyness, and, 203–206
  leadership as performance and, 206–208
  negotiating and, 220–221
  networking and, 214–216
  self-love and, 223–224
  strengths with, 205–206
  triggers for and reactions to, 213–223
  when it gets in the way, 208–210
social comparison, 109
social phobia. *See* social anxiety
social radar, 205–206
Sotomayor, Andrew, 93
So What? exercise, 158–160
Stossel, Scott, 29, 42–43, 167
stress
  definition of, 27
  habits and, 122–123
  health effects of, 65–66
structure, 173–174
substance use, 2, 129–130
success
  anxiety in creating, 20–22
  documenting your, 191
  impostor syndrome, 189–190
  mental health and, 35–38
  metrics for, 173
  public speaking and, 222

superpower, anxiety as, 7, 11–12, 40–41,
    43–46
  hyperawareness and, 167
  leadership and, 63, 72, 76
support, 37
survival, 44, 94, 101
Suzuki, Wendy, 39–42, 215–216
sweetheart method, 153
systemic factors, 24. *See also* family systems
    theory
  in impostor syndrome, 191–194
  racism, 24
systems thinking, 75–77

Taitz, Jenny, 216–217
Talks at Google, 147
Tarr, Tanya, 191, 220–221
TED talks, 151
TEDx talks, 206
tells
  definition of, 49
  playing detective to find your, 49–53
temperaments, 25
therapy, 44–45, 90–91, 226
Think Act Be podcast, 124–125
thoughts, accepting as just thoughts,
    198
thought traps, 99–119
  all-or-nothing thinking, 102–103
  catastrophizing, 105–107
  common, 102–112
  definition of, 99
  discounting the positive, 107–108
  emotional reasoning, 112
  filtering, 107
  jumping to conclusions, 104–105
  labeling, 103–104
  leadership style and, 112–114
  loosening the grip of, 114–117
  perfectionism and, 151–154
  personalization and blaming, 109–110
  ruminating and overthinking, 110–112
  "should" statements, 108–109
  when they come true, 117–119
  why they occur, 100–102
threat appraisal, 30–31, 101
  mindfulness and, 139–140
  rumination and, 111
  trauma and, 166
Todobebé, 190
trait anxiety, 2
transparency, 49
trauma, 43–45, 166. *See also* family history

triggers, 47–63
  automatic reactions and, 60–62
  changing habits and, 137–138
  common, 54
  definition of, 53
  identifying your, 54–56
  from insight to action and, 63
  knowing your, 53–56
  mindfulness and, 138–142
  playing detective to find, 49–53
  for social anxiety, 213–223
  in the workplace, 70–73
  your typical responses and, 56–59
trust, 227–228
  check-ins and, 185
  insecurity and, 84–85
trusted advisers
  for decision-making, 128
  in fighting perfectionism, 155
  for thought traps, 102–103, 105
Tulshyan, Ruchika, 192, 193

uncertainty
  addiction and, 130
  managing through, 9–10
  threat appraisal system and, 30–31
underfunctioning, 78, 79–80, 82
urgency, false sense of, 55, 83, 178–179

values, 85, 229–230
  grounding yourself in your, 210–213
  identifying your core, 212
  questions to center, 229–230
visual effects, for thoughts, 199–200
visualizations, 74–75
vulnerability, 49, 227–228

Wallace, Christina, 19
warmth, 48–49
what-if lists, 42
Wildfang, 227
Winchester, Susan Schmitt, 70–73
wing persons, 215
Women Online, 4, 19, 20
Work Friend column, 177
work hours, boundaries around, 176
workplace
  boundaries at, 175–182
  control needs in, 168–170
  as a family system, 75–77
  recovering from your past in, 70–73

worry
    control and, 164
    impostor syndrome and, 46
    impulsivity and, 128
    perfectionism and, 149
    planning and, 21
    problematic anxiety and, 2
    rumination and, 111

    So What? exercise and, 159–160
    as unhelpful reaction, 133–136
worst-case scenarios, 163

Yale Center for Emotional Intelligence, 67
Yates, Chris, 114
your greatest hits, 56–59

ACKNOWLEDGMENTS

Thank you to Alicyn Zall, Kevin Evers, and Melinda Merino at HBR Press, who made this book a reality!

This book would not have been possible without Catherine Knepper. Catherine, thank you for being my editing and writing partner.

By the age of forty-six, one has far too many people to thank in life than could possibly fit in a list of acknowledgments. But as I reflect on the first half of my life, I am so grateful to everyone who helped me through my mental illness and helps me with mental wellness. Jeanine Brescia, Bob Ditter, Wilma Selenfriend, Steve Cunningham, Jillian McDonough, Ellen Donaldson, and Laugharnananda Ray helped me stay healthy in mind and body.

I want to thank all the women's networks that have powered my career and lent amazing counsel through the years. Rachel Sklar, your impact in my life has been monumental. Gina Glantz, thank you for everything.

Carolyn Glass, my dear friend and clinical adviser, made sure this book was sound from a therapeutic and clinical perspective and made editing fun along the way. Thank you and much love to Rebecca Harley for all the growth we've achieved together since Isis Parenting.

Mary Dooe has produced *The Anxious Achiever* podcast from the beginning, and I wouldn't be here without her and her amazing team. Mary, thanks for being my partner and creating amazing audio and for trying to figure out how to work less.

Thanks to Carol Franco and Kent Lineback for helping me shape my proposal and helping find a home for the book at Harvard Business Review Press

The team at HBR Press adopted me and helped me bring *The Anxious Achiever* to life. Maureen Hoch, Adi Ignatius, Amy Bernstein, Adam

Buchholz, and Anne Saini, thank you for helping launch the podcast. Amy Gallo and Gretchen Gavett, you've been such wonderful editors and thought partners in my writing of this book. And to the wonderful HBR marketing and publicity teams for building a launch plan with oomph.

Jessi Hempel at LinkedIn, thank you, thank you, thank you! Mike Nussbaum, Rhian Rogan, Sarah Storm, Amanda Peña, and David Giongco, working with you is a joy, and I love seeing *The Anxious Achiever* grow.

To all the guests on *The Anxious Achiever* and people who lent their wisdom to this book, I am so grateful. Thanks to Harley Finkelstein, Kathleen Smith, Christine Runyan, Andrew Sotomayor, Alice Boyes, Alyssa Mastromonaco, Roxane Gay, Judson Brewer, Wendy Suzuki, Scott Stossel, Andrea Parra, Jason Miller, Jerry Colonna, Amanda Clayman, Marc Brackett, Susan Schmitt Winchester, Paul English, Steve Cuss, Esther Perel, Ashley C. Ford, Jess Calarco, Amy Edmondson, Chris Yates, Rebecca Harley, Danny Bernstein, Jason Kander, Poppy Jaman, Zev Schuman-Olivier, Thomas Greenspon, Angela Neal-Barnett, Sharon Salzberg, Bob Pozen, Amelia Burke-Garcia, Emma McIlroy, Christina Wallace, Vikas Shah, Christopher Barnes, Erica Dhawan, Joel Gascoigne, Melissa Doman, Amelia Ransom, Paul Greenberg, Robert Glazer, Amy Gallo, Priska Neely, Lee Bonvisutto, Jyl Johnson Pattee, Andy Johns, Andy Dunn, Aarti Shahani, and Julie Lythcott-Haims.

Kelly Greenwood and the team at Mindshare Partners, it's been awesome collaborating with you and learning from each other. I'm looking forward to the evolution of workplace mental health.

My team at Women Online, you are the 100 percent bestest. Jen Vento, Christine Koh, and Melissa Ford, love you and thank you.

To Nicco, A, T, and J, I love you more than anything. Thank you for putting up with me and supporting my dreams for *The Anxious Achiever*.

Rev. Claire Feingold-Thoryn inspires me weekly. I'd like to close with an excerpt from a poem she introduced me to, by Wisława Szymborska. It's called "Life While You Wait."

Performance without rehearsal.
Body without alterations.
Head without premeditation.

I know nothing of the role I play.
I only know it's mine. I can't exchange it.
I have to guess on the spot
just what this play's all about.

Ill-prepared for the privilege of living,
I can barely keep up with the pace that the action demands.
I improvise, although I loathe improvisation.

ABOUT THE AUTHOR

MORRA AARONS-MELE hosts *The Anxious Achiever*, a top business podcast that was a 2020 Webby Awards Honoree. She is one of the ten thought leaders selected as LinkedIn's Top Voices in Mental Health for 2022. She's passionate about helping people rethink the relationship between their mental health and their success. She consults frequently with *Fortune* 500 companies, startups, and US government agencies.

Aarons-Mele is an entrepreneur and communications executive. In addition to her work in workplace mental health, she founded the award-winning social impact agency Women Online, which she sold in 2021. She has helped three US presidential candidates and countless mission-driven organizations create digital marketing and fundraising campaigns.

Since 2004 Aarons-Mele has covered the campaign trail, the White House, the office cubicle, and even the lactation room, and has written for publications ranging from the *New York Times* and the *Wall Street Journal* to *Fast Company*. Her first book, *Hiding in the Bathroom: How to Get Out There (When You'd Rather Stay Home)*, was published by Dey Street Books in 2017.

Aarons-Mele has degrees from the Harvard Kennedy School and Brown University. She and Nicco Mele live outside Boston with their three children.